GOVERNMENTAL ARTS IN
EARLY TUDOR ENGLAND

Governmental Arts in Early Tudor England studies the representational strategies through which government and dissent were performed during the English 1530s. Polito argues that the reign of Henry VIII saw the emergence of new forms of secular government. Through innovative legislation, the dissemination of propaganda and conduct literature, the appropriation of ecclesiastical and pastoral modes of rule and new and sometimes spectacular rituals of statecraft, this monarch and his counsellors worked on the intimate territories of conscience, desire and speech, as intention, sexual practises and verbal performatives were brought into the domain of public discourse and the juridical sphere. The book suggests that the conundrum of government was its assumption that its objects of government were 'sovereign' enough to deploy the kinds of self-temperance and circumspection required for the security of the realm. The same subject, however, governors understood and feared, would be deep and complex enough to alienate intention from action and, in the interest of liberty, to 'perform' as another if necessary. Tudor governmentality's notion of the self-conscious, self-divided, free subject/actor is therefore both the condition for, and the limit of, a pre-liberal form of government

The case of Elizabeth Barton, the nun executed for treason in 1534, supports Polito's argument that gender was key to the humanist-inspired epistemological approach to the art and science of government. The book also provides an examination of the new drama that was the Tudor secular interlude and finds that these plays both model and mock the governmental arts that linked self-temperance, freedom and prosperity. When the drama joins the government in worrying about the necessity and danger of dissimulation in the public sphere, actors, ironically, work to show that actors can be dangerous. Thus Polito shows Henrician theatre to be as complex, compromised and interesting as the Elizabethan public stage it helped to foster.

Mary Polito is an Associate Professor in the Department of English at the University of Calgary, Canada.

'Lucretia Romana,' the printer's device of Thomas Berthelet, royal printer to Henry VIII, taken from *Apomaxis Calumniarum*, by Richard Morison, 1537. By permission of the British Library, Shelfmark 851.i.11.

Governmental Arts in Early Tudor England

MARY POLITO
University of Calgary, Canada

ASHGATE

© Mary Polito 2005

Published by
Ashgate Publishing Limited
Gower House
Croft Road
Aldershot
Hants GU11 3HR
England

Ashgate Publishing Company
Suite 420
101 Cherry Street
Burlington, VT 05401-4405
USA

Ashgate website: http://www.ashgate.com

British Library Cataloguing in Publication Data
Polito, Mary
    Governmental arts in early Tudor England.—(Studies in Performance and early modern drama)
    1.English literature—Early modern, 1500–1700—History and criticism 2.Didactic literature, English—History and criticism 3.Great Britain—Politics and government—1509–1547
    I.Title
    820.9'358'09031

Library of Congress Cataloging-in-Publication Data
Polito, Mary, 1949–
    Governmental arts in early Tudor England / Mary Polito.
        p. cm.—(Studies in performance and early modern drama)
    Includes bibliographical references and index.
    ISBN 0-7546-3420-5 (alk. Paper)
        1. English drama—Early modern and Elizabethan, 1500–1600—history and criticism. 2. Politics and literature—Great Britain—History—16th century. 3. Political plays, English—History and criticism. 4. Politics in literature. I.Title. II.Series.

PR649.P6P65 2005
822'.309358—dc22

2004052543

ISBN 0 7546 3420 5

Printed in Great Britain by Antony Rowe Ltd, Chippenham, Wiltshire

STUDIES IN PERFORMANCE AND EARLY MODERN DRAMA

General Editor: Helen Ostovich, McMaster University

This series presents original research on theatre histories and performance histories; the time period covered is from about 1500 to the early 18th century. Studies in which women's activities are a central feature of discussion are especially of interest; this may include women as financial or technical support (patrons, musicians, dancers, seamstresses, wig-makers) or house support staff (e.g., gatherers), rather than performance per se. We also welcome critiques of early modern drama that take into account the production values of the plays and rely on period records of performance.

To Philip and Jeanne Polito

Contents

Preface

This book represents research that began as a doctoral dissertation; therefore many thanks are owed. I owe a great debt to my dissertation committee at York University: Ian Sowton, Marie-Christine Leps, Doug Freake and Doug Hay. They generously and with great wisdom guided my development as a reader of literature, theory and history. Linda Woodbridge was an encouraging and thought-provoking external reader and she generously advised a plan for development of the material that has influenced the shape of this book. From York, I also thank Heather Ross, James P. Carley, Yvonne Vera and Jennifer Henderson. I remember, with gratitude, my many mentors, colleagues and friends at Trent University, especially Zailig Pollock and Molly Blyth.

I am very grateful to the Department of English and the Faculty of Humanities at the University of Calgary, who had confidence in me and this research and who have supported the work in many ways. Jim Ellis, a friend and fellow student of the Renaissance at York, is now a cherished colleague and astute reader of my work at UofC. Among other UofC colleagues who deserve special thanks are Susan Bennett, Susan Rudy, Penny Farfan, Murray McGillivray, Lou Knafla Jacqueline Jenkins, Stephen Guy-Bray, Aruna Srivastiva, Doug Peers and Eric Savoy.

Some of this research has been presented as conference papers at University College, London, the University of Alberta and to meetings of the Canadian Society for Renaissance Studies and the Pacific Coast Conference on British Studies. I am grateful for the thoughtful responses of audiences in those venues. Material from chapter two originally appeared in *Mosaic* as "Wit, Will and Governance in Early Modern Legal Literature," Special Issue ADVERSARIA Literature and Law, Vol. 27.4: 15-34. A version of chapter four appeared as "Governing Bodies Tempering Tongues: Elizabeth Barton and Tudor Treason," in *Law and Literature: Current Legal Issues.* Volume 2. Eds. Michael Freeman and Andrew Lewis. Oxford: Oxford University Press, 1999. 603-21. I thank *Mosaic* and *Current Legal Issues* for permission to reprint this material. I have received financial support from the Social Sciences and Humanities Research Council, the Independent Order of the Daughters of the Empire, the University of Calgary Research Grants program, the University of Calgary Faculty of Humanities and the Killam Trust. At Ashgate thanks go to Erika Gaffney, Ann Donahue, Ann Newell, Pete Coles and Helen Ostovich. Invaluable assistance in the preparation of the manuscript came from Glenn Mielke, Amy Britton and Jennifer Keneyers.

My greatest friend and toughest interlocutor is Roz Kerr and I thank her for a thousand conversations. Among other friends and relatives who have sustained me over the last few years are Mary Lou Trinkwon, Lisa Lowe, Carl Trinkwon, Jane Doel, Kathy Polito, David Bateman, David Ramsden, Tiffany Neddow, Janice Grant and Tim Westbury. I thank my sisters Anne Polito, Maggie Fry and their families for their support and my daughters Annie Rogers (a fellow student of Foucault from whom I have learned a great deal) and Elizabeth Rogers (who packed up and moved west with me when she might have made other journeys). My parents, Jeanne and Phil Polito, have been nothing but loving and proud.

General Editor's Preface

Helen Ostovich,
McMaster University

Performance assumes a string of creative, analytical, and collaborative acts that, in defiance of theatrical ephemerality, live on through records, manuscripts, and printed books. The monographs and essay collections in this series offer original research which addresses theatre histories and performance histories in the context of the sixteenth and seventeenth century life. Of especial interest are studies in which women's activities are a central feature of discussion as financial or technical supporters (patrons, musicians, dancers, seamstresses, wig-makers, or 'gatherers'), if not authors or performers per se. Welcome too are critiques of early modern drama that not only take into account the production values of the plays, but also speculate on how intellectual advances or popular culture affect the theatre.

The series logo, selected by my colleague Mary V. Silcox, derives from Thomas Combe's duodecimo volume, *The Theater of Fine Devices* (London, 1592), Emblem VI, sig. B. The emblem of four masks has a verse which makes claims for the increasing complexity of early modern experience, a complexity that makes interpretation difficult. Hence the corresponding perhaps uneasy rise in sophistication:

Masks will be more hereafter in request,
And grow more deare than they did heretofore.

No longer simply signs of performance 'in play and iest', the mask has become the 'double face' worn 'in earnest' even by 'the best' of people, in order to manipulate or profit from the world around them. The books stamped with this design attempt to understand the complications of performance produced on stage and interpreted by the audience, whose experiences outside the theatre may reflect the emblem's argument:

Most men do vse some colour'd shift
For to conceal their craftie drift.

Centuries after their first presentations, the possible performance choices and meanings they engender still stir the imaginations of actors, audiences, and readers of early plays. The products of scholarly creativity in this series, I hope, will also stir imaginations to new ways of thinking about performance.

Introduction

Minds of State and States of Mind

How to govern oneself, how to be governed, how to govern others, by whom the people will accept being governed, how to become the best possible governor — all these problems, in their multiplicity and intensity, seem to me to be characteristic of the sixteenth century.
(Michel Foucault, 'Governmentality' 87–8)

The King's most Royal Majesty...cannot...tolerate or suffer any such ordinance as might by any mean hinder the advancement...of the Knowledge of the seven arts liberal...as be expedient to be learned for the conservation of...good policies and the breeding of discrete and prudent personages to serve and administer in his commonwealth.
('An Act concerning the exoneration of Oxford & Cambridge from payment of their first fruits and tenth,' *Statutes of the Realm* 27 Hen. VIII, c 38)[1]

Thomas Elyot's 1539 *The Castel of Health* presents to his English readers the Galenic theory of the four humours (the choleric, melancholic, phlegmatic and sanguine) as causative agents in human behaviour and health. While reading an excerpt from this text with my sixteenth–century literature class, an article appeared in a local daily about the use of the same model for categorizing and managing difficult co–workers. The director of the Petroleum Institute for Continuing Education in our Canadian prairie city offered a 'seven step program' to deal with difficult employees.[2] A forensic tool prescribes that if co–workers are 'dominating, directing, decisive, driving, demanding, determined, doer[s],' they should be deemed choleric; if 'cautious, competent, compliant, calculating, careful, contemplative,' they must be melancholic; if 'steady, stable, shy, security–oriented, submissive,' phlegmatic; and if 'inspiring, influencing, interactive, interested in people,' sanguine. Following from this diagnosis by alliteration, formulas are offered for dealing with each of the types and the director concludes: 'If situations with people are properly resolved, the difficult person will ultimately feel important, understood and appreciated.' Thus managers and workers are urged to understand themselves and their workplace in terms of personalities, feelings and relationships and to invest their soul in the company store.

When I brought the article to the attention of the class, several students, to my surprise, knew of the humours in a self–help context. One had encountered the scheme while working part–time for a major department store. Another related that a friend recommends this learning as a form of alternative medicine because she does not trust the medical establishment. I offered that while the theory of the humours is now considered unscientific learning, it had been endorsed by the early modern medical establishment. On the other hand, in Elyot's day it was often women medical practitioners who were the empiricists, devising skills and remedies from experiment and observation. While such practices may appear rational to us, they were prohibited by legislation in the reign of Elyot's employer, Henry VIII. And today, despite their bad science, the humours have been legitimated once more in institutional contexts. Such are the vicissitudes of knowledge and power.

But why the humours as an egalitarian form of self–help in the development of a workforce in a late twentieth–century context? In fact a perusal of Human Resources material employed for such purposes reveals that the tools of this trade are randomly selected: social scientific, pseudo–scientific; eastern, western; in this case new age, and as such old age. What is at stake for the corporations and self–help writers who are encouraging such behaviour modification is clearly not the truth told about the nature of humans. Rather, what is important is the efficacy of the method and the method involves exhorting workers to believe in and pursue their own empowerment and fulfillment through work.

In spite of the eclecticism of the new managerial discourse and the historical distance between Elyot and the educators at the Petroleum Institute, I suggest that there is a logic in the revival of this ancient Greek diagnostic and transformational tool in the periods we name early and late modernity. *Governmental Arts in Early Tudor England* argues that it is in the early Tudor century that we can first locate secular strategies by which English subjects were exhorted to know themselves through expertise in order to succeed in the public sphere. The new sixteenth–century 'human sciences,' as represented by books such as Elyot's *The Castel of Health* and his highly popular *The Boke Named the Governour*, counseled civil subjects to understand and then to manage themselves and others for the promise of happiness and profit. The mode of leadership and rule at work in the detailed designs for governing in both the reign of Henry VIII and in the sphere of human resources management of our time is essentially liberal, in that the primary object of governance in each case is that paradoxical entity, the free but self–regulating individual.

Not that Tudor England was a liberal society. Rather, I find that in the English experiments in new and secular forms of government in the 1520s and 30s, we can locate winning and losing experiments in the intimate governance of individuals and the technical rule of populations that anticipate and indeed provide the conditions of possibility for the rise of liberalism in the centuries that follow. As Jennifer Henderson explains:

> In liberal societies, the activity of government forms the practical underside of liberalism's avowed philosophical foundations of liberty, equality, and freedom...[and includes] [s]chemes for inculcating fitting dispositions and for shaping forms of subjectivity that are merely presupposed by the theories of contract and individual right of classical liberal political philosophy. (19)

The 1536 statute cited above in my epigraph — 'An Act concerning the exoneration of Oxford & Cambridge from payment of their first fruits and tenth' — provides an Henrician example of the liberal impulse to govern more by governing less. Introduced by a two thousand word preamble, the act promises to release the major educational institutions from their obligation to pay taxes in the form of 'said first fruits and yerely rent of the tenth,' formerly sent to the Pope but since 1534 to the King (600). The tax break is tied to curricular reform towards particular and pragmatic ends, however. Oxford, Cambridge and several colleges are told to desist in their preoccupation with the obscure problems of the scholastics and canon law and instead to stress the 'seven arts liberal,' the trivium and the quadrivium (599). This emphasis has a very explicit utility in the 'reviving and quickening of the courage of Students to the intent they should the more joyously and gladly bend their wits and wholly give themselves to the attaining of learning and knowledge' (599). 'Youth and good wit[s]' will be educated in a 'virtue and learning' that will be acceptable to God, a source of joy and prosperity for the student governor and 'profitable for the King's public wealth' (599). This student body will provide the wealth of their own expertise as they are transformed into a class of civil managers who will themselves, the act tells us, 'breed' future governors, a full complement of 'discrete and prudent personages to serve and administer in his commonwealth' (599). These civilly prudent governors were to be a product of 'good policy' just as they in turn would serve in the 'conservation and maintenance of policy and common justice' (599). The King governs more by governing less when he cuts taxes but also when he disperses the sites of governance. While the institutions of governance in the Henrician period are ever more centralized, the actual practices of governing move centrifugally into the sphere of education, into increasingly complex and ever more rationalized bureaucratic structures and indeed into the private place where subjects and governors were to govern themselves.[3]

This new mode of governance comes with the offer of freedom. Henrician students, the statute implies, were to receive some of the financial benefit provided by the remission of the tax. Troubled by hardship, the statute explains, such students might have 'withdraw[n] and give[n] their minds to...other things and fantasies,' not expedient for the health of the kingdom (599). Through the efficacy of this law, however, students will be freed from the 'tenuity of living' and this freedom will allow them to concentrate more fully on their studies (599). Henrician student–governors, like our contemporary petroleum industry employees, will achieve and utilize expertise as they themselves become managers of human resources, ready to take part in the 'inculcation of fitting dispositions' in themselves and others, to the promised end of further liberty and both personal and corporate satisfaction.

Governmentality Studies

In the last several years, a body of scholarship has been devoted to an analysis of such modes of governance. Governmentality studies have built on the later work of

Michel Foucault to explore how we have come to be governed in ways we do not recognize because such governance does not operate, in any simple way, against our freedom. Primarily based in the social sciences, these studies argue that a new approach to the present and its history is required in order to account for the decline and perhaps even death of the welfare state in the west during the last twenty years. The Marxist narrative of capitalist domination versus the proletariat freedom of futurity, for example, does not provide a full and adequate account of the complexities of 'late capitalism.' Foucault's lecture 'Governmentality,' given at the College de France in 1978 and published in English in 1979 in the journal *Ideology and Consciousness*, was, argues Mitchell Dean, a 'startling development' that modeled an approach capable of addressing the problem of our present (*Governmentality: Power and Rule in Modern Society* 1).[4] In his essay 'Governmentality', as well as in 'Omnes et Singulatim: Towards a Criticism of "Political Reason,"' 'The Subject and Power,' 'Two Lectures,' and sections of *The History of Sexuality Volume I: An Introduction*, Foucault sketched out a grid by which we might begin to understand governance in a very broad sense, beyond the juridical modes of what he named 'sovereignty' and the regulatory mechanisms of 'discipline.' Governmentality scholars are building on this work to describe the present proliferation of a form of neo–liberalism that appears to have colonized thinking on both the left and the right and operates within and beyond the sphere of partisan politics and state forms of rule (such as the business self–help industry).[5]

While sixteenth–century governors incorporated classical and Christian epistemologies and practices into their design for the intimate governance of the individual in the name of freedom, we have returned to such rule by way of the social sciences that arose in the nineteenth century. We have come to understand ourselves in terms of a set of surfaces and depths and narratives of oppression/repression/liberation that are developed by way of often bowdlerized notions of Freudian science. In recent years, such romance narratives and the therapeutic practices which they enable have proliferated dramatically and can be found in such diverse sites as social service directives, international policy and, as we have seen, corporate professional development schemes. While the free and self–actualizing individual is invoked as the principal site of governance, the same individual is deemed entirely responsible for the ills that might befall him or her. Increasingly, unemployment, poverty and even poor health are figured as solely personal failures rather than political or structural ones.[6] This is the promised end of a liberal rule that would govern without governing. It is one contention of this book that the neo–liberal governmentality of today shares with the earliest manifestations of this mode of rule in the sixteenth century an orientation to the individual as the principle governmental object as well as a certain promiscuity of techniques and domains of operation.[7]

Sixteenth–century Governmentality

Foucault provides us with a useful narrative[8] within which to consider the interrelation of identity, freedom, government and ethics.[9] In this account, "sovereignty" is figured as the juridical and military form of rule that arose in the medieval period; established by the shedding of blood and transmitted through bloodlines, sovereignty maintains 'a right of seizure: of things, time, bodies, and ultimately life itself' (*History of Sexuality* 136). Henry VIII is most remembered in popular culture as just such a bloody and absolute sovereign, although that is not the unsubtle aspect of the reign that is my primary focus. The "disciplinary" society emerges in the generalized ordering of social life, in the production of habituated and passive bodies. Early modern disciplinary measures are signified vividly in the imperative that women of all classes ever busy themselves with the complex techniques of the distaff, the spindle, the needle and the thimble, not only as a contribution to the economy of the household and as an assurance of their virtue, but also as a form of temperance that would accrue, conduct manuals suggest, to the strength of the realm. By contrast, "governmentality" refers to the ways in which theories of corporate entities such as the state or the city, along with accounts of human nature, serve the 'how to' of a rationalized, future–oriented and utopian mode of government. Governmentality studies do not focus on over–arching ideologies but rather on the local details, the heterogenous modes of understanding that inform the day–to–day human practices designed to 'conduct the conduct' of people and populations. The theories and practices with which such strategies are entangled often live beneath the roar of war and religious schism, though they are not unaffected by them. Thus, for example, we find in sixteenth–century Europe, across the boundaries erected by incendiary differences of faith and across the borders of enemies, an exchange of ideas about managing both the poor and the bureaucracy of workers charged with governing them.

Foucault, as my epigraph demonstrates, finds in his studies of the European sixteenth century an intensification of thought about and experiments in government.[10] He observes that 'governance as a general problem seems...to explode in the sixteenth century' ('Governmentality' 87). His contention is that early modern Europeans were heir to two models of governing that become linked for the first time in this period in new governmental practices. The first, from antiquity, offers as its object the free 'city–citizen;' the second appropriates from Christianity the pastoral 'shepherd–flock' relationship. Each model defines an ethical orientation between those who have and those who need. The ancient city–citizen regarded himself as possessing rights and responsibilities; the former involving his freedom, the latter his ethical obligation to temper his character in accordance with the needs of the polity and to give freely in some way to the city. The Christian pastoral model taught that the rich need the poor as much as the poor need the rich, since through the poor the rich receive grace for giving alms and thereby earn their way to heaven.

In each case, there is a differently articulated, certainly imperfect, yet nevertheless ethical imperative by which elites were enjoined to act in the interest of others. Governmentality studies examine the ethical implications of the union of city–citizen and shepherd/flock governmental practices, a union that Foucault describes as potentially 'demonic' in its modern state form, in that the ethical imperatives of each mode of governing have become obscured ('Omnes' 239).[11]

The gender and class divisions inherent in the classical city–citizen model of course remain viable in the early modern European context. A way of understanding such divisions, suggests Foucault, is to see them as working to divide city–citizens from those judged incapable of managing their freedom. At the same time, the citizen/subject is divided from him or herself 'in so far as the condition of mature and responsible use of freedom entails a domination of aspects of the self' (Dean 133). Pastoral rule is intimate in its practices; it is the rule that keeps close watch, that will shepherd the domains of self–rule. The shepherd governor (whether Christian or secular) must know both the flock as a totality and each individual sheep, its propensity and weakness and its inner existence. Moreover, he must devise particular strategies in relation to such knowledge, the strategies of daily rule: the calculation of risk, the management of 'men in their relations, their links...wealth, resources...customs, habits, ways of acting and thinking...accidents and misfortunes, such as famine, epidemics, death.' ('Governmentality' 93). Belonging to the good citizen flock provides more than the amelioration of danger, however. Governmentality comes with what Colin Gordon calls 'startlingly ambitious promises' of prosperity and happiness (12). In the sixteenth century, it is significant that the promised Eden was to be achieved in this life, rather than the next.

As Foucault describes the complication of government processes from the sixteenth century: 'one has a triangle, sovereignty–discipline–government, which has as its primary target the population and as its essential mechanism the apparatuses of security' ('Governmentality' 102). These modes of rule each employs the law in distinctive ways. Foucault observes that while law and sovereignty are "absolutely inseparable," governmentality instead employs tactics, "even...using laws themselves as tactics — to arrange things in such a way that, through a certain number of means, such and such ends may be achieved....the instruments of government, instead of being laws, now come to be a range of multiform tactics" ('Governmentality' 95). Alan Hunt views early modern European sumptuary laws as being such governmental tactics, in that they were enacted with 'little or no attention to the possibility of enforcement' (Hunt, "Governing the City: Liberalism and Early Modern Modes of Governance" 181). Rather, he suggests, they were 'a form of public exhortation' designed to address a variety of concerns about governing (181). Such a move is exemplified in the "Exoneration" statute as well; it is a law that is not punitive nor preventative but rather productive in its aims and it aims to produce a governing class. It will do so personage by personage, linking the identity and cultivated qualities of governing subjects to their profession. As such, the law is also individualizing in its strategies. I attend in particular to similar instances in which the law is employed as government by indirection and to the novel and various ways in which modes of rule take as their object of government the individual.

Importantly, sixteenth–century governors are not excluded from the government that they set in motion. They must be especially self–knowledgeable and prudent and they must also work hard to appear as good shepherd governors, no matter their sphere of activity. As such, the monarch, as represented in the Exoneration statute, is to stand as an exemplar to the 'youth and good wit[s]' who would benefit from his educational reform:

> His Majesty of his most abundant and special grace, ha[s] conceived such hearty love and tender affection to the continuance and augmentation of all honest and virtuous learning arts and sciences, wherewith it hath pleased almighty God so abundantly to endow His Highness as in Knowledge and wisdom he far exceedith any of his most noble progenitors. (599)

Just as a king is a better king for having loved learning, so will lesser governors be better governors for their exposure to the humanist curriculum. Thus, the ever more absolutist Tudor monarch is figured in government discourse as not different in kind but rather in degree from his objects of governance. Henry VIII needs subjects and governors like himself, sovereign masters of themselves, subjects who can be made to bear the burden of history. In England, as elsewhere in Europe, ideas about civil prudence and the ideal governor are developed in opposition to Machiavelli's *The Prince*. Fairly or not, Machiavelli's prince comes to function as the foil of the good and prudent governor, the governor who is to be profoundly concerned with his own character, with the 'oeconomy' of the household and with an increasingly complex and technical form of state rule. I show that in the English case, *The Prince* becomes one of many warning tales about the true tendencies of overly ambitious men, tendencies each man must account for and temper. Yet, as Henry signals in his statute, the state needs ambitious men to serve in the newly rationalized bureaucracy. Men are exhorted both to be ambitious and to generate and conform to prudential checks on that ambition.

To describe early modern state forms of governmentality, Foucault employs the phrases 'reason of state' and the 'theory of police' and each phrase proves resonant in the early sixteenth–century English case. 'Reason of state' is that which understands the nation as a functional entity and 'the doctrine of police defines the nature of the objects of the state's rational activity; it defines the nature of the aims it pursues, the general form of the instruments involved' ('Omnes' 242). Foucault finds the earliest fully realized 'theory of police' to have been developed in Germany in the early seventeenth century and named at the time 'Polizeiwissenschaft.' Colin Gordon suggests that 'Polizeiwissenschaft' might better have been translated into English as 'policy' rather than 'police' (10) and in fact the *Oxford English Dictionary*, in defining 'police,' collates its earliest English usage with 'policy' and 'civil administration' and finds that usage first in the 1530s. One of the earliest usages cited by the *OED*, in fact, is found in the "Exoneration" statute. What I have modernized as 'policy' is rendered in the original printed text alternately as 'polices' in the case of the learning that will conserve 'good polices' and as 'pollicie' in the case of the liberal arts that will conserve and maintain 'policy and common justice.'[12] While the Henrician experiments in policy/policing are in no way fully realized, nor even particularly successful, they are nevertheless instructive in their novelty, in their use of representational strategies, in the responses they evoked in their objects of governance and in terms of what they make possible in the future.

As "policy/police" comes into the language to describe the novel union of thought and action to the end of governance, so does the word 'state' itself, as the description of a political entity, emerge in the period. As David S. Kastan has observed, the first English usage of the word 'state' as '[a] particular form of polity or government' occurs in Thomas Starkey's 1538 *Dialogue Between Pole and Lupset* (Kastan 270). This text is one of several books of the 1530s on the nature of government that would be offered to the king as a kind of 'job talk' (in this case for both Starkey himself and his soon–to–fall patron Cardinal Pole). Starkey anatomizes the 'common weal' by way of the metaphor of the body, even likening the problems of England to humoral imbalances. The *OED* finds a novel use of the term 'state' in his figuration of the perfect commonweal as occurring when 'the multytude of pepul & polytyke body ys helthy beutyful & strong...ther ys the veray & true commyn wele, ther ys the most properouse & perfayt state, that in any cuntrey cyte or towne by pollycy & wisdom may be stablyshyd & set' (Starkey 38). Here is the utopian vision that policy would achieve.

Starkey employs another novel usage of the word 'state' in his dialogue, during a discussion of the nature of 'prosperity.' While the Lupset persona appeals to the traditional notion of prosperity as a deterrent to heavenly reward, Starkey's Pole offers the argument that 'When prosperyte ys wel vsyd, hyt ys a mean to set mannys mynd in that state, wherby he schal attayne hyar felycyte' (Starkey 30). The *OED* categorizes this usage of 'state' under the definition, '[a] condition (of mind or feeling); the mental or emotional condition in which a person finds himself at a particular time.' Starkey suggests that the right use of wealth will provide the conditions in which an embodied nation state with 'states of mind' properly disposed will generate mutual 'helth.' Minds of state seek states of mind for mutual reward.

Governmental Arts

This book presents a historical argument about the development of new forms of government in the sixteenth century, as revealed in forms of representation designed to 'conduct conduct,' often by indirection. As a literary scholar, I aim as well to contribute to the now substantial body of scholarship that provides a new valuation of the Henrician period, not only as it has been valued in the past, that is as the precursor to 'the great Elizabethan age.' As Peter C. Herman observed in 1994, in his introduction to the first anthology of essays on Henrician literature, 'Even though practically all of the older constructions of the Renaissance have been challenged [in the last thirty years] ...the dismissal of pre–Elizabethan literature still holds, as does...[the] view that it represents the inept first stirrings of what will later bloom into the glories of Elizabethan and Jacobean verse' (4). I work to foreground the complex cultural context out of which this literature emerged and to demonstrate that the interrelated themes which have engaged historicist literary critics in their studies of the Elizabethan and Jacobean periods — gender and politics, erotic friendship, class conflicts, the birth of imperialist imperatives and the rise of self–fashioning — first emerge in their early modern forms in the early sixteenth century and are compelling and important in that context as well.

Foucault's scholarship has certainly influenced early modern literary studies, most often in the service of New Historicism and studies of the Shakespearean stage. The spectacles of sovereignty and the surveillance and regulation of discipline, however, have been of more interest than the micro techniques by which the nascent liberal subject and populations were managed. An exception is David Glimp's important study of governmentality, population and subjectivity: *Increase and Multiply: Governing Cultural Reproduction in Early Modern England.*[13] Glimp's historical focus is on the many novel strategies and technologies developed in the sixteenth and seventeenth centuries to enumerate people for the purpose of governing them; he observes that 'Foucault's concern is to understand the very terms and practices through which the population comes to be available as a way of understanding the world, and as a way of conceptualizing the work of government' (xvi). Glimp also articulates the activities and techniques involved in 'making up' the right kind of subjects, with the aim of assembling an English population from which the wrong kinds of people would be excluded.[14] He examines such governmental strategies in a wide range of political documents as well as in the work of Sidney, Shakespeare and Milton in order to consider 'how early modern literary practice acknowledges, contributes to, resists, or disavows the dynamics that have as their unanticipated and unplanned outcome the development of population as a theoretical and practical construct' (xii). *Governmental Arts* identifies similar modes of understanding as they emerge in the 1520s and 30s. This interest in the new totality that was England is revealed in the early sixteenth century in novel attempts at census taking; in utopian visions such as Thomas More's; in the struggle over and the work of such words as commonweal, public weal, realm, empire, body politic, nation and John Bale's beleaguered and feminine dramatic character 'England' from his interlude *King John*. Nevertheless, I contend that the early sixteenth–century experiments in the government of the individual are particularly intense and productive (though certainly not always in the way governors hoped), and that the government of the individual contributes to the creation of conditions within which the government of populations can be thought about and acted upon.

I also argue that drama and spectacle are revealed as more than powerful tools of government and dissenters. Government discourse reveals the assumption that its objects of government are 'sovereign' enough to deploy the kinds of self–temperance and circumspection required for the security of the realm. The same subject, however, will be deep and complex enough to alienate intention from action and, in the interest of liberty, to 'act' as another if necessary. I show how performance is thus figured as the surface beneath which subjects learn to know and hide their 'true natures,' free from the ever watchful eyes of the intrusive king and his administrators. Tudor governmentality's notion of the self–conscious, self–divided, but free subject/actor is therefore both the condition for and the limit of liberal government.[15]

The first chapter approaches the topic of change in the 1530s, both from the perspective of the debates on this topic among historians and in relation to my investigation of the governmental arts. The chapter title, '"That lovely bond": Binding England,' derives its name from a rationalization of the relationship between nation and subject found in *An Exhortation to Styre All Englyshe Men to the Defence of Theyr Countreye* by Richard Morison, a prolific government propagandist whose works are put to use in each chapter of this book. Morison instructs his audience in how to avoid breaking 'that lovely bonde, which god hath...sette in nature' to unite subject and sovereign 'in justice, temperaunce, modestie, and honest lybertie.' He maintains that the king has heroically liberated his people from that unlovely bond to Catholicism, 'the chyenges, that our soules laye tyed in, slaves and bond to Romishe tyranny'(56). The King's 'lovely bond' links rhetorically the 'all and each' in a totalized 'flock' of now liberated subjects. We will see as well that the metaphor of the shepherd king and his flock is employed by both Thomas More and Morison as a means to describe the nature of that bond.

The forces of totalization can be seen as Henry VIII declares in an Act of Parliament in 1533 that Rome has no further right of appeal to any jurisdiction in England and that 'this realm of England is an empire,' thereby defining England as both a discrete nation and the centre of an imperialist imperative (Elton, *The Tudor Constitution* 344). In the same period, the ancient concept of 'commonwealth' is newly employed to define the amalgamation of secular and spiritual jurisdictions under the 'monarch in parliament.' Both individualizing and totalizing strategies are accomplished in the ascendance of the conciliar courts — the court of Chancery takes on novel functions and the court of Requests and the Star Chamber are created. These courts dealt with complaints on a case–by–case basis and developed a wide jurisdiction. Star Chamber developed its jurisdiction by defining the category of 'misdemeanours,' many of which involved the prosecution of speech acts and criminal intent: '[c]riminal libel, forgery, perjury, subornation of perjury, conspiracy and attempts to commit crimes, were largely the creation of the Star Chamber' (Baker, *Introduction* 137). Chancery, in particular, finds a swelling jurisdiction in property disputes as the Chancellor, no longer necessarily a cleric, appropriates for civil purposes what had been seen historically as 'a transcendent form of justice' functioning as 'the temporal counterpart of the confessional' (Baker, *Introduction* 122–3). I detail these juridical, administrative and social strategies by which the new regime aimed to enter into a personal relationship with each English subject, in what could be seen as an appropriation and redeployment of relations of feudal fealty for national purposes.

Chapter two is a study of humanism and governance. English humanism quickly abandoned its vision of a united Europe under the rule of an enlightened prince and began to occupy itself with serving secular rule by conceptualizing the nature of the objects to be governed and the methods for such governance. Women and men were bidden to take part in the domestication of women and in what we could call the 'publication' of men, as men were fitted for public life in the newly rationalized Tudor bureaucracy. I attend to the discourses produced by and about humanism upon which the Henrician administration could draw, beginning with humanism's account of itself as a liberationist, transformational and democratising movement and proceeding with recent commentary on this narrative. Critics such as Lisa Jardine, Victoria Kahn, Lorna Hutson and Alan Stewart suggest that humanism should be approached, not by way of its accounts of itself, but by way of 'the social relations that it facilitates, maintains and transforms' (Stewart xx). In this light, I examine self–help manuals specifically for governors and would–be governors and find that essential to the arguments of such works as Elyot's *The Boke Named the Governor* and Christopher St German's *Doctor and Student* is the premise that masculinity desperately needs temperance but that fortunately men are governable.

Thus, one of the relationships the English humanists worked to encourage was between men and their masculinity. Understanding their weakness, men would learn to be 'circumspect' about what they show to the world of that weakness, and work to both transform and perform their natures. Just as men wrote self–help books for other men, so was male friendship conscripted to the end of checking excess male ambition. And just as women were conscripted as governors of governors, so was a proper orientation to abstract notions of the 'feminine' essential to the tempering of masculinity. Indeed the feminine is presented in several documents as the tempering influence itself. Gender is thus revealed as a specific rationale for the understanding of the self and as one crucial element through which management is made possible. Men were trained to manage first and foremost themselves; then their peers through the virtue of 'amity;' then their wives as managers of their households; and finally the 'public weal,' as Elyot conceives of the totality of England. Through all of these complex forms of government, the subject would be freed from what Elyot calls the 'bondage' of his own nature (*The Boke Named the Governor* 120).

Chapter three argues for a distinction between the late medieval morality play, which was interested in the Christian struggle for salvation, and the 'secular interlude.' In the latter, the allegorized characters are virtues and vices related more to humanist and secular values than to theological ones; there is a change of emphasis from sin to civil imprudence; and a deflection of concern about cause and effect from the next life to this life. These works appear to fulfill a variety of functions. As historians of the theatre have demonstrated, many are topical editorials on current political issues. As St German and Elyot's male readers are exhorted to accept counsel from other men, so even is the king, and these plays functioned as such counsel. I demonstrate that they also generate and contest the kinds of disciplinary and governmental imperatives that are found in the juridical maneuvers and the conduct books, making and mocking the links among self–temperance, freedom and prosperity.

A representative selection of such interludes written or played between 1516 and 1538 provides a mirror onto the multiple anxieties of subjects and government. The first such play — *Magnyfycence* — is by the former tutor of the king and poet laureate John Skelton and the last I consider are by the rabid reformer John Bale — *The Three Lawes* and *King John*. These products of humanism provide advice to the prince and demonstrate the earthly rewards of a self–governed life. They also warn of the temptations of the senses and the flesh. Ironically, not the least of this drama's worries is a concern with the ability of the subject to dissimulate, to 'act' as another. Actors work to show that actors are dangerous, claiming that the flesh is a liability to the state in theatrical pieces that are full of titillation and sensory pleasures. We see such a conundrum when John Skelton's character 'Counterfeit Countenance' offers a 94 line catalogue of dangerous dissimulators (*Magnificence* 417–72). The theatrical text and its performance thus prove to be slippery mediums for these playwright/courtiers, who present 'acting' as a grave threat to the nation. And while these plays, without exception, attempt to warn their audiences about the dangers of carnality, the contradiction between their didactic and their theatrical imperatives finally renders both theatre and sex tremendously compelling, inevitably interlinked and almost impossible to resist.

The final chapter evaluates how new strategies of government in the Henrician period affected the lives of women in particular ways. Through juridical means, the range of women's freedom was curtailed and redirected. In fact, however, women's freedom within the domestic sphere was necessary to particular forms of government. Indeed, women and marriage are conscripted to the project of governing men. And despite efforts to privatize women in the domestic sphere, women figured prominently in the political life of the nascent nation state, from the parade of queens and unwanted princesses to the mystics, prophets and rebels actively protesting against government imperatives.

I look closely at one particular case, that of Elizabeth Barton, the nun or Holy Maid of Kent. The extant narratives about Barton exist in a wide range of government documents, (including Richard Morison's nasty, anti–Catholic rant *Apomaxis Calumniarum*). I argue that her case, which generated so much government anxiety about treason and the word, allows us to observe the emergence of the conditions within which the early modern juridical and 'sovereign' subject was to be limited as a thinking, speaking and acting being. While Barton speaks from a pre– and anti–sovereigntist position, offering ritualized performatives saturated in history, the king attempts to sever her speech from the long history of English political prophecy by citing her words as individual acts emanating from a sovereign, autonomous, treasonous personage. The council of justices assembled by Henry, however, refused to grant that Barton's words were treasonous and the King was forced to turn to Parliament for a Bill of Attainder against her.

In the preamble to that Act of Parliament, Barton is accused of performing the role of a saint and prophet. While she presented herself as an instrument of divine communication for the throngs who gathered to see and hear her, she and her followers are accused of treasonous duplicity, of criminal 'feigning' (a key word in the Barton archive) — in short, of acting. In that this "performance" presented a great threat to the security of the realm, the theatrical is granted great potency in the official record, demonstrating how a kind of agency can arise unpredictably out of limits. Barton's case reveals the irony in which the mark of an individualization that allows for the prosecution of speech acts in treason law becomes the ability to suppress one's identity and to take on the trappings of another.

In explaining his approach to history, Foucault suggests, 'Let us give the name genealogy to the union of erudite knowledge and local memories which allows us to establish a historical knowledge of struggles and to make use of this knowledge tactically today' ('Two Lectures' 83). Thus, doing history in governmentality studies means writing a 'genealogy' or 'history of the present,' in that there is an acknowledgement that the questions we ask of history can be usefully rooted in our own 'problematics' around ethics and justice and freedom, that every present moment provides, even demands, a new perspective on the past. There is, however, often a dearth of direct evidence of 'local memories' and counter–knowledges to be had when one attempts early period study. This is certainly true for the Henrician period and for the case of Elizabeth Barton in particular. While there are references to many documents generated about her by her and her followers, such documents were banned and burned; not one remains for our perusal. Nevertheless, through close attention to the strategies of the governmental arts, as evidenced in these state papers we have been left, I work to show that we can still learn something about the 'counter–knowledges' and tactics of those subjects who engaged with and contested their roles as satellite governors of themselves and each other.

Berthelet's Lucretia

I conclude this introductory discussion by drawing attention to the image that appears in the frontispiece of this book: the ideal, though sexually violated, ancient Roman wife Lucrece, pictured in the moment of her self–annihilation. In that this image is the printer's shingle of Thomas Berthelet, Henry VIII's official printer from 1530, it literally hovers over the acts of political communication in the period.[16] The first title attributed to Berthelet is the highly popular *Lyttylto[n] Tenures*, which appears with the following inscription: 'In edibus Thome Bertheleti Reg. impressoris, in Fletestrete prope aquagiumsitis, sub signo Lucrecie Romane.' Indeed, Henry Plomer claims that the shop was itself call 'the Lucrece" (*Wynkyn de Worde & his Contemporaries* 179). This evocative Lucrece figure witnesses the flow from Berthelet's shop of mass printings of propagandist pamphlets, proclamations, circular letters, sets of injunctions, sermons and statutes themselves with their polemical preambles. But what did this image mean and what governance could it accomplish in the early Tudor context?

I suggest that one way that the Tudor Lucretia can be understood is by way of Stephanie Jed's argument about the function of the Lucrece narrative in early modern Florentine political discourse. In *Chaste Thinking: The Rape of Lucretia and the Birth of Humanism*, Jed demonstrates how a group of fourteenth–century Florentine civic authorities appropriated the quasi–historical Roman narrative of the 'rape of Lucrece' in order to suggest an ideological connection between these Florentines and the Brutus of that story — the founder of Roman republicanism. Raped by the son of the tyrannical emperor Tarquin (who was inflamed by the obvious chastity of the Roman wife as he observed her weaving), Lucrece lives to tell the story to her male relatives and then falls on her knife, annihilating her dishonour with herself. Brutus and her menfolk oust the Tarquins, declare Rome a republic and thus liberate all Romans from tyranny. Putting to use the rich etymology of the word 'chaste' Jed links the word's obvious reference to sexual value and its distant Indo–European root (skeri–) 'meaning to cut, separate, sift.' The famous knife, employed by Lucrece in the enactment of her self–sacrifice, is linked by Jed to many kinds of severance and 'castigation,' the modus operandi she names as symptomatic of the humanist enterprise. 'Chaste thinking' is the figure of rarefaction and division that spawned the humanist disciplines themselves and which serves to delimit the function of writing and authorship. Such modes of thought, Jed argues, are necessary to the project of state–making.[17] Jed sees the knife of Lucrece as the figure of 'chaste thinking' as the story is cut off from the woman who told it and transformed into a political narrative to drive the republican impulse. 'Humanism itself,' Jed concludes, 'is an effect of chaste thinking' (8).

Presiding over the government's print shop in the English 1530s, Lucrece certainly stands for Jed's chastenings and dividing practices. The virtuous, disciplined weaver represents the model of household economy upon which the state was to build itself. She, like the Tudor housewife, can also be read as an ideologically motivated alibi for certain acts that might otherwise be construed as ambitious or ethically questionable.[18] But Berthelet's Lucrece is also a figure of liberty. Her willing and very classical Roman self–sacrifice for the honour of the family is a performance of the autonomous, free, city–citizen self that this government needs. The iconographic Lucretia thus stands not only for the sacrifice of women within patriarchal ideology; she also enacts a complex of government by which men and women were to manage self, household and each other for the good of all. And by providing Rome with the justification for the expulsion of a tyrannical, perhaps to the English Machiavellian, ruler, Lucrece warns even supreme governors themselves to follow her model, to be shepherds of the political experiments in which they find themselves.[19] Thus, when we find the image standing as a frontispiece in the Morison pamphlet about Elizabeth Barton, it points ironically to the limitation of sovereign rule.

As a model for the practice of self–castigation in the service of liberty, the image of Lucrece is a governmental art. I name as governmental arts those similar forms of representation (whether printed word, visual image, theatrical performance, spectacle or public address) that aim to conduct conduct and to produce 'personages' (as the 'Exoneration' statute puts it). Berthelet's books make promises and provide technique and Lucretia exhorts the heroic action of the free self. I will show, however, that these governmental arts did not necessarily determine the kinds of conduct that they had in mind. As Nikolas Rose suggests, while governmentality 'multiplies the points at which the citizen has to play his or her part in the games that govern him...it also multiplies the points at which citizens are able to refuse, contest, challenge those demands' (xxiii). Both small acts and large scale struggles illustrate this point. The representational armature employed by the rebels in the self–named 'Pilgrimage of Grace' and by Barton the prophet of Tudor doom, for example, reveals the sophistication of such subjects, and in particular their understanding of the religious, political and social implications of this new complex of government.

Notes

1. I have modernized the spelling and expanded the contractions from *Statutes of the Realm Printed by Command of His Majesty King George the Third in Pursuance of an Address of the House of Commons of Great Britain from the Original Records and Authentic Manuscripts* (London: Dawson of Pall Mall, 1963. Reprint. Originally published: London: G. Eyre and A. Strahan, 1810–1828).
2. See Vicki Barnett, 'How to Deal with Difficult People,' *Calgary Herald* 4 Sept. 1999: WS1.
3. The instrumental nature of the links between humanism and government in the sphere of education has been well recognized by such studies as Joan Simon's *Education and Society in Tudor England* (Cambridge: Cambridge UP, 1966) and Michael Van Cleave Alexander's *The Growth of English Education: 1438–1648* (University Park, Pennsylvania: Pennsylvania State UP, 1990).
4. I refer to both Foucault's essay 'Governmentality" and to Mitchell Dean's book, *Governmentality: Power and Rule in Modern Society* (London: Sage, 1999).
5. On this point, see the introduction to *Foucault and Political Reason: Liberalism, Neo–liberalism and Rationalities of Government*, by the editors, Andrew Barry, Thomas Osborne and Nikolas Rose, (Chicago: U of Chicago P, 1996) 1–18.
6. See Alan Hunt's recent *Governing Morals: A Social History of Moral Regulation* (Cambridge: Cambridge UP, 1999). For Hunt's work in the early modern period, see *Governance of the Consuming Passions: a History of Sumptuary Law* (New York: St. Martin's Press, 1996).
7. The business self–help industry certainly makes frequent use of early modern model governors. Shakespeare's model leaders have spawned an industry and Queen Elizabeth I is herself presented as an exemplar in Alan Axelrod's *Elizabeth I CEO: Strategic Lessons from the Leader Who Built an Empire* (Paramus, New Jersey: Prentice Hall Press, 2000). For examples of Shakespearean self–help, see Norman Augustine and Kenneth Adelman, *Shakespeare in Charge: the Bard's Guide to Leading and Succeeding on the*

Business Stage (New York: Hyperion, 1999); Paul Corrigan, *Shakespeare on Management: Leadership Lessons for Today's Managers* (London: Kogan Page Ltd., 1999) and Richard Olivier, *Inspirational Leadership: Henry V and the Muse of Fire: Timeless Insights from Shakespeare's Greatest Leader* (Rollinsford New Hampshire: Spiro Press USA, 2001).

8. In an interview Foucault acknowledges what New Historicists will call the "textuality of history": "'I realize full well that I have never written anything other than fictions...One can "fictionalize" history starting from a political reality that makes it true; one can fictionalize a politics that doesn't yet exist starting from a historical truth'" (cited in and translated by Lesley Higgins and Marie–Christine Leps in "'Passport Please": Legal, Literary, and Critical Functions of Identity.' *College Literature*. 25.1 (1998): 94–138.

9. For Foucault, ethics is figured 'as the arena of the government of the self, as a form of action of the "self on self"' (Dean, *Governmentality* 13). Thus the analysis of the discursive schemes within which we have learned to practice such 'forms of action' will be an engagement with the ethical. Dean continues: 'The analysis of the ethical government of the self, or of an attempt to govern the self, involves four aspects....First, it involves ontology, concerned with *what* we seek to act upon, the *governed or ethical substance*. This may be the flesh in Christianity, the pleasures in ancient Greece, or the "soul" of the criminal in modern penology...Second, it involves ascetics, concerned with *how* we govern this substance, the *governing or ethical work*. This may include the spiritual exercises... the procedures of surveillance, management and normalization applied to deviant individuals. Third, it involves deontology, concerned with *who* we are when we are governed in such a manner, our 'mode of subjectification', or the *governable or ethical subject*...Fourth, it entails a teleology, concerned with *why* we govern or are governed, the ends or goal sought, what we hope to become or the world we hope to create, that which might be called the *telos of governmental or ethical practices*'(17).

10. Foucault's histories of European government are sometimes dismissed in terms of the English case as wrong and/or irrelevant; yet, while Foucault is notorious for avoiding the academic decorum of signaling historical sources, there is evidence that he did read widely in the English sixteenth and seventeenth centuries. Evidence for such reading emerges much more clearly in the College de France lectures that are now being published in several volumes. See the first volume, *Michel Foucault: Society Must be Defended Lectures at the College de France 1975–1976*, ed. Arnold Davidson. (New York: Picador, 2003) and in particular Lecture five, 4 February 1976. As well in terms of the English case, when Foucault talks about the emergence of new experiments in government that he will describe as 'governmental' or 'pastoral' (to supplement what he described as the sovereign power of the law and the crown and the disciplinary power of social regulation and education) he is observing some of the same empirical evidence that, for example, Geoffrey Elton did in his study of Cromwell's administrative innovations and that feminists have observed in terms of early modern women's conduct literature. His contribution is to inscribe such phenomena in different, sometimes quite contrary, but nevertheless intriguing, and useful narratives.

11. Dean observes that 'We are used to questioning the attributes of welfare recipients and of the poor...However the ethical orientation of those from whom national governments seek to raise the funds for social benefits and services is rarely called into question' (*Governmentality* 83). Looking historically at this state of things Dean argues that 'An analysis of the ancient inheritances of the welfare–state...reveals the novel way in which it tries to fuse Roman civic culture and Christian charity, and the manner in which it

neglects a crucial aspect of both these cultures, the cultivation of the motivation to give' (83). On the same problem, see Dean's *The Constitution of Poverty: Toward a Genealogy of Liberal Governance* (London: Routledge, 1991).

12. All definitions and usage histories are taken from the *Oxford English Dictionary Online*: http://dictionary.oed.com/ (August 6, 2002).

13. See also Richard Wilson, 'The Quality of Mercy: Discipline and Punishment in Shakespearean Comedy' in *Will Power: Essays on Shakespearean Authority*, (Detroit: Wayne State UP, 1993) 126–68 and 'Prince of Darkness: Foucault's Shakespeare' in *Measure for Measure* a title in the Theory in Practice series edited by Nigel Wood (Buckingham: Open UP, 1996) 134–81. Wilson tracks the shift from discipline to a "bio–politics" of populations as a strategy of governmentality in the comedies.

14. Glimp borrows the phrase 'making up people' from Ian Hacking's 'Making up People,' in *Reconstructing Individualism: Autonomy, Individuality, and the Self in Western Thought*, ed. Thomas C. Heller, Morton Sosna, and David E. Wellberry (Stanford: Stanford UP, 1985) 222–36.

15. Katharine Eisaman Maus observes that, by the late sixteenth — and early seventeenth — century, 'the sense of discrepancy between "inward disposition" and "outward appearance" seems unusually urgent and consequential for a very large number of people' (13). She observes that she is 'inclined to seek an explanation in the far–reaching political, religious and economic realignments that constitute the English Reformation' (15). This book works to provide such an explanation.

16. While the Lucretia image is included and Berthelet is mentioned in several studies of early printing, the provenance of the image and the origin of Berthelet himself have not been established. Plomer suggests, in *Wynkyn De Worde & his Contemporaries from the Death of Caxton to 1535*, that Berthelet was Welsh and that he was one and the same with 'Thomas Bercula or Berclaeus' (London: Grafton & Co., 1925) 224, while Marjorie Plant, in *The English Book Trade: an Economic History of the Making and Sale of Books* calls him a foreigner (London: George Allen & Unwin, Third edition, 1974). Plomer observes that the Lucrece device 'was one of the most artistic of any found before the time of John Day. It was a metal block with the figure of Lucretia Borgia. The pose of the figure, the draperies, and the background point to the work of a skilful foreign engraver' (227) though I can find no other evidence to suggest that the model was Borgia.

17. An excellent example of humanist 'chaste thinking' in the early Tudor context is elucidated in Linda Woodbridge's chapter 'Humanism against the Homeless' in her *Vagrancy, Homelessness, and English Renaissance Literature* (Urbana: U of Illinois P, 2001) 109–48. Humanist thinking saw the poor as either deserving or undeserving; in the latter category were the vagrants who 'tried the limits of humanism' (109). Vagrancy for the humanists stood on the other side of a divide, a threat to the flock.

18. I rehearse Lorna Hutson's argument about the Tudor housewife as an alibi for humanist business practices in chapter two.

19. Ian Donaldson concurs in *The Rapes of Lucretia: a Myth and its Transformation*, that the tale reads as a warning to early modern princes and that for this reason English writers who employed the narrative were cautious when relating the incident of the expulsion of the tyrannical monarch (Oxford: Clarendon, 1982). As Quentin Skinner argues in *Liberty Before Liberalism* (Cambridge: Cambridge UP, 1998), in the seventeenth century, the English worked out their notions about the freedom of subjects and states in relation to their understanding of ancient Rome.

Chapter 1

'That Lovely Bond:' Binding England

Among all the societies in history, ours — I mean, those that came into being at the end of Antiquity on the Western side of the European continent — have perhaps been the most aggressive and the most conquering; they have been capable of the most stupefying violence, against themselves as well as against others. They invented a great many different political forms...[and] they alone evolved a strange technology of power treating the vast majority of men as a flock with a few as shepherds. They thus established between them a series of complex, continuous, and paradoxical relationships.

(Foucault, *Omnes* 230–1)

[E]mongest a great flocke of shepe some be rotten and fau[l]ty which the good sheperd sendeth from the good shepe...[as in the case of Cardinal Wolsey] for his graces sight was so quike and penetrable, that he saw him, ye and saw through him, both within and without so that all thing to him was open.

(*Hall's Chronicle* 764)

Change

The topic of change in the English 1530s has been hotly debated in the last forty years. How broadly did the reformation of the Church effect the everyday life of everyday English people? And, in relation to the change that did occur, what or who exactly was the origin or cause of that change? The arguments of Geoffrey Elton have dominated the field since the fifties and still hold authority. He maintained that the degree of change was very great indeed — 'revolutionary' in fact — and that its direct cause was Henry Tudor's chief minister: 'the rapidity and volume of change, the clearly deliberate application of one principle to all the different sections of the central government, and the pronounced success obtained in applying that principle, justify one in seeing in those years a veritable administrative revolution...caused by the personality which appears in every aspect of it' (*Tudor Revolution* 415) and that personality was Thomas Cromwell. Though Elton died in December 1994, he certainly still wields influence. He has his defenders and detractors who contend with him on his own terms.[1] Other scholars find considerable verity in the argument made by Elton and others of his generation about the magnitude of change, but their focus is less on origins than on effects. The sociologists Philip Corrigan and Derek

Sayer argue that 'the Henrician revolution was of immense importance in developing the national state forms and political culture within (and in part, through) which capitalism was eventually able to triumph' (43). John Guy makes a sensible intervention into this debate, arguing that it cannot be denied that 'the break with Rome was a jurisdictional...[and] cultural revolution of the first magnitude' (157). Guy argues, however, that the significant shift is not to be found in Cromwell's modern bureaucratic machinery, which he demonstrates was neither entirely modernized nor lasting; but rather in the capacity of leaders in the period to attempt 'conscious state planning' (*Tudor England* 158). Guy also makes the important observation that 'the word "revolution" in Tudor speech did not mean the sudden overthrow of an established order of government, but merely signified the completion of a cycle or a "turning back" to earlier practice' (158). As we shall see, those who struggled over the direction that change would take all make a claim on history as precedent; all present their movements rhetorically as just such a turning back, such a 'revolution.'

The debate initiated by Elton's thesis has invited careful analyses by a number of historians of the elements of this particular administrative apparatus that were in fact not novel to the period. The English state, for example, was by the reign of Henry VII already highly centralized. David Loades asserts that '[l]ate medieval England was the most centralised and unified monarchy in Europe' (*Power in Tudor England* 1), and S.J. Gunn calls the administration an 'ordered, formalized, professional, parchment–bound thing of proper forms and channels' (Gunn 12). The extension of the king's direct influence was enabled in particular by his expanding demesne, or land holdings, procured principally through the forfeiture of land by wealthy nobles attainted for treachery (Gunn 32, Guy, *Tudor* 7–10)[2] and Gunn argues that the subsequent swelling of the royal administration by non clerics constituted a laicization of rule well before the Reformation. Further, Christopher Haigh notes that '[i]n 1485 Chief Justice Hussey declared that the king of England was superior to the pope in his own realm...[and that the common] lawyers' combination of practical self–interest and theoretical self–justification proved powerful — and dangerous to churchmen' (73). Both Guy and Gunn show that, for the most part through attainder and forfeiture, the crown's income from land increased by tenfold from the reign of Edward IV to that of Henry VIII, despite the fact that the land seized was often strategically restored to the families of such traitors, a move that secured the debt of future loyalty.[3] Here is a blatant example of the rule of law depending on transgression for its own reproduction.

The rise of influence of both common and civil lawyers at court, widespread anti–clerical sentiment and the attack on church court jurisdiction by king's bench and common pleas also predate the reign of Henry VIII. However, the advance of the printing press, the pastoral infrastructure of the Roman church and the public nature of English legal rituals all worked to create the conditions of possibility for what I argue is finally a significant shift in the nature of governance in the early sixteenth century. The change that I study is the new focus on the highly strategized government of the individual English subject.

To demonstrate the principle gestures of such individualization and intimate rule as realized in rhetoric, I begin with an analysis of the last political pamphlet produced in the 1530s, *An Exhortation to Styre All Englyshe Men to the Defence of Theyr Countreye* and a discussion of some of the events and examples of written discourse to which the piece is responding. *An Exhortation* was composed by the Cromwellian protégé Richard Morison in 1539, in response to a set of volatile current events. Morison was among a group of state–sponsored scholars studying abroad at Padua with Melanchthon. He returned to England, as did Thomas Starkey, summoned by Cromwell to serve their country by writing propaganda to counter dissent.[4] His tract is part of the body of propagandist pamphlets that Elton describes as 'the first such campaign ever mounted by any government in any state of Europe. Not that propagandist writing was new, but an intensive and government organised campaign of printed propaganda was' (Elton, *Policy* 206–7). J. Christopher Warner has described the pamphletting more recently as 'the first time in England's short printing history that...men used the equipment of the new learning in systematic, public attempts to steer the ship of state' (4). And certainly, *An Exhortation* falls within the category of propaganda that was ad hoc, a response to the strategies of dissenting subjects (*Policy* 174). In this case, Morison's task is to respond to the northern rebellions of the latter part of the decade and to the government's anticipation of military interference by a union of continental Catholic countries. The tract is a reactive response to current events through which notions about the nature of both England and Englishness are put to use in an attempt to govern conduct. But this governance appeals to the free subject who is invoked, not commanded, to respond in the service of liberty.

While I agree with Guy that there is significant evidence of 'conscious state planning' in the period, I think it is important to note that the rationalizing, nationalizing and centralizing impetus does not generally include examples of constitutional thinking; the planning itself is seldom long range, but most often reactive, improvised and compromising. Henry Tudor took a vigorous interest in learning. As we have seen, he supported the universities towards pragmatic ends. He also patronized several young men (including Morison) studying on the continent. His interest is not in tapping humanism for its ability to formulate theories of state, however; rather, he is interested in how such learning can be put to immediate use to fulfill particular ends. Thus we have in the person of Morison and the document he produces an example of the 'social relations that [humanism] facilitates, maintains and transforms' (Stewart xx 28).

In *An Exhortation*, Morison elevates the monarchy, the nation state and citizenship to the top of a hierarchy of institutions through which God will become immanent to each member of the populace. In fact, claims Morison, it is God's 'polycie' 'that some rule, and some obeye. Obedyence undoubtedly is the knotte of al common weales, this broken they muste nedes runne al heedlonge to utter destruction' (17). But, together, as a totality, a 'flock,' claims Morison, they will powerfully show forth as 'one realme, so our enemies shall fynde us of one harte, one fydelitie, one allegiance' (39). Morison thus conscripts the behaviour of each for the reward of all: 'love and dewtie bynd all englyshemen, both to say and do, al that they judge to be for noble Englandes honour, welthe, and safetie' (1). On the other hand, says Morison, it is with the pope and his cardinals

> a gay schole poynte, without any drede of god, to breake that lovely bonde, whiche god hath ordeyned and sette in nature, to holde togyther, to preserve and maynteyne a thynge in this worlde for mans welth and safetie moste nedefull, civyle ordinaunce, obeysaunce of the membres to the heed, of the Subjectes to theyr soverayne. What thynge is more beneficiall unto mannes lyfe, then polytike order, then mutuall socyetie of men, knitte together in justice, temperacie, modestie, and honest lybertie. (16–7)

Morison employs the metaphor of the 'bodye polytike' (3) to further exhort the population in defense of itself: 'We see nature hath taught the handes, whan a strooke is offered unto the heade, to caste theymselve betwene the strooke and the heed, even in greattest jeoperdies' (3). In this way, he celebrates the mutuality that is the pastoral link, 'that lovely bond' of king and subjects: 'Certes, it were a great yoke for a kynge, to be bounde to defend his people, if they were not joyntlye bounde to obeye, hym...not only for feare of punyshement but for consciences sake, there is no doubte, but as subjectes are to be kepte frome injuryes, perylle, and slaughter by their kynge...so muste they all be redy, not onely with bodies, but with their goodes also, to see their...countreye defended' (3). Morison's employer wants loyalty, love, obedience and taxes.

Morison's exhortation to arms is clearly a call to a particular form of militaristic masculinity that he measures against the femininity of Rome. This tale becomes a means for Morison to invoke willing conscripts. His first rhetorical move is his citation of the recent words of a foreign ambassador who makes the claim that although the military 'actyvitie of Englyshmen hath ben greate...if I maye judge by any conjectures, it is nothynge so nowe, I se[e] neyther harneyes, ne weapons, of manhode' among Englishmen now. Those men 'of good hartes, couragyouse, bolde, valiant in marciall feates...are deade' (20). These are fighting words, claims Morison, a 'spytefull tale' that should induce Englishmen to prove that 'as long as Englyshe bodies remayn in Englande, they shal also fynde Englyshe stomackes, Englyshe handes, Englyshe hartes' (20–21). (Morison's polyptoton repeats words relating to 'England' ten times in one paragraph). He calls on history to shame and inspire both men and boys, whose education should include the many historical examples of the English winning battles against great odds, including of course the battle of Agincourt: 'It were ryghte expedient, that yonge Jentyll men dydde ofte reade theyr fathers noble actes, wherby undoubtedlye they may bothe be encouraged, to the like, and also know the weakenes of their enemys' (34).

Morison, the motivational speaker, promises rewards for the good subjects of a re–unified realm:

[W]as there ever prince, that dyd, or coulde better rewarde the servyce of his subjectes, than our moste bountifull soveraynge? have not all we, that be Sotherne men, good cause to shewe our selfe harty, courragious, valyaunte, seinge that we knowe, the Northen men, woll do what they can, to make a large mendes, for theyr laate fau[l]te? I doubt not, but they have moche desyred, some suche occasyon, to testyfye their hartes and fydelytie, to the kynges hyghnes. They have sene, howe mercyfully his grace gave theym theyr lyves, whiche the lawes chalenged as forfayte and loste. We may all truste...that he rather lente them lyves, than gave them any. (39)

Morison deploys the performative force of both love and terror in his muster call here, making plain the tactical nature of the mercy this king himself had deployed in his recent dealings with northern rebels.

The text appeals to subjects' fear of foreign invasion as well, claiming that Henry, who certainly was a lusty soldier/king in his younger days, has personally produced the security of all: 'I praye you, what kynge, sythens kynges ruled fyrste this realme of England, hath made greater provision for the saftie of our bodies? Is it possible, that any of his gracis subjecte, can refuse peyne, whan his hyghnes rydeth about from haven to haven, from castell to castell, dayes and nightes devysynge all the wayes, that wytte can invent, for our assuraunce?' (52). Morison offers a litany of some thirty–seven fortifications which, he implies, have been secured personally by this mercurial monarch: 'Caleys, Hammis, Guysnes...Dover haven, Dover castel...bulwarkes in the Downes, bulwarkes at Folkestone...' (52). When the king is done with his fortifications, England, Morison declares, will be absolutely enclosed and more 'liker a castel, than a realme' (53).

Morison sustains a dizzying rant of rhetorical questions. If this good shepherd king 'thus diligentely watche, that we maye safely slepe, spend his treasure thus largely, that we maye surely kepe our goodes, were it not our great shame, to suffer his highnes to travaile alone? Is it not our partes, in this oone thynge, even to contende with his grace, that is, to love his honour, his prosperytie, more than he canne love our welth and safetie?' (53). Morison muses that he and others had even wished an enemy had set on England during the recent northern uprising, because such a challenge from without might well have united the English against a common enemy. The performative effects of actions, he goes on to argue from this hypothetical example, are not determined by the intentions of acting subjects: 'Men ofte tymes fayle of theyr purpose, and turne thinges quyte contrarye to that they intended' (23) he argues, citing the case of a 'good wyfe' who poisoned her husband twice, little knowing that each poison would prove an antidote for the other.

Morison makes a metonymical link between the woman and her poison and a tale of Roman sodomy and rape. His warning tale begins with this treasonous wife and ends with that 'whore of Babylon' the Catholic Church, thus linking femininity and sedition even as he had earlier linked masculinity and military honour: 'Poyson hath put me in minde, here to tell a story done in our tyme, not longe sythens, by a noble man of Rome. I shall lytell digresse from my purpose, for ye maye also lerne by this storye, that men ofte tymes have great hurte, where they loke for great pleasure' (40).

He relates the story in sordid detail, of an Italian — Petrus Aloisius — a Captain 'of the Romyshe churche' who becomes a house guest of the bishop of Phane. The bishop entertains the captain '[s]parynge neyther labour, in provydynge all suche deynties as myghte make his chere the better, ne cost in dressyng of them' (42). After leading the captain to his bedchamber, 'he made hym the courteyse offer of the Italyan, desyrynge hym, if there were any thynge in all his house, that his phantasie stode to, that he wolde thynke it his owne, and so to take it. And that he, his body, his harte, and all his, was at signior Aloisius commandement' (43). Morison interjects hyperbolic praise for the bishop, even as he casts him in the feminine role in this courtly tale. This suspiciously omniscient narrator proceeds to relate that the captain called several of his men to him 'tellynge them all of the bysshops offer, sayinge, I lyke well this parte of the offer, that his body is at my commandemente, I intende to morowe in the mornynge to prove, whether he be a man of his worde or noo. If I canne not obteyne by fayre meanes, I intende to use your helpe, and have it by force' (43–4). In the morning, the captain makes his desires known:

> thoughe there be manye thynges here, which I fansy wel, yet I purpose to take that parte of your offer, where ye sayde your person is at my commaundemente. Certes I woll sease upon that and leave all other thynges to you. (44)

The bishop, in virginal horror, 'sore astonished, knew what his abomynable demaunde ment, and sayde: Syr I knowe ye can lytell fansye, thynges soo fylthy...I woll be torne in peces, rather than you, or any lyvyng creature, shal make me willyngly to fall into so brute and unnaturall a synne' (44). The captain calls his men and with their help, 'enforced the byshop, [in] spite of all his strivinge, to kepe his promyse' (45).

Morison records the response of the bishop: 'Sodom & Gomorra sunke for this synne...woll not the emperour one day se[e] lawes made for such syn executed?' (45) and the allusion is likely to the 1533 English statute against buggery. But the bishop is soon poisoned by the captain and this captain, Morison boldly claims in his moment of narrative disclosure, is the son of the pope. Could such a church, he asks rhetorically, be the 'dere darling unto Christ?...Dothe not god rather admonyshe all princis, howe lyttell he setteth by this strompet of Babylon, whom he hath left in suche mens handes?' (45). Thus, concludes Morison, the Catholic church is a whore, her captains are sodomites and the English are well rid of them all. As he put it earlier in the tract, they are all better off, 'sithes this good father, with this trumpery and baggage departed hens...to dispatche his wares in some other markets of fooles' (10–11).

Besides casting out feminized men and men who desire feminized men, Morison's narrative, beginning as it does with the seeming non sequitur about the poisoning wife, is symptomatic of the way in which women are viewed by governors in this period. First of all, women's presence is powerfully registered in the political events of the day, while at the same time, as I will show in chapter four, legislation and an array of discursive practices militated to keep women out of the public sphere, ignorant and thus impotent actors. The wife's malevolent intent is similarly rendered impotent by her ignorance of the effects of the substances she administers to her husband. Yet, despite the legislative and discursive practices aimed at marginalizing women, we will see that such women were clearly far less impotent than Morison's poisoning wife.

In his tale, Morison is also reiterating one of the principle strategies used by the government to justify the dissolution of the monasteries, that is to claim that the Catholic clergy (including the nuns) were sunk in sexual depravation. Such proofs had been elicited by the inquisitorial visitations that produced the *Valor Ecclesiasticus*. In an earlier pamphlet, *A Lamentation in Which Is Showed What Ruin and Destruction Cometh of Seditious Rebellion*, Morison refers to this visitation:

> The world hath spied them. I would scarce believe that men could teach nature a new way, except it had been proved to their teeth and uttered by their ownselves. They that be learned know what I mean...They that be unlearned will much marvel (except they have been brought up with monks and friars) how young novices may stand instead of young wives. I have said enough. It stinketh too sore to be stirred too much...I cannot think that the putting down of abbeys, that is to say, the putting away of maintained lechery, buggery, and hypocrisy, should be the cause of this rebellious insurrection. (*Statutes at Large* 94–5)

'The world hath spied them': sexual 'abomination' is driven into discourse, the product of an investigation that sets out to find it. The stage had been set for this inquisition by the buggery legislation (5 Hen 8 c, 6), which reads:

> Forasmuch as there is not yet sufficient and condign punishment appointed and limited by the due course of the laws of this realm, for the detestable and abominable vice of buggery committed with mankind or beast...the same offence be from henceforth adjudged felony, and such order and form of process therein to be used against the offenders as in cases of felony at the common law...such pains of death, and losses and penalties of their goods, chattels, debts, lands, tenements and hereditaments, as felons be accustomed to. (267)[5]

Sexual practice enters civil jurisdiction and thus the commissioners of inquiry can demand to know of the Catholic religious '[w]hether the master, or any brother of this house, useth to have any boys or young men lying with him?' (Berkowitz 106). Since there were no prosecutions of any cleric on such charges at any point during the dissolution, the law is clearly a tactic in the interest of ideological and economic restructuring. Morison's rant against the church is ideological in that it works to influence belief and public opinion. It is also governmental in that it brings sex into public speech and the juridical sphere; thenceforth, can sexual practice return to the cloister?[6]

Morison is compelled to move towards the conclusion of *An Exhortation* by circling back to the link between the king and God and he does so by including a particular genre of truth production that was a vibrant tool of various dissenters — prophecy. As Sharon Jansen demonstrates in her careful study, *Political Protest and Prophecy under Henry VIII*:

> [M]ost political prophecy was really history disguised as prophecy...the prophecy was made to seem as if it antedated the historical events it narrated...Although new prophecies do appear, reworked versions of older predictions are far more common, and even 'new' compositions include familiar symbols and long passages adapted from earlier pieces. A prophesier went to great lengths *not* to be original. (15)

While prophecy and prophesying were ancient modes of discourse in Britain, Jansen argues that they begin to serve a novel purpose in the fifteenth century during the Wars of the Roses, when Yorkists and Lancastrians exploited traditional prophecies, producing competing interpretations of them in their own interests: 'By the sixteenth century...political prophecies are not simply a way of understanding the present. They have become a way of shaping the present. They have become weapons, wielded deliberately, if sometimes wildly, by a very different class of person' than the factionalised aristocrats who 'produced and distributed politically expedient prophecy in manuscript in the medieval period, such as Geoffrey of Monmouth' (Jansen 18–19). 'By the 1530s,' Jansen continues 'those who chose the weapon of prophecy were those who had few other weapons to hand' (19) including Elizabeth Barton and the many women and men who, during the Pilgrimage of Grace, deployed prophecy as a performative force in the enactment of the future. Thus, political prophecy becomes an historical discourse, a means to struggle for a hold on the authority of both the past and the future, a struggle against the alternative mythmaking of the Tudor administration.

Prophecy is a weapon employed vigorously during the Pilgrimage and it is clearly taken very seriously by the government, who seize both the prophecies themselves (that circulated in written form) and those who were discovered disseminating them. In February 1536, the Duke of Norfolk sends Cromwell a copy of such a prophecy:

> A little boke was made in dede
> By the cownsaill of Marlin and Bede —
> Who so it doth rede writen shalbe
> That a litle cuntrey called Braytin
> Shalbe brought in such caas certayne
> And be compelled to begyn agayne,
> At A.B.C. thait saide not Christes crosse
> Therfore I like it the woorse...
>   (qtd. in Jansen 41–2)

The prophecy calls on the ancient authority of the historical Bede and the mythological Merlin, who foretell the destructive interventions of A.B. and C., Anne Boleyn and Cromwell, and call for armed struggle to bring Cromwell 'in lawe' because, foretells Bede, punning on Cromwell '"More ill cumethe of a smal note / As Crumwell set in a mans throte"' (42).

Morison's counter–prophecy, he claims, carries the authority of both English history and scripture in that he finds it in both Welsh narratives and the Old Testament (the Book of Esdras):

> a proude Egle...toke upon her, [so much] that al princes, all kyngdomes were troden under her fete. What and whom this Egle figureth, we can not doubte...the kyngdome of Antichriste, the reigne undoubtedly of the byshoppe of Rome. All thynges spoken here of the Egle, agree with hym as just as may be. This byrde, sayth the texte, made al the erth afrayde, al men trembled, at her syght, all thynge became subjecte to it. (56)

The pope is feminized again, transformed in Morison's allegory to a she–eagle, though the saviour/English lion remains properly masculine, 'But at the laste...there came out of a woode a Lion...roring a lowd, and sayde to this saucye and mysproude Egle...[once] gone, the erthe may be refreshed...thy kyngedome ones fallen, men may turne ageyne to freedome' (56). He asks, rhetorically, 'What if I contende, noble Henry the VIII to be this Lyon? May I not have many conjectures, to leade me this way?...as the Egle hath always ben the Romains badge, so hath kynges of Englande ever more gyven the Lyon in their armes: so that it can so welle be applied to none other prince' (56). The lion is soon transformed, however, by Morison's overblown rhetoric, into air — a 'wynde' capable of defeating the eagle in her own element: 'This Lion, saith the text, is a wynde, wyche the lorde hath kepte in store, for these later days, bothe to tosse the Egle and her byrdes, and also to refreshe, refrigerate, and comfort our consciences...Hath not our couragious Lyon... blowen up a blast, that refreshed us all, whan he by his prechers, by his proclamations, brake the cheynes, that our soules laye tyed in, slaves and bond to Romishe tyranny?' (56). Henry's subjects are to understand themselves as enslaved and their king as a heroic liberator.

Morison concludes his pamphlet with the offer of more, even, than freedom, for subjects who would run with the lion: 'let us therefore worke lustely nowe, we shall play for ever hereafter. Let us fight this one fielde with englysshe handes, and englysshe hartes, perpetuall quietnes, rest, peace, victorie, honour, welthe, all is owers' (58). Morison's weighty 'owers' signals a conceptual and ideological totalization of the English as a race and the territory of England as a realm, bound so carefully by Henry's forts and so conveniently by the sea. As such, we can see the initiation of a process that will finally subordinate a concern about governance of territory to a concern about the governance and security of the totality of those 'handes' and 'hartes.' Morison gives us such security in his promise of 'perpetuall quietnes, rest, peace, victorie, honour, welthe.' Now the happiness of each English political subject is not simply the product of good government but rather has a bearing on the strength of the state.

Centralization, Reformation and the Rule of All and Each

The centralization of the institutions of royal rule actually allowed those institutions to expand their sway far and wide. Just as Morison, in *An Exhortation*, aims to unite the realm of England against the threat of foreign invasion, so was one of the principle aims of late medieval centralization to strengthen the king's defenses against both external threats and internal rebellions. Yet, in relation to continental Europe, England was highly centralized well before the efforts of Edward IV and Henry VII to strengthen (and in fact to recover) that centralization. England's ancient jurisdictional divisions and encompassing institutions of government worked and endured.

In the fifteenth century, in the disruptive civil turbulence of the Wars of the Roses, many of the centralizing links were weakened and the Crown was running a deficit (Guy 5). It was the task of the Yorkist Edward IV (1461–83) and then Henry VII (1485–1509) to restabilise the realm and their own positions, while seeking measures to prevent further disruptions. Attaining more direct control over wealth and military potentiality was crucial, and doing so meant establishing more direct control than the nobility had ever had over landed estates and the human military capital that went with them. As John Guy asserts about both France and England, 'The aims of Charles VII, Louis XI, Edward IV, and Henry VII can be summarized in a sentence: they wished to control their realms and to create administrative machinery to channel disposable wealth into royal coffers' (13).[7] Henry VIII inherited a reinvigorated, centralized and to some degree secularized judicial and administrative system and he and his ministers aimed to maintain the trend.

Two of those socially mobile talents who formed part of the new managerial class were Thomas Wolsey, son of an Ipswich butcher, who rose through the church and Thomas Cromwell, son of a Putney clothworker, who appears to have been self–educated on the continent. Many of the accomplishments that marked the careers of both these men can be described as managerial. For example, Wolsey drew up a code of practice, the 'Eltham Ordinances' for the too big and amorphous royal council of fifty or sixty men who were to advise the king, calling for the reduction of the core council to twenty. By 1540 it had become the efficient administrative unit, newly named (and still named) the Privy Council (Loades *Tudor* 25).[8] Cromwell was certainly the first king's secretary to organise the council's work and his successors, claims Gunn, 'did play a role unmatched by those who went before' (53). The huge administrative households of these principle bureaucrats also provided the infrastructure that constituted a crucial strand of continuity throughout the period (Gunn 33).

As the law began to supplant the church as a means to political power, there was a significant expansion of membership in the inns of court, the institution that would come to fulfill the King's wish for a training ground for professional 'personages.' A generalized production and dissemination of legal knowledge was aided by the printing of the legal texts that were very popular among early printed books (Gunn 93, Haigh 73). Certainly the collating of information in 'year–books' about pleadings, judgements and arguments at English law had been carried on since the twelfth century and lawyers cited these medieval texts (eventually printed in abridgements) as precedent, '"vouch[ing] the record"' into the seventeenth century (Baker *Introduction* 152). The first printed legal text that laid out the technicalities of land law was *Littleton Tenures* (printed more than twenty times between 1482 and 1547). In the sixteenth century, there was an array of printed texts — abridgements of the year–books, books of 'entries' (examples of special pleadings), formularies (sample writs), such texts as John Rastell's *Termes de la Ley*, and Anthony Fitzherbert's manual *New Boke of Justices of the Peas* — that aimed to inform and guide law students and lawyers about how this ancient and complex machine, the common law, worked (Baker, *Introduction* 160, Haigh 73). Baker argues, however, that there persists into the sixteenth century a conspicuous lack of treatises that demonstrate an interest in thinking about English law constitutionally, with the exception of St German's *Doctor and Student* which Baker calls 'a remarkable enterprise' (*Introduction* 164) and which Gunn calls a 'general masterpiece' (15). The law, for the most part, was busy with doing.

Such an egalitarian disbursement of learning among potential men of law and government is part of the governmental aim to conscript each and all in the laicized governance of self, others and the 'common weal.' As Richard Morison puts it in *A Remedy for Sedition*, if governance is put into the hands of those 'that cannot skill thereof' then the common weal would 'go to wrack' (*Berkowitz* 116). Young men trained at the inns now brought back home to the farthest reaches of the realm both a knowledge of the common law and a conviction about the supremacy of the central courts and their procedures over local borough and church courts. Such men were now poised to take on many administrative and judicial functions, some involving the day–to–day drudgery of 'police' work, such as the gathering of evidence for the equity courts and for the dissolution of the monasteries.

A principle obstacle to the workings of government, however, was the over–bureaucratized formalisms of the common law. The principle reward for obedient subjects must be above all a sense that justice is there to serve them, that justice is the reward, even the right, granted them by the benevolent king, now their own personal monarch. The rationalization of medieval administrative structures and judicial labour involved circumventing or overriding some medieval bureaucratic forms almost entirely. One problem was the rigidity of the 'blank charters,' forms that had long been in use by both domestic and papal administrative bodies in the pre–printing press era. These common law writs were standardized bills in Latin, naming actions that could be taken by a plaintiff and that judicial officers used to set cases in motion by filling in the blank 'window' with the names of plaintiff and defendant. As Gunn observes, 'by the 1330s several thousand writs a year arrived at the office of the sheriff of each county, were enrolled and were copied for forwarding to the appropriate hundred bailiff, while the originals were retained to be endorsed with a reply and returned to the various central government offices that had issued them' (12).[9] Two hundred years later, the same Latin writs were proving inadequate to the task of representing each and every case of perceived injustice. The courts were also bogged down by other procedural problems, with, for example, how to secure the appearance of the accused, how to deal with corruption and the sheer numbers of cases. When a case did get to court, it could easily be lost on a technicality, such as a mistake in the wording or spelling of a writ. Less than one case in ten reached a judgment. The courts were corrupt, slow moving and hindered by their forms of action and processes. This was not a centralized judiciary that appeared to be functioning for all and each.

Justice needed rationalizing. More than this, the people needed to perceive that the king's justice was a personal justice, that their security was guaranteed. The most important development to this end and the most governmental is clearly the appropriation and expansion by the king's council of the jurisdiction of 'equity.' John Rastell defines 'equity' as 'the correction of a law, generally made in that part wherein it fails, that correction taking two forms, the one doth abridge and take from the letter of the law, the other doth enlarge and add thereunto' (*Termes* 199). The necessity of an equitable jurisdiction speaks to the rigidity of common law forms, to the burden of the already written, to the notion of the inadequacy of writing itself.

Equitable justice, like many of the innovations of the period, was not novel in function, but rather novel in form, in its appropriation by the enlarging central superstructures. Arbitration had frequently been practised as a supplement to the common law. Fourteenth– and fifteenth–century noblemen, bishops, gentlemen, lawyers, urban guilds and most interestingly high status women had regularly negotiated settlements in disputes between their social equals or inferiors. For example, from her palace at Collyweston in Northamptonshire, Henry VII's mother, Lady Margaret Beaufort, wielded an equitable jurisdiction often over cases referred to her by the king's council. The councils of the great feudal magnates operated like local equity courts as well, as arbitrators imposed equitable solutions on quarrelling parties. The jury itself, in fact, at points applied equity in both criminal and civil cases, often to modify the 'stark rigour of the law,' through a number of strategies. For example, they might undervalue stolen goods to save a convict from the noose (Gunn 85).

In Henry VII's reign, conciliar tribunals led by the chancellor began to proliferate 'at the boundary where justice and administration met' (Gunn 87). Specific bodies were set up to administer justice in specific settings: to punish corrupt jurors, to enforce royal proclamations, and in particular to attend to the details of the king's demesne holdings; and even in these early days vernacular bills were used. But it increasingly fell to the court of Chancery to parcel out equity, using as a model continental civil law and driven by both lay and clerical chancellors with civil law training such as Cardinal Wolsey, Thomas More (the first layman and common lawyer to be chancellor), Thomas Audley and Thomas Wriothesley (Gunn 78).

In the 1520s and thirties, Chancery, whose function in English legal history had served various administrative and judicial needs, was developing an independent equitable jurisdiction. It was highly attractive to litigants for several reasons. The chancellor was one of the king's leading ministers and his presence provided a powerful sense of proximity to the king's transcendent power. Importantly, plaintiffs in Chancery did not have to attempt to manipulate their case to make it apply within the limited range of Latin formulaic writs and the fixed 'forms of action,' demanded by common law. Rather, for the first time in an English court of law, plaintiffs could state their particular grievance in a bill in the vernacular. The chancellor also developed an efficient means to ensure the presence of the defendant at the proceedings: the 'subpoena writ,' which promised a steep fine for non–appearance. With the greater freedom of his office, the chancellor could attempt to work out a compromise solution, rather than being bound to common law processes. Chancery also had the power to hear appeals of common law decisions and to inhibit common law actions by injunction: '90 per cent of its commercial contract cases under Wolsey came on appeal from inferior jurisdictions' (Gunn 78–9).[10] For these reasons, the volume of cases in Chancery increased tenfold between the early sixteenth and the early seventeenth centuries (Erickson 31).

If Chancery functioned as an instrument of personal mercy, offering considered compromises that might well serve to compensate both parties in a dispute, Star Chamber weilded terror, particularly for men of law themselves. Wolsey used Star Chamber as an instrument for the reform of law–enforcement and for the discipline of corruption at common law courts, bringing earls, knights and JPs to court on charges of corruption, even inviting complaints from individuals. As Guy conceives it, 'To throw open the doors of the courts was a bold and radical move; in an age when the slogan was "Justice is a fat fee", Wolsey proclaimed the notion that the people should have justice as a right' (91). Wolsey touted the workings of equity as the application of '"thindifferent ministracion of Justice"' (qtd. in Gunn 82). As in Chancery, Star Chamber process involved the English bill, the subpoena, depositions by witnesses under oath and interrogatories (lists of questions furnished by the parties to be put to their opponents or to witnesses) and this body gradually accrued a specific portfolio in criminal cases. Among Wolsey's contribution to administrative centralization was his calling into London of all JPs and sheriffs annually to Star Chamber, where they were '"new sworn' and received instruction on the workings of the new courts (Guy, *Tudor* 172).

From Wolsey's time on, Star Chamber applied an at times particularly cruel if individualized punishment, as in the case in 1556 of the convict who was sentenced to 'ride through Westminster facing backwards and wearing pieces of paper which detailed his misdeeds, before being branded on each cheek with the letters FA for false accusation' (Gunn 98). The Court of Requests grew up in the same period, taking the overflow business from the growth of Star Chamber and Chancery and hearing the petitions of the poor. Like Star Chamber, it began as a tribunal established by Wolsey in the 1520s, gradually losing its link with the royal council. It busied itself with defending customary law against encroachers on copyhold land.[11] The Court's administrators researched manorial records and took the testimony of elder tenants as evidence about local practices.

Under the Cardinal, Requests was one of the instruments deployed against enclosure of common lands, along with parliament (where laws were passed against enclosing in 1489 and 1514–15) and the equity side of Exchequer which Wolsey approached 'from the perspective of equity rather than economics' (Guy, *Tudor* 92). There were proceedings against 264 landlords or corporations under Wolsey, including against the good Thomas More himself. In its check on enclosure, Requests defused potential enclosure riots and other demonstrations of popular unrest, and as such, was clearly providing good, strategic government.

Chancery, Star Chamber, Requests and the equity side of the Court of Exchequer were all extensions of the king's personal governance:

> Royal equitable justice won such ready acceptance because in execution it so resembled and subsumed private arbitration...the royal equity courts brought the king's power to bear effectively in every locality...[and] increasingly used local commissioners — peers, bishops, abbots, gentlemen and lawyers — to interview witnesses and extract answers from recalcitrant defendants...The more people sued in the equity courts, the tighter the king's grip on his subjects became; the tighter the king's grip on his subjects became, the more attractive it was to sue in the equity courts. (Gunn 85–6)

While Tudor courts of equity served to situate a broad range of jurisdictions in the figure of the personal monarch, the actual administration of equity took place in satellite locations around the country, including at York and in Ireland, which underlines the argument that the king's equity courts were powerful and personal, universal and local.

Jurisdiction was plastic in this period and there was a jockeying for the shrinking jurisdiction of the church courts among the king's old central courts, the new equity courts and the local borough and manor courts. And the old royal central courts — King's Bench and Common Pleas — were themselves reformed in light of the rise of equity. To sustain its share of cases and to ameliorate the inefficiencies of common law forms, the court of the King's Bench devised new actions (some 39 between 1498 and 1549). One of its most important innovations was the elastic 'action on the case,' with its writ formula that was brief and non–specific enough to allow the plaintiff to describe their problem in detail, much like they could in an equity bill. In the phrase 'action on the case,' the significant word for the history of common law is 'case,' as this word is used here in a novel fashion to indicate the unique nature of the breach in question, in which some kind of contract with the plaintiff is alleged to have been 'trespassed' against by the accused. The 'action on the case' utilized a number of legal fictions to achieve its ends and increased the King's Bench jurisdiction in a variety of areas, including the broadly defined area of promises made and broken (and thus debt) that formerly had been the jurisdictional territory of the ecclesiastical courts.

In the struggle for the supremacy of the crown's jurisdiction in the courts, churches and hearts of English subjects, the crown happily used strategically the emotions stirred up by the famous case of Richard Hunne versus the church court of St Mary Magdalen. Hunne's baby son died in 1511 in this parish and when the parish priest made the customary demand of the child's christening robe as a mortuary fee, Hunne refused and was brought to trial before the archbishop's Court of Audience, Hunne denying that the mortuary was owed. When the court found in the clerics' favour, Hunne defied the order and then boldly attended a parish mass where the priest stopped the service, cursed and then expelled him. Hunne sued the priest in the King's Bench for slander, alleging loss of credit and reputation. He also 'sued out a writ' that alleged the original mortuary had been a praemunire offence. The case offered a potential threat to church court jurisdiction over defamation and it was making very slow headway through the courts when, in December 1514, Hunne was found hung in his jail cell. Church officials claimed that his death was a suicide, brought on by Hunne's own despair as a heretic, but in 1515 a London coroner's jury found that Hunne had been murdered and named the church official Dr. Horsey and two jailors as the killers (one of the jailors having confessed). Haigh argues that Hunne becomes a 'martyr for secular interests' (80) and that 'Hunne's case' is a crucial one in the erosion of both the legal and emotional hold of the church over parishioners. Edward Hall's report of the event, as reconstructed from evidence offered at the trial of Horsey 'woorde for woorde,' claims that Hunne was 'counted of honest reputacion, no man to the sight of the people more vertuous' (573), and thus were the clerics revealed as all the more despicable.

Town oligarchies and manorial courts attempted to hang onto and increase their sway over issues of social regulation, where pressures of rapid population growth drove local authorities to regulate vagrancy, prostitution, gambling and alehouses (Gunn 94). It is in this period that such courts employed such punishments as the stocks, the pillory and the cucking–stool, modes especially useful for the punishment of those too poor or too indigent to be fined (Gunn 94).Yet borough courts themselves lost to the central courts as litigants understood the power to hear appeals held by those central courts and began to go straight to the top.[12]

The judicial apparatus was being rationalized at every level. With the closing of the monasteries, where the poor, the ill and the orphaned were often ministered to, the state found itself formulating a range of policy that was, by necessity 'pastoral,' even as its motivations for filling the gap were at least partially the avoidance of riot and rebellion. It thus found itself with a burgeoning jurisdiction over social problems and was becoming more and more interested in the intentions, the health and the productivity of English subjects. There were novel attempts to control epidemic disease, for example, such as the quarantine measures ordered in London and Oxford in 1518. The Cardinal also initiated raids to arrest vagrants, prostitutes and other criminals; a proclamation in 1513 called for the branding of prostitutes caught 'within the King's host' of armed retainers (*Tudor Royal Proclamations* 113). Wolsey, like Cromwell, was interested in the strategic production of bodies of information. To this end, in 1522 he had surveys taken of military resources, including the skills of the 128,250 men — the 'manred' — who were available for conscription. To the end of disciplining this potential armed force, 'morally tainted' leisure pursuits such as gambling and football were proscribed in the 1520s. It was purported that such games distracted men from the military discipline of archery, thereby threatening the kingdom's military preparedness. Attention eventually was turned on alehouses as 'the natural centre of disorderly activity' (Gunn 177).

Cromwell continued to attempt to regulate at least the size of enclosed estates, although parliamentary statutes were hard to come by, parliamentarians being themselves landowners interested in their right to enclose. Tudor administrators also operated in parallel with old 'communitarian' forms of poor relief such as the 'help–ale,' by which those in need brewed ale for their more fortunate neighbours to buy at 'charitably inflated prices' (Gunn 180). Provisions for the poor gradually increased; legislation in 1531 called for begging licenses that could be issued by justices of the peace and provisions were made for both parochial collections and taxation or 'poor rates' that could be levied when the need was great in any one area (Gunn 181). A sign of the radical shift in the state's ability to rationalize its relation to its 'flock' is clearly evidenced in Christopher St German's sweeping legislation, proposed in a twenty–two page draft in 1531 (but never made law), St German called for a 'nationwide scheme of combining parochial relief; employment for vagabonds on public works, and an investigation into the causes of inflation and poverty' all to be coordinated by a '"great standyng counsayll"'(Gunn 180). Attitudes towards the poor included then (as now) the sense that poverty is to be blamed on the poor, or at least blamed on those categorized as 'undeserving.' As for the others, John Guy argues that the 'assurance of labour discipline was as fundamental to the new outlook as provision of public doles for the deserving poor' (*Tudor* 43).[13]

The most important legal instrument of the Reformation was clearly parliament. The king used parliament to legitimate his agenda and as a result, parliament itself gained a power and status that it would never lose. To the end of reform, law–making power was rationalized as being situated in a triad of equal partners: king, lords and commons. This 'governing body' is itself charged by Christopher St German, in the *New Additions* to his dialogue *Doctor and Student*, to take care 'not onely charge on the bodies, but also on the soules' of English subjects (327). Thus, in the early 1530s, parliament made law that would make possible the care of these state–invested English souls. The 'Supplication of the Commons' (1529) transferred from the church to the king the power to make ecclesiastical law and over the ecclesiastical courts themselves, with the clergy, after some protest, registering their acquiescence with the document, 'Submission of the Clergy.' In 1533, the 'Act in Restraint of Appeals' was passed, its preamble (composed by Cromwell) containing the declaration that England was an 'Empire.' As such, it claimed jurisdiction (disqualifying Rome's) in legal appeals to do with 'matrimony, testaments and tithes' (Dickens 117–18). In 1534, Cromwell wrote and guided through parliament several key pieces of legislation: the 'Act in Restraint of Annates' and the 'Dispensations Act,' both of which stopped payments to Rome, the former also declaring that Rome had no more authority to appoint English bishops; the 'Act of Submission of the Clergy,' which established a licensing system for clerics; the 'First Succession Act,' declaring that Anne Boleyn's children (and not Katherine's) would be heirs to the throne; the revised treason legislation of 1534 extending the law's jurisdiction over what subjects both said and did not say (an example of such misprision of treason being Thomas More's unendured silence); and the 'Act of Supremacy,' declaring the royal headship of the church to be already in existence. With this act, the king was annexing the power 'to correct the opinions of preachers, to supervise the formulation of doctrine, to reform the canon law, to visit and discipline both regular and secular clergy, and even...to try heretics in person' (Dickens 119). These acts clearly do not represent the unfolding of a plan, but are improvised moves as Reformation policies are worked out in often unforseen ways. John Guy concurs that 'no settled policy existed during the crisis years 1529–32; instead competing policies were advocated by rival factions' (124).

The already highly centralized infrastructure of the late medieval state was the condition of possibility that allowed Tudor administrators to further refine the system in the interest of the intimate governance of all. To successfully intervene in the intimate pastoral way that it wished, however, the state required ever–increasing amounts of specific information as well as many means to disseminate its own prescriptions, proscriptions, promises and warning tales. To achieve this end, propagandist pamphlets, proclamations, circular letters, sets of injunctions, and statutes themselves with their polemical preambles were printed in London to be distributed in a variety of ways for the consumption of specifically targeted subjects. When the 'Act for First Fruits and Tenths' directed all tithes to the crown, Cromwell conducted the assessment that produced the *Valor Ecclesiasticus*, increasing the royal coffers by over 40,000 pounds per annum. In what was Cromwell's most massive bureaucratic undertaking, six canon lawyers toured every religious house in the country with eighty–six articles of inquiry and twenty–five articles of injunctions; the information gleaned would be collated in the massive document *Valor Ecclesiasticus* (Guy 147). As Alan Stewart demonstrates, the information produced in the *Valor* was far broader than mere economic statistics, although those were painstakingly calculated. The commission was also highly interested in evidence of sexual transgressions by nuns and male clergy and monastics which it could use as justification for seizing the wealth and pastoral jurisdiction of the religious houses. This institution of demographical knowledge production is clearly a disciplinary move as the overseer — Cromwell the vice–gerant — sought confessions about sexual practises, which he entered in files for future use.

As well, means were devised to record and calculate information about the general population. In 1538 an injunction was distributed to all bishops requiring that every parish should record every birth, marriage and death in new parish registers. Cromwell claimed that the exercise was designed "'for the avoiding of sundry strifes, processes and contentions rising upon age, lineal descents, titles of inheritance, legitimation of bastardy, and for knowledge whether any person is our subject or no...also for sundry other causes'" (qtd. *Policy* 259–60). It was just such 'sundry other causes' that worried the people.

The administration sought to know especially about what they saw as counter–information being disseminated by dissenting subjects. A proclamation of October 29, 1536 commanded authorities 'to take and apprehend all and every such person and persons that they can prove to have bruited or set forth any forged false rumors, tales, and lies whereby any commotion, sedition, or encouragement of unlawful assemblies hath, or might be, among our people to the disturbance of our peace.' If any persist in seditious actions (including assembling or seditious speaking) the King warns, 'we will withdraw our eye of mercy and clemency...and proceed...with all our royal power, force, and minions of war which we now have in a readiness, and destroy them, their wives, and children, with fire and sword, to the most terrible example of such rebels and offenders' (*TRP* 245). Henry Tudor would discipline the speech and the modes of public assembly of his subjects, reminding them that their reward for being so governed would be his benevolent 'eye of mercy and clemency' for minor transgressions. Their punishment for disobeying his proscriptions against sedition, however, would be the full force of his sovereign privilege.

A key communication tool was the proclamation, an old technology put to novel use after the development of the printing press. These documents are printed for the first time in June 1530, but as early as the 1520s they had been used to administer censorship of the printed word. Their first target was Lutheran heresy; Elton claims that this campaign amounts to the closest thing to an inquisition in English history (*Policy* 219). One issued on March 6 1529 personally exhorts every subject 'that all favor, affection, and partiality laid aside, they effectually with all diligence and study' should help enforce the laws against heresy; a list of specific commands includes a table of banned books (in particular English ones coming in from Europe) which it would be illegal to import, own or read (*TRP* 182). A proclamation a year later concentrated solely on the heretical book trade, calling them 'worthy to be damned and put in perpetual oblivion' (*TRP* 194). Cromwell's proclamation of 1536 was against Catholic heresies, but contained no index for fear, suggests Elton, of advertising the enemy (*Policy* 220). The proclamation of November 16 1538 is directed once again against reformers; it announces that the printing and selling of books was to be henceforth controlled by the crown.

Just as the government aimed to temper the rhetorical force of such documents by acting on who would distribute them, so did the centralization and personalization of government depend to a new degree in the Henrician period on the deployment and the control of many forms of representation. The monarch attended first to representing himself as a transcendental king within a number of discursive practises. One such practice was the discursive production of the English past. While there was a tradition in which the monarch claimed to be taking advice from noble forefathers as a justification for present strategies, Henry Tudor's commission of Edward Hall's *The Union of the Two Noble and Illustre Famelies of Lancastre & Yorke...to the Reigne of the High and Prudent Prince Kyng Henry the Eight, the Undubitate Flower and Very Heire of Both the Sayd Linages*, published in 1548, represents Henry as the culmination of history. The chronicle relates in detail, year by year, a narration of the reigns of the last Yorks and Lancasters up until Henry VIII's own reign. While, as John McKenna demonstrates, God had been 'an Englishman' in English discourse from the reign of Edward III (1330–76), Henry VIII made the leap to declaring that an Englishman (himself) was very nearly God. Edward III had claimed that England was God's promised land, the English were God's chosen people and that he, as clearly evidenced by the miraculous cures he performed, was God's chosen king; from this period, chroniclers and kings themselves propagandized this position by claiming against others the title of 'most Crysten kyng.' Thus, for McKenna, Henry VIII's acquisition of the title 'Defender of the Faith' from the pope in 1521 was 'the very end of a two–hundred–year search for an outward symbol of England's sovereign aspirations' (41). But the superlatives appropriated by Henry go beyond 'most Christian king' in the 1530s. He is head of state, of church, of each and every subject and their daily private practises and, importantly, of empire: his presence is increasingly everywhere.

Henry defined the realm as an empire in his 1533 statute, but he had employed the lexicon of empire as early as 1513–14, when he named ships the *Henry Imperial* and *Mary Imperial* (Gunn 164). Henry's team of researchers, at work to justify the divorce, provided historical evidence that previous English kings had exercised the same supremacy as had Roman emperors, even aligning Henry with the codifier Justinian. This claim to an historical and superlative jurisdictional autonomy is made in the act's preamble, which declares that 'divers sundry old authentic histories and chronicles [showed that England] so hath been accepted [as an Empire] in the world' (*English Historical Documents* 738). Such rhetoric was blended with the iconography of Old Testament kingship, as in the depiction on Henry's psalter of King David with Henry's features. In this way, the Reformation is presented as a return of the English church to an original pristine alignment with the state and its interests. As images of Catholic saints were destroyed and disqualified from the repertoire of English worship, they were increasingly replaced by those of the king and his symbols, to the point in Edward VI's reign, when carved scenes of the crucifixion began to be replaced at the focal point of churches by boards painted with the royal arms. Henry VIII also commissioned Hans Holbein to create flattering images of himself that showed up on 'panel–paintings and palace murals... plea rolls, the great seal, the coinage, and the frontispiece of the Great Bible placed in every parish church' (Gunn 196). This 'political messianism' (Gunn 197) clearly aimed to harness the performative force of visual representation and the authority of an array of histories to do its ideological and governmental work.

Yet, ironically, the necessity of harnessing the power of imperial signifiers speaks to the fragility of the claim to incontestable power. As David Loades argues, the English medieval monarchy 'exercised authority within a firmly established network of constraints' (*Tudor Government* 2). There was an implied contract between ruler and ruled and while the Reformation produced the Tudor state as sovereign, 'in the face of the outside world...its internal order depended upon a *de facto* concordat or understanding between the monarch and the political nation...increasingly identified with parliament...[which] embodied the concept of consent' (6). Even as Henry declares his and the realm's imperial status, he only does so through the consent of parliament and in fact parliament is strengthened by its use as the principle tool of reform. Thus the king could only assert his absolutism by allowing a check upon it.

Arts of Government, Arts of Dissent

The Tudors made use of a wide range of governmental arts and the authority of these forms (as we saw in the case of prophecy is itself the site of struggle). The government attempts to appropriate grass roots prophecy just as the people will redeploy elements of government strategy against the government. Spectacle was used by the court in innovative ways. Henry VII evoked the past, reviving the old medieval practice of public 'crown–wearings' (Gunn 196), as part of the rhetoric of dynastic magnificence. Henry VIII (guided by Wolsey) used theatrical spectacle for diplomatic purposes, the most famous events being the 'Field of Cloth of Gold' in 1520 and the entrance of the emperor Charles V into London in 1522. As well, this administration took spectacles through the streets and onto the river in newly designed rituals of 'choreographed joy' such as the fascinating case of 'corporate idolatry' (Ives 218) that was Anne Boleyn's coronation. This was the last of the Henrician mega–spectacles; polemicism was to replace splendour as a tactic in the solicitation of the acquiescence of the people.

The four day celebration of Boleyn's coronation is described by a range of eye witnesses in the *Letters and Papers* as well as by Edward Hall. The coronation was staged amid much public opinion against the marriage; as one of Cromwell's clerks puts it, 'many of the inconstant commons be not therewith satisfied. And though they forbear to speak at large for fear of punishment, yet they mutter together secretly; which...doth not a little embolden the King's adversaries without the realm' (*Letters and Papers* 6: 738). It was a question of national security that the people be brought to demonstrably accept the marriage and Boleyn's coronation was designed to have an effect in this regard. The event will be examined in detail in Chapter four.

In order to secure the loyalty of subjects, another kind of ritual was newly fitted for purposes of statecraft: the public performance of oaths. Certainly oaths of fealty were not new, and there was also the recent precedent of oaths sworn by conquered Frenchmen in Henry's campaigns in France. But the 'oath of succession,' sworn by English subjects in 1534, historians agree, was novel in kind and scope: 'the first employment...of a spiritual instrument of commitment as a political test' (Elton, *Policy* 222) and 'in scale ...entirely new' (Gunn 181). By this 'corporal oath,' English subjects swore that 'they shall truly, firmly and constantly without fraud or guile observe, fulfil, maintain, defend and keep to their cunning, wit and uttermost of their powers the whole effects and contents of this present act' (Elton, *The Tudor Constitution* 12). Despite the compliance with the oath swearing, how truly such speech acts reflected the intent or determined the action of those who swore is questionable. Bishop Hugh Latimer wrote to Cromwell that "'If you might make progress throughout England, you should find how acts declares hearts'" (qtd. in *Policy* 6); the implication, argues Elton is that the 'universal acquiescence beloved by historians' is doubtful; we can infer that 'acts' did not necessarily 'declare hearts' at all.

As the king attended to his visual representation and his subjects' consent and loyalty were represented orally (and, he hoped, felt in the heart) in the form of the oath, so was his policy transformed not only into law but also into rhetoric, aiming to convince, seduce and compel (as well as to threaten) his subjects into compliance. Berthelet had become the king's official printer in 1530, and from that date there flowed from his shop mass printings that reached 'deep into Tudor society' (Gunn 189).[14] As we have seen, one very important purpose of some of these communications was to require and facilitate the bringing of information back to London. Documents dispersed, Cromwell kept in close touch with the civic and ecclesiastical authorities to monitor the reception of these documents and their directives. As A.G. Dickens notes about these documents, the sheer volume of Cromwell's papers 'leave an impression of laborious omnicompetence hardly rivalled by any other minister in English history' (112).

It is before Cromwell is on board, however, that Henry launches the systematic propaganda campaign. Henry himself published a pamphlet — 'The Glass of Truth' — in 1532, in which he aims to convince a wide range of readers of the legitimacy of the divorce and calls on Parliament to exert its "'wits and good will'" to dissolve the marriage (qtd. in *Policy* 178). Stephen Gardiner's 'The Oration of True Obedience' followed, savaging the pope and exhorting support for the king's ecclesiastical supremacy. With the outbreak of rebellion in October 1536 the king's press was occupied with decrying the folly of rebellion with the aid of polemicists such as Morison.[15]

A discussion of the 1536 rebellions known as the Pilgrimage of Grace will serve to demonstrate how subjects both used the government's methods against the government and indeed determined the direction of government tactics. The Pilgrimage rose up at first in Lincolnshire, in 1536 in response to the presence of three government commissions at work gathering information for the Valor and taxes. One commission was collecting a subsidy tax to aid in military preparation, another was assessing the moral and educational 'fitness' of the clergy and a third was administering the first actual dissolution of the smaller monasteries. Cromwell was employing the pastoral and Catholic 'visitation' of religious houses to new and clearly rationalized ends. As Alan Stewart observes, '[w]hile the "visitation" was a tested means of internal policing by the Catholic Church...never before had it been employed by a secular authority; and whereas the Church's usual visitations could include hundreds of questions to each resident, this Cromwellian intrusion was brief and to the point' (47). And the point, as we have seen, was to record evidence of sexual transgressions in order to justify the closing of the monasteries, while simultaneously determining their monetary value. The commissions found what they were looking for:

> Even with the partial extant records of the visitation, covering only north and east of England, the 153 houses mentioned in the reports register 239 confessions of incontinence with women [by men], 161 of voluntary pollution (masturbation), and 60 of possessing relics. Many nuns confessed to having been or being pregnant; several even allegedly admitted to abetting in the killing of their children. Most shockingly, as far as Parliament was concerned, there were 105 accounts of sodomy. (Stewart 48)

While the government employed notions about the transgression of sexual boundaries as a weapon, ironically those from the lower orders who drove the northern rebellion employed notions about the transgressions of class boundaries by the Court as one of their rallying cries. One such transgression to which the pilgrims objected was the presence of non–noble persons — 'villeins' (specifically Cromwell) — in the king's privy council.

The first rising occurred at Louth on October 2, 1536, when the registrar arrived from the bishop to carry out the visitation; the commons, led by a shoemaker named Nicholas Melton — soon to be famed as Captain Cobbler — seized the registrar, burned his papers and forced the registrar and the assembled priests to swear an oath to be true to the rebels and their cause. They then marched to Legbourne nunnery and took captive the royal commissioners who were at work there. Soon after, there were similar risings in Lincolnshire and Yorkshire, the commons persuading the gentry to lead them (Fletcher 22). One such member of the gentry, Robert Aske, reluctantly assumed the principle leadership and it was he who began to speak of the rising as a 'pilgrimage.' All rebels swore the 'oath of honourable men' (composed by Aske) on October 17, 1536. They swore to fight, for the 'common wealth,' and in no way for their own profit or personal motivation; for the Holy Church (of

Rome); for 'the preservation of the King's person and his issue,' for the purifying of the nobility; and 'to expulse all villein blood and evil councillors against the commonwealth from his Grace and his Privvy Council' (Fletcher 122). This oath swearing clearly mimics and renders void the oath of succession. All sympathetic to the cause wore badges upon which was embroidered the symbol they claimed for themselves — the five wounds of Christ. (Who did this embroidery was never revealed, despite extensive questioning of the rebel leaders about this matter). As well, there were ballads and marching songs composed and widely circulated for the occasion, and as we have seen, prophecies proliferated. The principal captains took the names Charity, Faith, Poverty and Pity. Like the government, the rebels had to make their case rhetorically as well as militarily.

On October 15, the rebels also articulated sets of demands, the York Articles, and then the Pontefract Articles in early December. Among the concerns of the rebels were the social effects of the closing of the monasteries, including the loss of local care of the poor as well as the destitution of the nuns. They expressed their fear of taxation, called for the revoking of the new treason act, with its new category of treasonous words, and, as we have seen, demanded the expulsion of Cromwell and his 'villein blood' from the King's privy council. They accused two commissioners, a Doctor Leigh and Doctor Layton, of stealing from the monasteries during the visitation and of 'abhominable actes by them comytted and done' (Fletcher 129). In this charge, they are appropriating the language used in the *Valor* itself to describe the sexual vice that they counter–claimed such commissioners themselves had committed.

Yet the rebels were not in any simple way pro–Rome. As Fletcher notes '[t]he commons expressed dissatisfaction with many of their priests; in a remarkable outburst of radical thinking they went so far as to suggest that they themselves might take the initiative in replacing inadequate or non–resident ministers...[thus demonstrating] the extreme complexity of the movement Aske managed to hold together' (44). These subjects of this self–styled emperor, Henry VIII, clearly declared their right to have a say in their own governance to the point of claiming a veto power over the composition of the body of the king's advisors, even, ironically enough, as the non–nobles among them were supporting a conservative agenda that would delimit their own social mobility.

As to the application of the law in the case of the Pilgrimage of Grace, the government won and the rebels lost. The rebel leaders were executed, the monasteries were closed. Yet government is clearly made acutely self–conscious by these events, recognizing the need for strategies that supplement the strong arm of sovereignty. One sign of such a recognition is the government's sensitivity to the rhetorical power of prophecy and other forms of representation, as evidenced in a commission, in 1536, to all local courts in the country. Its tone, argues Elton, displays 'an urgent, almost hysterical, concern':

Ye shall...enquire of tale–tellers and counterfeiters of news that import any hurt or damage to the King's person, or to any of his nobles and councillors...[or to anyone who might stir up] the infamy and slander of the common people. These kind of people be to be abhorred and hated of any honest man. They go about utterly to extirp love, concord and quiet whereby any commonwealth flourishes. (qtd. in *Policy* 46)

The very fact that the king answers the Yorkshire rebels' petition demonstrates their sway (despite his derisive tone): 'We marvel therefore much that ignorant people will go about to take upon them to instruct and teach us...what the faith should be' (Berkowitz 177). He feels compelled to defend his actions, calling on historical precedent, 'Did not King Henry V suppress above one hundred monasteries, taking the great benefit of the same to his own proper use and behoof?' (Berkowitz 178) and attempts to represent the changes his administration has so far accomplished in a positive light, 'there was never...so many wholesome, commodious, and beneficial acts made for the commonwealth as have been made in our time' (Berkowitz 179). The king continues:

> What king hath kept his subjects so long in wealth and peace...so indifferently ministered justice to all estates both high and low, so defended them from all outward enemies, so fortified the frontiers...hath given among his subjects mo[re] general or free pardons? What king hath been loather to punish his subjects, or showed more mercy amongst them? (Berkowitz 180)

This is the shepherd king who keeps close watch. As to the composition of his council, the king calls on statistics to prove that the balance of nobles around the king had not altered in his reign. He dares anyone with any proof of wrongdoing to come forward, promising that he will bring the offender to due process. Dissent was clearly determining to a significant extent the material being produced in Berthelet's print shop.

Sermons were probably the most important vehicle for the king's rhetorical exhortations. To the end of controlling preachers and reaching the most humble subject in the farthest reaches of the realm, in 1533, Archbishop Cranmer revoked all existing clerical licenses and ordered new ones to be issued with instructions embodying the king's council's resolutions about reform. Instructional 'circular' letters with the royal seal were sent out to local officials of both Church and state, conscripting them in the enforcement of the government's policy. This strategy, claims Elton, 'better than any other method could mobilise the whole force of the state in support of the King's policy' (*Policy* 231). Guy observes that the letters were strategically personalized, 'letters were individually handwritten, the printing press being avoided so each thought his own letter unique'; in this way Cromwell could tell recipients that they had been "especially elected and chosen" (qtd. in Guy 137). The intention of the circular was not necessarily to identify local transgressors and command that they should be brought to justice however; rather the circulars' function was primarily a means of collecting information for future discretionary use. Like other innovations, the letter was to function as a centripetal force between subject and monarch.

During the rebellions, bishops received letters about what to say and not to say about these events: they must not themselves express any dissent, even privately, and they must send up for punishment anyone around them "'that will not better temper his tongue'" (qtd. in Elton, *Policy* 251). In 1536, a letter to the bishops commands them to find the means to 'remove out of men's hearts such abuses as by false doctrine...have crept into the breasts of the same' (qtd. in Elton, *Policy* 244). This task could neither be accomplished by those preachers who had been 'seduced with filthy and corrupt abominations of the bishop of Rome' nor by 'the setting forth of novelties and the continual inculcation of things not necessary' (qtd. in Elton, *Policy* 244). Instead, the bishops were to 'have their instruction tempered with such mean and be taught with such discretion and judgement as little by little they might perceive the truth' (qtd. in Elton, *Policy* 244). Here we have the promotion of the tempered tongue and the uncankered heart through the achievement of the mean between Rome and radical reform.

The bishops themselves, however, were to be monitored by officers of the law and to this end, sheriffs and justices of the peace received their instructions in June, 1535. They were to make

diligent search, wait, and espial, in every place of your sheriffwick, whether the said bishop do truly, sincerely, and without all manner cloak, colour, or dissimulation, execute and accomplish our will and commandment...[if they see any bishop that] do coldly and unfeignedly use any manner sinister addition, wrong interpretation, or painted colours...[they are to] make indelayedly, and with all speed and diligence, declaration, and advertisement to us. (*TRP* 231–2)

In the setting of the sheriffs and justices as watchdogs over the bishops, effectively a reversal of roles, 'the laicisation of the realm could not have been more plainly demonstrated' (Elton *Policy* 239). This document appeals as well to these judicial officers as individuals 'unto whose wisdom, discretion, truth, and fidelity we might commit a matter of such great weight, moment and importance as whereupon the unity, rest, and tranquillity of our realm doth consist and is stabilized' (*TRP* 232). Should they fail and 'halt, stumble, or wink...be you assured that we like a prince of justice will so extremely correct and punish you for the same that all the world besides shall take by you example' (232). On the other hand, obedience would ensure the fulfilment of the governmental promise of great earthly reward to all and each: 'an inestimable weal, profit, commodity, unity, and tranquillity [will come] to all the public and common state of this our realm, whereunto both by the laws of God, nature, and man you be utterly obliged and bound' (232).

Another innovation that came out of the transfer of ecclesiastical authority to the Crown was the appropriation of the 'injunction,' traditionally a set of orders following a bishop's 'visitation' to the regular clergy in his diocese. As Vicar General or vicegerent, a top ecclesiastical post, Cromwell exercised his authority of inspection and direction by issuing two sets of injunctions (in 1536 and 1538) to every bishop in the realm. In the first set, the directions are principally to do with educational imperatives about the supremacy and the reformed liturgy. The clergy are ordered first to comply with all orders themselves 'to the uttermost of their wit, knowledge, and learning, purely, sincerely, and without any colour or dissimulation' (Gee and Hardy 270). They then must in their sermons 'declare [and] manifest [the same truths] for the space of one quarter of a year...every Sunday, and after that at the leastwise twice every quarter' (270). The demotion of the saints would involve 'seeing all goodnes, health, and grace...to be...only of God, as of the very Author of the same, and of none other' (271). Another injunction calls for the redirection of the time, devotion and money that once had gone to the saints and pilgrimages to subjects' immediate families as well as to 'the poor and needy' (Gee 271). Thus, the family (and its pleasures and responsibilities) was to be the site of an investment, even as the state (through the person of Cromwell) conscripted individuals to the aid of the poor, who, as the northern rebels observed, were suffering with the suppression of the monasteries. Injunction five calls on the bishops to discipline their parishioners by having them memorize the Paternoster, the Articles of Faith and the Ten Commandments. Clearly 'disciplinary' as well is this article's prescription to parents to educate their children, or to set them up in apprenticeships, because

> through sloth and idleness divers valiant men fall, some to begging and some to theft and murder, which after, brought to calamity and misery, imputed great part thereof to their friends and governors, which suffered them to be brought up so idly in their youth; where if they had been well educated and brought up in some good literature, occupation, or mystery, they should, being rulers of their own family, have profited as well themselves, as divers other persons, to the great commodity and ornament of the common weal. (272–3)

The clergy themselves are instructed, for the 'profit of the commonwealth' to stay out of taverns, to give both to the poor and to scholars at Oxford and Cambridge and to see to the good repair of church property.

The second set of Injunctions, more extensive still, besides establishing record–keeping in the form of registration, reiterated the campaign against all things Roman. Clergy were to publically confess to their parishioners if they had transgressed any of the first injunctions and to spy on their parishioners. These injunctions also demanded that there be English Bibles placed in every church and called for rote learning in English of the Creed, the 'Pater noster' and the ten commandments, this skill to be tested in the Lenten confession. A follow up letter (*L&P* 13:1304) instructs the clergy to inform parishioners that if they are puzzled or worried over anything they read in their English Bible, they are not to give 'too much to your own minds, fantasies and opinion...[nor discuss it with others] in your open taverns and alehouses;' instead, they are to look to their betters and those learned for advice. As Elton suggests, the Bible was being employed as 'an instrument of social peace and moral improvement' and as a means to transform 'central resolve into local action' (*Policy* 261–2). The injunctions and the practices they describe are clearly tactics of governmentality that involve the deferral of government to the governed. The injunctions were also a technology for surveillance as this network of watchers and producers and disseminators of information was mobilized. Yet how effective were such prescriptions and proscriptions? Elton writes of 'a Warwickshire curate who was so sick of reading the injunctions he says they are "as light to learn as a boy or a wench should learn a ballad or a song...here is a hundred words ...where two would serve...it cometh in like a rhyme, a jest, or a ballad"' (*Policy* 259). It appears such discipline was at times tedious, at best ineffectual and at worst, counter–productive.

Change did not happen from the top down, from the command of the king or the rationale of Thomas Cromwell. As Gunn suggests:

> [S]ociety interacted with the state: the ambitions of monarchs and the projects of their ministers were at times welcomed, at times obstructed or diverted, according to the perceived self–interest or duty of those who held power locally, from the greatest nobleman to the constables, churchwardens and jurymen who held sway in village life. By their appropriation of governmental initiatives for their own purposes, selective cooperation, evasion, and at times outright revolt, they played their part in the development of the Tudor state. (Gunn 203)

And as Steve Hindle has argued, 'early modern English government was not, indeed could not be, an arcane or remote "royal mechanism": it was something in which subjects were involved, something they learned to manipulate, to criticise and even to change' (*Renaissance Law and Literature*, Abstracts 1). The change that was called the 'Tudor revolution' was arbitrated not only by those in positions of power but by those without official power: the commons, including women, played their role as well.

This historical review of the representational strategies employed by governors and dissenters has revealed two aspects of the government of individualization that I would like to emphasize. First, individualization is designed to work as an alienating process, as subjects are urged to subject themselves and those under their authority to suspicious scrutiny. Yet the forces of fragmentation and appropriation — the dividing practices of individualization — are not, in any simple way, exercised from above. Rather, although such forces may be administered from above, power is dispersed in a network and exercised by subjects on themselves and each other even if there is finally an 'immanence to the state' (Foucault, 'Governmentality' 91). Rather than demonstrating that such forces are all the more determined and impossible to confront, Tudor history shows that power depends on the complicity of subjects for its enactment and that English subjects engaged vibrantly with the governmental arts.

'The numbered of his flock'

I began with a document from the end of the 1530s; I will conclude this chapter with one from the beginning of that decade — a speech made by the then chancellor Thomas More on November 3, 1530 at the opening of parliament, as reported by Hall. As Morison would figure forth the king as a lion, hungry to show his prowess for the protection of his people, More sets forth the king as that quintessential figure of governmentality, the 'good shepherd.' More had employed the same trope in *Utopia*. His character Raphael Hythloday opines that 'the king ought to take more care for the wealth of his people than for his own wealth, even as the office and duty of a shepherd is in that he is a shepherd, to feed his sheep rather than himself' (119). More declares in parliament that Henry as shepherd not only,

> kepeth and attendeth well his shepe, but all so forseeth & provideth for althyng, which either may be hurtful or noysome to his floke, or may preserve and defende thesame agaynst all peryles that may chaunce to come. (*Hall* 764)

To this end, the shepherd is also a prophet 'vigila[n]tly forseyng thinges to come' and what he sees are laws that need reforming: 'divers lawes before this tyme wer made nowe by lo[n]g co[n]tinuance of tyme and mutacion of thinges, very insufficient, & unperfight' (764). Because of the 'mutation of things' over time, as well as 'the frayl condicion of man, divers new enormities were spro[n]g amongest the people, for the which no law was yet made to reforme thesame, which was the very cause why at that tyme the kyng had somoned his high court of parliament' (764).

Hall reflects on More's use of the metaphor of the shepherd: 'if a prince be compared to his riches, he is but a richeman, if a prince be compared to his honour, he is but an honourable man: but compare him to the multitude of his people and the numbre of his flocke, the[n] he is a ruler, a governor of might and puissaunce, so that his people maketh him a prince, as of the multitude of shepe, commeth the name of a shepherd' (764). The prince needs his people just as the people need their prince and his 'numbering' of them is the operation by which the 'multitude' is transformed into representation, into 'a flocke' of individualized subjects. Further, the 'frayl [moral] condition' of the populace justifies the increased level of intervention in the lives of English subjects.

This shepherd has a policy for strays, More continues, in a thinly veiled account of the case of that stray sheep Wolsey:

> [A]s you se that emongest a great flocke of shepe some be rotte[n] and fau[l]ty which the good sheperd sendeth from the good shepe, so the great...late fallen as you all knowe, so craftely, so scabedly, ye & so untruly juggeled with the kyng, that all men must nedes gesse and thinke that he thought in him self, that he had no wit to perceive his craftie doyng, or els that he presumed that the kyng woulde not se nor know his fraudulent Juggeling and attemptes: but he was deceived, for his graces sight was so quike and

penetrable, that he saw him, ye and saw through him, both with in and without so that all thing to him was open. (764)

The shepherd sees all, knows all, both the deeds and thoughts of each member of his flock. The transgressive sheep Wolsey, More declares, 'hath had a gentle correction...but...that whosoever here after shall make like attempt or commit like offence, shal not escape with lyke ponyshment,' as Chancellor More himself would soon see (764).

The king is an absolute sovereign, an imaginative disciplinarian and a gentle shepherd. The governmental arts and the counter–arts are put to evermore novel and imaginative uses in the public affairs of the English nation. The king tells the story of his free subjects, who need to guide and be guided in his name, whose happiness and productivity are to accrue to the strength of the state. They respond with their own imperatives about government and about modes of being in the world. The next chapter will look at the principle designers of the Henrician arts of government, those students of the state and human nature — the humanists, and show how, foe this class of men, governing itself becomes a form of governance.

Notes

1. See Geoffrey Roberts for a recent valorization of Elton's 'sustained defence of what may be called a human action account of the past: the view that history was not the result of social structures, objective forces or (as some postmodernists argue) linguistic discourses, but of autonomous human agents' (29), in *The Historian* 60.2 (1997): 29–31. For an argument against Elton's contention that Cromwell was the force of change see G.W. Bernard's 'Elton's Cromwell,' in *History* 83. 272 (1998): 587–607. Bernard argues that 'Elton was wrong above all in minimizing, as have so many of the historians who have followed him, the independent role of Henry VIII, so misrepresenting the relationship between king and minister' (590).

2. *Black's Law Dictionary* defines 'demesne' as 'Domain; dominical; held in one's own right, and not of a superior; not allotted to tenants. In the language of pleading, own; proper; original' (297). John Rastell in his *Les Termes De La Ley: or, Certain Difficult and Obscure Words and Terms of the Common and Statute Laws of England, Now in Use, Expounded and Explained* locates the origin of the term in 'a certain tenure whereby all manors belonging to the crown in the days of William the conqueror were held' (30). All revenue from the land held in demesne was directly payable to the king and all subjects living on that land were subject to the common law procedures of the king's court (and not as in areas held 'of the king' but not directly by him where various lesser and local courts held jurisdiction).

3. *Black's Law Dictionary* defines 'attainder' as '[a]t common law, that extinction of civil rights and capacities which took place whenever a person who had committed treason or felony received sentence of death for his crime.' The effect of 'attainder' upon such a felon was, in general terms, that all his estate, real and personal, was forfeited. (85). An 'act of attainder' could also be passed by parliament, thereby avoiding the necessity of a

trial at common law; here the function of parliament as a court, and indeed as the highest court, is made evident. The family of the convicted felon lost all right to the land and goods held by that felon, the blood of the family being 'attainted' by the conviction.

4. For a lively narrative about the Paduan English humanists and their later role in government, see W. Gordon Zeeveld's *Foundations of Tudor Policy*, (Cambridge, Mass: Harvard UP, 1948).

5. The 1533 statute (25 Hen.8 c, 6) called for the death penalty for sodomy. This statute is repealed under the more reactionary Henry in 1541; reenacted under Edward VI, in 1548, (excluding forfeiture for convicts); repealed again under Mary. In 1563, Elizabeth I reinstated the law with the original Henrician terms (5 Eliz. c, 17) and the death penalty for sodomy remained on the books until 1861. I have summarized Jonathan Goldberg in *Sodometries: Renaissance Texts, Modern Sexualities* (Stanford: Stanford UP, 1992.).

6. Alan Stewart provides a discussion about whether the buggery law was consciously part of the strategy that would culminate in the suppression of the monasteries. It was certainly, from its inception, part of a campaign against monastics, its enactment directly associated with the issue of sanctuary and the 'benefit of clergy.' Both the latter were limited by legislation in the same parliamentary sitting.

7. S.J. Gunn relates that '[i]n a sample of counties studied using the taxation returns of 1522–5, the gentry and the church each held about a third of the land, the nobility's share was between 1 and 7 percent, and the crown's equalled or exceeded it, at between 4 and 6 percent.' Looking at the effect of the dissolution of the monasteries in one riding, after 1535, 'the nobilities share...rose only from 8 to 9 per cent, and the gentry's rose from 40 to 48 per cent, the crown's tripled from 9 to 27 per cent' (26). Clearly the point was for the crown to control the nobility, either by tempering their numbers or by ensuring a body of loyal nobles through patronage. By the year 1558 (the first of Elizabeth Tudor's reign) of the total number of peers in the realm, 23 percent were first–generation noblemen and a further 23 percent second generation (Gunn 57).

8. Loades notes, concerning the Cromwell, 'revolution' thesis, that since it was not in Cromwell's own political interest to have made the Council more efficient than it had been under Wolsey by reducing the power of one strong councillor, then it must have been the king's and not Cromwell's initiative.

9. There was also the precedent of the blank forms issued by Rome — papal indulgences and confessional letters. If a person had to pay a fine, a papal tax or a fee for membership in a confessional guild, they had to both make the payment and purchase a receipt as demonstration of payment and it is clearly a sign of an irrational bureaucracy that by the pre–Reformation years, the receipt cost more than the original fee or fine.

10. For a discussion of Thomas More's role in the entrenchment of an equitable jurisdiction in
  ·   Chancery and of Chancery's right of injunction over common law actions, see J.H. Baker's *Introduction to English Legal History*, 3rd ed. (London: Buttersworths, 1990)124–5.

11. Copyhold is a feudal form of land tenure; Rastell calls it that for which 'the tenant hath nothing to shew but the copies of the rolls made by the steward of his lord's court' (*Les Jermes* 119). It was administered according to the customs of the local manor court, not the common law, and did not indicate ownership of land but rather rights to the lord's land. Those rights, even to the issue of whether land was transferable to heirs, varied and were determined by custom.

12. Inflation as well served to bolster the jurisdiction of the central courts since borough courts could only hear cases having to do with sums of money below a certain level (two

pounds in the early sixteenth century). As business relationships boomed, more cases involving debts arose and as the centralization of business in the largest centres increased, the populations of the boroughs themselves began to shrink

13. Henrician treatises on poverty and attempts to govern vagabonds and the poor would influence Edward VI to donate Bridewell Palace to the city of London as a 'house of occupations.' There, under Elizabeth, a full program was developed in which the poor, sex trade workers and the homeless and unemployed were incarcerated for retraining.

14. Statutes, by the 1540s, were run off 500 at a time for public proclamation and display, enough to deliver one copy to every market town in the country. Proclamations increased in volume and were printed in runs of 1200 by this period.

15. For a detailed examination of Henry VIII's printing program in the 1520s and early thirties see J. Christopher Warner, *Henry VIII's Divorce: Literature and the Politics of the Printing Press* (Woodbridge, Suffolk: The Boydell Press, 1998). Warner argues that during the divorce crisis the King attempted to craft an image as benevolent philosopher/king. This supports my argument that the experiments in pastoral government in the same period required an anti–Machiavellian orientation to the image of leadership.

Chapter 2

Governing Bodies:
Humanism and the Bureaucrats

A traitour, whether he be so taken or nat, can lacke no scouringe, whan he is most alone. He hath his wyppe in his bosom, and playeth the tormentour him selfe for lacke of an officer.
(Richard Morison, *An Invective Agenste the Great and Detestable Vice, Treason*)

thou shalt always be mery and...alwayes have inwarde peace.
(Christopher St German, *Doctor and Student* 93–5).

Humanists on Humanism

In the last fifteen years, historians and literary critics have worked to usefully problematize the category of early modern humanism. Alistair Fox observes that since the contemporary study of English humanism began in the 1930s there has seldom been consensus on even the basic criteria by which a figure could or could not be labelled humanist: '[o]n the one hand [the modern student] will be told that humanism was "arrested" with the deaths of More and Fisher...then on the other hand that the Henrician religious settlement was the fulfilment of Erasmianism, and that northern humanism "grew up largely in the service of the Reformation"' (*Facts and Fallacies: Interpreting English Humanism* 9–10). Similarly, as Erika Rummel observes,'Modern scholars are divided on whether humanism acted as retardant or a stimulant to the development of Renaissance philosophy. Some see it as an impediment in the linear path leading from scholasticism to the scientific revolution, others think it breathed life into a moribund system' (153). Fox concludes that humanism was 'a multifarious phenomenon' (32), certainly having something to do with the revival of classical learning and the reform of education; but that finally 'most of the prevailing generalizations about English humanism need to be either discarded or radically revised' (33). I agree with Lorna Hutson that '[w]e should not collude with Renaissance humanism's account of itself' in our reconsiderations of this category, although of course, accounting for themselves was one of the humanists' favourite occupations (3).[1] Nevertheless, to set the stage, I will begin by offering a brief sketch of some humanist accounts of the birth of humanism.

Liberationist if not revolutionary, humanism represented itself as liberating the trivium from its emphasis on logic, as exercised in dialectical argumentation based on a strict formal procedure derived from Aristotle. For 'the scholastics,' rhetoric was suspect and only an accruing of logical inference could and would lead to objective truth. The humanists charged that the scholastics' conclusions were often nonsensical and though an opponent in a debate might be vanquished within the bounds of the process, they may not in fact be persuaded to believe in the premise of the victor. As Erika Rummel summarizes Juan Vives' complaint in *De causis*, '[d]ialecticians played a fatuous mechanical game in which victory went to the person who left the opponent without a counterargument. Thus: the response of the opponent was elevated to a criterion of truth...Everything else, however senseless and paradoxical, must be accepted because the contestant cannot refute it' (Rummel 172).[2] Here is Erasmus' satirical take on scholasticism in *The Praise of Folly*; he speaks of:

> the philosophers who are reverenced for their beards and the fur on their gowns. They announce that they alone are wise, and that the rest of men are only passing shadows...One would think that they had access to the secrets of nature, who is the maker of all things, or that they had just come from a council of the gods. Actually nature laughs uproariously at them all the time...They know nothing at all, yet profess to know everything. They are ignorant even of themselves...[the] subtlest of subtleties are made more subtle by the methods of the scholastic philosophers. It is easier to escape from a maze than from the tangles of Realists, Nominalists, Thomists, Albertists, Occamists, and Scotists. (404–5)

The humanists associated losing their 'ignorance of themselves' with the privileging of the place of rhetoric in dialectical/logical processes as they worked to tie all their studies to the practical life. 'Logic,' argues Vives, should be 'an art which is learned not for its own sake, but in order to serve as a basis for the other arts, and be their handmaid, so to speak' (Vives, *In Pseudodialecticos* 80). This validation of 'artificial proof' in argumentation, argues Lisa Jardine, is the fundamental contribution of humanism to the history of logic: its recognition that 'oratio may be persuasive, even compelling, without its being formally valid' ('Humanistic Logic' 175).This shift in emphasis to the perlocutionary potential of the sign had a variety of important consequences of course, from a new emphasis on reading the classics in the original, to a rise in importance of the genre of dialogue (as a perfect marriage of inquisition and pleasure), to a call for a return to what they saw as a standardized language for dialectical reasoning. As Vives put it: '"In the simple, genuine, true, and direct manner of speaking there is no room for caviling, which is the primary goal of [the scholastics'] investigation"' (qtd. in Rummel 181).

As well, the new valuation of the rhetorical raised the instrumental value of 'poetry.' Literary texts could be culled for their rhetorical strategies as models to be emulated. Jardine makes the critical point, however, that for the humanists, encounters with pedagogues and classical texts offered more than the accruing of information about right method. Rather, such encounters were productive; they were capable of accomplishing a reformation of the intellect, the very consciousness of the student in such textual engagement. Linking humanism and social praxis, Victoria Kahn argues that the quintessential humanist virtue was prudence, and that prudence could similarly be achieved through the mental exercise provided by reading for rhetoric:

> [Humanists] go beyond their classical mentors in conceiving of literature not only as the cause and effect of prudence and right action...but as a form of prudence itself. Rhetoric here is not primarily conceived of in terms of style or ornament, but in terms of its capacity to exemplify and encourage the activity of practical reasoning...Praxis in the sense of political action can be the fruit of reading because the practice of interpretation educates our ability to deliberate about such action. (Kahn 39–41)

Texts transform readers, not merely by convincing the reader of the efficacy of an argument, but also by converting the mental capacity of the reader to a prudential structure of consciousness. And a prudent man will operate within the bounds of decorum, a word with a positive moral valence in the period. Such was the power of good poetry, that reading decorous literature could render a man, not only eloquent and prudent, but also good. For Cicero and Quintillion 'the good orator is a good man...moral goodness and decorum...cannot conflict' (Kahn 34).[3]

Such was humanism's account of itself. It was a moral, even democratic movement that promised reform through encounters with literature and one class of subjects needing governance was the one to which they themselves belonged. Certainly humanists themselves believed in 'the Renaissance'; as Vives reflects: 'whenever reference is made to the rebirth of the humanities [*humanitas*], more particularly the origins of this revival, or to the state of the other higher disciplines, we cannot help feeling a certain pride in our age' (*In Pseudodialecticos* 26).[4] This new class of morally good, prudent, dialectical and eloquent orators began by 'managing' themselves through their 'human sciences' in order to earn the governance of household, trade, law courts, the king's administrative bodies and foreign affairs. These were trusty counsellors.

Lorna Hutson and Alan Stewart have recently offered 'counter accounts' of Henrician humanism with which I am largely sympathetic. Hutson's *The Userer's Daughter: Male Friendship and Fictions of Women in Sixteenth–Century England* and Stewart's *Close Readers: Humanism and Sodomy in Early Modern England* articulate the pragmatic economics of the professional humanists who depended on an essentially conservative system of patronage for their livelihood and status. And both explore the relation of gender and sexual practices to economic and literary relations. Hutson argues that marriage and the 'good housewife' become an alibi for the humanists' crude profit motive and Stewart sees marriage as an alibi for relations between men that flirted with those codes of the sodomical that were established during the campaign to suppress the monasteries. In relation to the pragmatics of humanism, Stewart argues that 'humanism deliberately created the perceived need for humanism' (xxv). While humanists theorized about egalitarian societies where free willing subjects would produce prosperity, humanist literature and its 'chaste thinking,' 'masks a more crudely pragmatic program with which individual humanists sought to infiltrate the very "feudal" structure they attacked, through their own and their children's marriages' (Stewart xxiii). Hutson observes, in a similar vein, that, unlike feudal relations of alliance, in which a system of credit and debt was created among aristocratic families through the exchange of gifts as 'surety' or assurance, the humanist 'gift' of powerful rhetoric and reasoning was 'a technology available to all men, a transferable instrument for the creation of credit' (76).[5]

Governing Bodies

Of particular interest to my argument is the way in which this flurry of textual production involved humanist men in the service of governing humanist men. They did more than 'deliberately create the need for humanism' by calling for the kind of educational reform their skills could address. One of the principal humanist tasks was the production of a discourse about masculinity — as wild, lusty and potentially treacherous — that would demonstrate the need for professional humanist interventions. It would take rhetoric and rationality to design and deliver an elaborate set of checks and balances through which a class of men could be rendered managers of themselves and others.

We see this ethic at work in another treatise composed by the humanist scholar and employee of Henry VIII and Cromwell, Richard Morison. Morison composed two treatises at the request of Cromwell after the uprisings of 1536, the one announcing itself as prescriptive — *An Exhortation to Styre All Englyshe Men to the Defence of Theyr Countreye* (examined in chapter 1) and the other proscriptive — *An Invective Agenste the Great and Detestable Vice, Treason, Wherein the Secrete Practises, and Traiterous Workinges of Theym, that Suffred of Late are Disclosed. An Exhortation*, I argued above, aimed to produce a totality of English subjects obliged by a 'lovely bond' to defend king and country 'with englysshe handes [and] englysshe hartes'; doing so would realize the promise of 'perpetuall quietnes, rest, peace, victorie, honour, welthe, all is ower' (58). In his *Invective*, Morison's strategies are more individualizing than they are totalizing and the individuals with whom he is most concerned are explicitly and implicitly male: he addresses only men and cites the cases of an array of exclusively male traitors — Roman, biblical and English — to demonstrate the bad end to which traitors inevitably come. *An Invective* is a vivid example of deliberative rhetoric and the construction of an argument that stands on an ethically and logically precarious set of artificial proofs.

As Morison proceeds, he produces a discourse, not about the personage of the traitor as congenital type, but rather about the self as a product of 'traytrous' thoughts. Being a traitor is thus not about politics, religion, or justice but about a dearth of self–temperance. He warns that a person who '[i]n harte...stylle feleth the stinge of treason must nedes at one tyme or an other, make the tonge and countenance partakers of his grefe' (A preface a iiii). True subjects therefore must exile treasonous thoughts from themselves as territories, even as they are bidden in *An Exhortation* to exile any threat of foreign invasion from the shores of England.

Further, Morison argues that his Roman examples, especially Nero, demonstrate that 'god pluckecth [the highly valuable attributes] wyt and prudency from malyciouse traytours' and as wit and prudence are exiled, subjects 'worke their owne confusion' (A preface ab i).

The vice associated with traitors is 'unkyndness,' as a turning away from one's 'kind': 'Unkyndnesse, is a fytte name for so unnaturall a vice: they that fal into it...lose that state and name, that nature put them in, and are tourned into cruell and unnaturall beastes' (B ii). Confused and less than human in their 'states' of mind, treasonous subjects also relinquish their autonomy: 'Treason can never lye alone in a traytours harte, it hath suche a rablemente with it, that deathe is pleasure, if it be compared with the gripes, the woundis, the tossynge and turmoylyng, the heavying and shovyng, that traitours fele in their stomackes' (Bb iv).

Morison's mind is on debt and credit. Concerning the recently executed Henry Corteney, Henry Pole and Edward Nevell, he asks rhetorically: 'what men were more endetted to man, than were all these thre[e] to his highnes?'(Aix). 'Gratitude' he continues,

> is a perpetuall memorie of benefittes receyved, and alsoo a defyse to recompense them [and is] a mother of many vertues, forasmoche as there commeth from her, love and feare of god, love and feare of our prince, love towarde our countreye, love towarde our parentes...frendshyp betwene man and man (Bii)

Here he addresses the totality of English subjects, as potential traitors: 'Englande, hathe thou no cause to folow David, to make himnes and ditties of thankes unto god?...whan wylte thou paye him thankes, if thou nowe deny thy self endetted to hym? thou must confesse dette, thou canste nat denie it, without thy greatte shame' (Aix).

The pamphlet's argument has so far been focussed on the self–producing, self–annihilating personage of the traitor and by implication the antithetical good subject. English subjects are rational and reading history will demonstrate the irrationality of treason. Treason itself, however, is crazy–making; it will lead to the decay of rational autonomous consciousness, to 'confusion,' to the confounding of 'wyt and prudence,' to 'shame,' finally metamorphizing the 'unkind' traitor to 'beastliness.' Through his appeal to pathos, Morison would bring his 'gentle reders' 'into hatred of treason' so that they 'maye at the laste fall in love with their duetie, and seke truly to serve, where god hath appoynted theym so to doo' (A Preface a ii). Traitorous English subjects, just as they make themselves into traitors, are doomed to self–infliction. Caught or not, they will be their own masochistic 'officer' of the law: 'A traitour, whether he be so taken or nat, can lacke no scourginge, whan he is moste alone. He hath his whyppe in his bosom, and playeth the tormentour him selfe for lacke of an officer' (Eb ii).

Morison has produced a conundrum: is the ideal subject to conceive of himself as entirely autonomous? It would seem that so doing would free him from the influence of the collectivity — the 'rablement of traytrous rebels' — and that individualization thus would be a means of ensuring the security of the state. But the word 'security,' in the sixteenth century, can slip into its own antonym, namely the obsolete sense of a 'culpable absence of anxiety, carelessness' breeding the kind of overconfidence and autonomy that could threaten the state (*OED online*, def. I, 3). One humanist solution to this problem is to be found in the promotion of the Ciceronian ideal of *amicitia* or as Thomas Elyot englishes the term — 'amity.' Through 'frendshyp betwene man and man,' Morison argues, two individualized men equalized within a humanist relationship would find solace and nourishment and economic gain (as Hutson argues) but their friendship also functioned as a check on the potentially traitorous and tyrannizing impulses of each (Morison Bii). Thus 'confessing debt,' in terms of friendship, becomes a mode of government.

Monetary debt and the related personal action of trespass had come to dominate late medieval litigation in every jurisdiction, but the Reformation heralded what Delloyd J.Guth calls the 'de–moralizing of debt,'as the age of debt gave way to the age of contract (69). Actions of debt and trespass relied on claims by witnesses that past promises had been made and had been guaranteed by the subject's sense of duty and Christian conscience. As debt came to be secularized, the issue was tied less to the debtor's conscience and 'actions of debt came to require what the lawyers labelled "consideration" the identity of a benefit, a material cause or *quid pro quo*...to explain why the debt existed' (84). Medieval subjects who owed debts were to examine their consciences, measuring past promises with deeds done or not done and viewed their shortcomings in relation to sin and made restitution both to God and, as the court dictated, to their neighbour; early modern subjects were coming to believe in their freedom to contract themselves, their duty and thus their conscience in terms of what could be demonstrated by evidence of 'consideration.'

A governmental mode of rule is evident in the displacement of old notions of debt and duty onto affective relationships with other men. Hutson suggests that humanist texts were a form of currency, their bestowal upon a patron a means of producing a credit. I would suggest further that the truck in cultural capital, patronage appointments and monetary rewards is implicated in the 'ambitious promises' offered by the operations of governmentality. Morison's figuration of debt as that which is owed to God and the king harks back to the feudal economy of knight's service, but it also points forward to a notion of debt that purports to transcend monetary concerns and in so doing enacts the management of behaviour in some measure through the generation of shame: 'thou must confesse dette, thou canste nat denie it, without thy greatte shame' (Aix).

As amity is a governmental institution, so clearly is marriage. Within the literary culture of humanism, argues Hutson, women are more than a sign of credit in marriage (as they were in medieval alliances): 'the claim to be able to "fashion" women by addressing them through persuasive fictions of themselves lent a special social credibility to the masculine activity of authorship' (7). Not only did a well–governed woman function as the sign of the man's 'good husbandry,' in such texts, she also took the rap for her husband's profit motive. The good 'housewife,' argues Hutson, becomes 'the subversive principle of her husband's economic plot' (11).

This paradigm, Hutson demonstrates, is vividly represented in a popular classical text — Xenophon's *Oeconomics* — first translated into English as *Xenophon's Treatise of Householde* in 1534 by Gentian Hervet. A dialogue between Socrates and Critobulus about estate management, this text defines such terms as wealth, value, surplus and property. Socrates holds up as an ideal manager one Ischomachus, whose principal talent is his ability to train and direct the activities of his wife. Hervet's text, says Sarah Pomeroy, was 'the first English translation of any of Xenophon's works to be published. It was reprinted in at least six editions' (Pomeroy 81). Hutson makes large claims for the historical significance of this text; she argues that it shifts the 'moral boundaries of economic thought (including those which determined Western attitudes to usury, and hence to capitalism)' (11) even as its central paradigm of the husband who fashions an unruly woman through rhetorical skill becomes a sign of the social transformations made possible by humanist literary culture; Xenophon 'replace[s] the notion of husbandry as necessary toil with the notion of husbandry as an art of existence which is both the sign and essence of the most fortunate, the rulers of the commonweal' (38). Isomachus gets the last word in the treatise: 'This grace cometh not [to] all of man, to rule and governe so, that men very gladly wil be obedient, but it is rather a speciall gyft of almyghty god: and [he] graunteth it unto theim that be indowed with vertue and temperaunce. But to rule men tryannousely against their willes, he putteth theim unto it...that be judgeth worthy [of] hell' (Hervet 63).[6] Clearly Xenophon's good husband governs himself and in so doing produces 'willing subjects' ready for his rule. Hutson agrees that good husbandry must be *done* and in fact it must be taught to be learned: 'Exemplarity does not, after all, mean learning by example; it means learning by *teaching* by example. The art of household is exemplary because it involves the man practising his own histrionic exemplarity in the training that will transform a "rude" and "wytles" partner into a womanly helpmeet' (34). Although Hutson does not cite Juan Vives' tract, *de Officio Mariti (The Office and Duty of a Husband)*, this text certainly supports her argument about the function of marriage within humanism:

> ...what a commodity the wife is unto the husband, in ordering of his house and in governing of his family and household, and by this cities are edified, and builded...[she] keepeth his goods as her own...This holy and sincere institution shall increase thorough the good example of the husband, the which to inform and fashion the woman's life and his family withal, is of no less value and force than the example of a prince to inform the public manners and customs of a city, for every man is a king in his own house. (Aughterson 431–33)

The implications of Tudor 'good husbandry' are many. Despite the indispensable myth of the division of labour in the household that is put forth as 'natural history' by humanist '*oeconomists*' (the man gets, the woman keeps), Hutson argues that in both literature and life women are implicated in a 'new economy of representation in ways that actually narrow the scope for positive representations of their agency' (11). I am interested here, however, in the figuring forth of masculinity in this 'new economy of representation.' Hutson explores how marriage was a means to mobilize idle aristocratic bachelors to the useful service of the state:

> The polemic common to the humanist texts...seems to oppose the idle household which maintains a retinue of bachelor younger brothers to a new, but hazily defined concept of nobility and gentry engaging in a kind of "husbandry" that involves matrimony, the persuasive mobilization of classical texts, and the remedy of the economic ills (underpopulation, the decay of towns, the export of raw materials and import of luxuries and trifles) that beset the realm. (69)

These texts, however, put forth more than polemics about sociological and demographical ills. They also link these ills to masculinity itself.

The misogyny of Vives' *Instruction of a Christian Woman* is frequently commented upon. But Vives' disparagement of men and masculinity in this text and in *The Office and Duty of An Husband* is striking as well. In *The Office and Duty*, Vives explicitly states the undesirable aspects of masculinity that marriage is to ameliorate:

> how many utilities and profits do spring and issue of matrimony? First...all controversies and debates are removed and do cease among men when lands be occupied and possessed...when the woman is lawfully married all such contentions do cease, which certainly would have grown among men, if women were common...[M]an..(if he followeth his natural affection and appetite) is a proud, a fierce and a desirous beast to be revenged, shall find many ways to accomplish his lust and to ensure and revenge, that he interpreteth to be an injury, and shall associate and gather many unto him, either for fear, or by some benefit enticed, whereby partakings and factions should first arise, and afterwards war, and cruel battle, both at home and abroad, as old auctors do report to have chanced for women ravished, as for Helen Lacona, Tindaras's and Leda's daughter and for Lucretia. (Aughterson 430)

For Vives, then, God 'hath put a measure to this immoderate luxuriousness, printing the law of matrimony not in paper only, but in every man's heart' (431). Marriage is thus charged as is amity to guard against Morison's 'rablement of traytrous rebels' who vie for rule in the hearts of men. Women are women, concludes Vives, and men cannot hope to change them from their 'proper and native nature;' and so are men men. Yet, he concludes, in this pre–marriage manual, 'the affections of women ought more reasonably to be supported and born withal, than the affections of men, the which are fierce, and can hardly be tamed, or ruled, and thorough a false spice of liberty the which doth teach them, they refuse and disdainfully cast off the bridle' (433). As the wife is well governed through the discipline of 'good husbandry' so is the good husband himself.

Policy and Practice

I now turn to two English humanist texts — Thomas Elyot's *The Boke Named the Governor* and Christopher St German's *Doctor and Student* — both interested in the good husbandry of wife, estate, friend, nation and self. Just as the 'good housewife' was to produce a profit by her good ordering of the man's household, so are notions about the feminine in these texts used to order a disordered masculine conscience and consciousness. I have chosen these particular texts in part because they have been recognized as important by historians as educational and constitutional documents respectively. Alan Stewart calls *The Boke* 'the first major vernacular articulation of an English humanism' (xxix) and its popularity is illustrated by the fact that it was reprinted at least seven times by 1580.[7] It is inevitably mentioned in histories of English education. Although St German's text did not achieve the kind of popular success he had hoped it would, recall that John Baker calls *Doctor and Student* a rare example of constitutional thinking, 'a remarkable enterprise' (164), and S.J. Gunn considers it 'a general masterpiece' (15). John Guy, as well, has argued for greater recognition of this text and its author. These texts, considered so central to the history of English thought, aimed to transform their readers in the name of English civil prudence and as such to transform theory into practice as an art of government.

Elyot's *The Boke Named the Governor* is directed to parents, educators, to ambitious young men themselves and generally 'to the reders...who perchance for the more part have nat ben trayned in lerning contaynynge semblable matter' and who might one day be in a position to govern and to whom 'the trewe signification of a publicke weale shall evidently appeare' (Elyot 1). Christopher St German's *Doctor and Student* was written, not just for the ambitious gentry, but for the everyman of Henry Tudor's England. Both books hold as their principle tenet the prescriptive injunction 'know thyself' and each provides a technique through which their readers can learn to do so. Elyot, in fact, argues that the acquisition of self–knowledge is crucial, not only for prospective governors, but for 'all men in a generality' and he advises: 'this sentence, know thyself, which of all other is most compendious, being made but of three words, every word being but one syllable, induceth men sufficiently to the knowledge of justice' (Elyot 164–7). Similarly, St German insists that '[t]here be many dyversyties of *men's* conscyence...but there is none better then that wherby a man trewely knoweth hym selfe...he that knoweth not hym selfe knoweth no thyng well. For to know other things and not to know oneself is nothing less than to condemn oneself the more grievously' (St German 93–5). I will illustrate the techniques for the achievement of self–knowledge put forth by Elyot and St German, the kinds of 'selves' that these writers suggest exist, as the a priori for the operations they propose, their detailed schemes for governing and the benevolent promises that they associate with successful self–government.

Elyot, a Middle Temple and Oxford–educated man, was associated in the 1520s with Thomas More's school. In 1526, he rose through the patronage of Wolsey, from his position as clerk of the Justices of Assize of the Western circuit to a position at court as clerk of the King's Council. He suffered a setback, however, with the fall of his patron in 1529. Alistair Fox narrates the events leading to the publication by Berthelet of *The Boke*: 'Elyot first sought to regain a place at court by attempting the route tried by almost every other ambitious scholar in the 1530s: he displayed his credentials by writing a book, and he attached himself to the rising star in Henry VIII's administration, Thomas Cromwell' (*Sir Thomas Elyot and the Humanist Dilema* 56). The sovereign and his chief advisor were to read the book as a prop for the theory of 'imperial sovereignty' and they apparently did; Elyot was appointed ambassador to the emperor Charles V. His brief was '"to fish out and know in what opinion the Emperor ys of us, and whether, dispairing of our old friendship towards him, or fearing other newe communication with France, he seeketh wayes and meanes that might be to our detriment or noe"' (qtd. in Fox 59). Elyot himself, however, seems to have been opposed to the divorce. And while his treatise calls enlightened governors to seriously consider the opinions and recommendations of all their good philosopher/councillors, an opinion against the divorce was unconscionable. On the one hand, claims Fox, Elyot the diplomat found himself equivocating by 'acting covertly on the Queen's behalf' (60), finally proving ineffectual to Henry, who recalled him in January 1532. On the other hand, he was to be no martyr, keeping quiet enough about his opinion to have been included as a 'servitor' at the coronation of Anne Boleyn. Fox sees Elyot's career as effectively over at this point; in Elyot's own words, he was '"rewarded only with the order of knighthood, honourable and onerous, having much less to live on than before"' (Lehmberg, *The Boke* v).[8] We find him in subsequent years assisting in the dissolution of the monasteries and in fact receiving monastic lands in Cambridgeshire. Fox reads Elyot's later publications for topical references registering his frustration and disappointment that his humanist ventures were not to be a means for the achievement of his own ambitions.

Significantly, in *The Boke Named the Governor*, it is the *book* that is the governor, the tempering instrument on the consciousness and actions of its 'gentle readers.' That Elyot's 'gentle readers' are explicitly male is made evident in several passages; early in the text he advises that when a student reaches the age of seven, he should be 'taken from the company of women' because they might ignite the 'sparkes of voluptuositie' within him (23). A most important piece of knowledge about such male subjects is that their selfhood is something to be subjected to epistemological consideration; that the self in fact needs to be governed, but that finally and fortunately men are governable. Elyot reiterates that of the varieties of rule a potential governor must learn to practise (including the rule of empire), the most important is the rule of the self: 'to hym that is a governoure of a publike weale belongeth a double governaunce, that is to saye, an interior or inwarde governaunce, and an exterior or outwarde governaunce. The firste is of his affects and passions, which do inhabite within his soule, and be subjectes to his reason. The seconde is of his children, his servauntes, and other subjectes to his autoritie' (224–5). In a section called 'Things to Premeditate' Elyot translates some advice–verses of the Roman poet Claudian to the emperors Honorious and Theodosius on this point:

Thou that thy powar stretcheth bothe ferre and large,
Through Inde the riche, sette at the worlde's ende,

Corrupte desire thyne harte hath ones embraced,
Thou arte in bondage, thyne honour is defaced.
Thou shalte be demed than worthy for to raigne,
Whan of thy self thou wynnest the maistry.

What thou mayst do delite nat for to knowe,
But rather what thinge wyll become the best;
Embrace thou vertue and kepe thy courage lowe,
And thinke that alway measure is a feste
Love well thy people, care also for the leste,
And whan thou studiest for thy commoditie
Make them all partners of thy felicitie.

For where the ruler in livynge is nat stable,
Bothe lawe and counsaile is tourned in to a fable. (120)

Fox does not discuss this poem in his essay on the topical allusions in Elyot's corpus — 'Sir Thomas Elyot and the Humanist Dilemma.' If he had, he would probably find in it, as he does elsewhere, an allusion to Elyot's opinion that it is King Henry's carnality as 'corrupt desire' that is his biggest problem at this pre–divorce political juncture. More important is the general comment that the temperance of masculine heterosexual desire is a crucial component of the conquest of both empire and self. The oxymoronic platitude 'measure is the feast' and the injunction to 'embrace virtue' rather than passively and 'in bondage' having his heart embraced by 'corrupt desire,' wrests sensual pleasure from 'what thou mayst do' and binds it rhetorically to manly activities fit for a free and virtuous governor.

The essence of self knowledge involves the assignation of terms of propriety: 'For a man knowinge him selfe shall knowe that which is his owne and pertayneth to him selfe...His soule is undoughtedly and frely his own. And none other persone may by any meane possesse it or clayme it. His body so pertayneth unto him, that none other without his consent may vendicate therein any propretie' (202). Elyot's subject precedes his body and soul and owns them as property (a prerequisite to contractual thinking) even as he must know others as similarly discrete and autonomous and all must guard against appropriation, or conversion from without, even as they must guard against falling prey to their sometimes tyrannous desires from within.

Importantly, Elyot declares that 'what governour in this wise knoweth him selfe he shall also by the same rule knowe all other men' (204). Elyot thereby reiterates that our subject's distinction as governor must not be regarded by him as signifying an essential difference in kind from those he rules, but only a distinction in degree. In the verse translation from Claudian, the governor is to reward his good subjects by making them 'partners of [his] felicitie' (120), just as he is offered the promise of empire if he too is well–governed. He is to stand as the model of temperance and the task of appearing and being thus is emphatically not a measure that allows him more liberty; on the contrary, 'authority, being well and diligently used, is but a token of superiority, but in very deed it is a burden and loss of liberty' (122). The mark of the governor is therefore not an interior mark in this discourse. The signifier of the governor is a piece of his wardrobe, a burdensome cloak:

> Thy dignitie or autoritie...is (as it were) but a weighty or hevy cloke, fresshely gliteringe in the eyen of them that be poreblynde, where unto the it is paynefull...whiles thou wearest it, knowe thy selfe, knowe that the name of a soveraigne or ruler without actuall governaunce is but a shadowe, that governaunce standeth nat by wordes onely, but principally by acte and example; that by example of governours men do rise or falle in vertue or vice. (203)

The cloak of authority is figured as a burden, just as governors, Elyot advises, (perhaps alluding to the sumptuous dress of the monarch) in planning their real wardrobes should have 'a discreet moderation in their apparaile...that they diminisshe no parte of their majestie, either with newe fanglenesse or with over sumptuous expences' (125).

A proper association to gender is key to the arguments about governance put forth by this book. Just as the governor must cultivate proper relations with both women and men, so must the governor's manliness be carefully managed through well–wrought relations between himself and what Elyot figures as feminine and masculine elements in his consciousness. While the governor in training must relinquish his association with the corrupt desire of the female, he gains the perk of association with the abstracted and idealized feminine as represented in the virtues he seeks to possess. 'Knowledge...[is] a perfeyte instructice and mastresse' (202). Similarly, 'sapience' is 'the science of things divine and humaine, which considereth the cause of every thing, by reason whereof that which is divine she foloweth, that whiche is humane she estemith ferre under the goodnes of vertue' (268). As he proceeds in the development of his argument, however, Elyot produces a familiar trope. The mean is the ideal; actual women endanger the achievement of the mean, while the abstract feminine itself is the mean: 'Temperance [states Elyot is]...a sad and discrete matrone and reverent governesse, awaitinge diligently that...any wyse voluptie or concupiscence have no pre–eminence in the soule of man' (257). Just as the good housewife guards the indoors of Ischomachus's estate, so in Elyot's taxonomy of masculine consciousness is the feminine the chatelaine figure to his male subject's 'palaice of manne's reason' (96).

The most explicit representation of the feminine as instrument of calculation and control is found in Elyot's extensive section 'On Dancing' where he presents 'the dance' as an allegory for the perfect 'concord' of qualities that would be present in an ideal and highly prudent governor.[9] Elyot begins to construct his analogy by cataloguing what he considers to be the untempered masculine and feminine attributes: 'A man in his naturall perfection is fiers, hardy, stronge in opinion, covaitous of glorie, desirous of knowlege, appetiting by generation to brynge forthe his semblable [read lusty]. The good nature of a woman is to be milde, timorouse, tractable, benigne, of sure remembrance, and sham[e]fast' (95). The dance, he argues, produces the mean between these qualities:

> And in this wise *fiersenesse* joined with *mildnesse* maketh *Severitie*; *Audacitie* with *timerositie* maketh *Magnonimitie*; *wilfull opinion* and *Tractibilitie* (which is to be shortly persuaded and m[o]ved) makethe *Constan[cy]* a vertue; *Covaitise* of *Glorie*, adourned with *benignitie* causeth honour; *desire of knowlege* with *sure remembrance* procureth *sapience*. *Sham[e]fastnes* joyned to *Appetite of generation* maketh *Continence*, whiche is a meane betweene *Chastity* and *inordinate luste*. These qualities in this wise beinge knitte to gether and signified in the personages of man and woman daunsinge do express or sette out the figure of very nobilitie. (95)

In the specific movements of the dance is figured forth the most important attribute of the noble ruler: 'the commodiouse vertue called prudence' (96), named by Aristotle, Elyot reminds us, as 'the mother of vertues; of other philosophers...[the] maistres of vertues; of some the house wyfe, for as moche as by her diligence she doth investigate and prepare places apt and convenient, where other vertues shall execute their powers or offices...[prudence is] the porche of the noble palaice of manne's reason, wherby all other vertues shall entre' (96). Thus the feminine Prudence performs a 'hymentic' function at the entrance to the palace. Elyot further taxonomizes the virtue of prudence, relating its parts to specific dance steps: 'honour' is seen in the curtsey and is made of 'feare, love and reverence'; a two step motion in 'celeritie and slownesse' denotes 'Maturity' as 'a mean betwene two extremities, wherin nothynge lacketh or excedeth...neyther too moche ne to litle, to[o] soon ne to[o] late, to swyftely nor slowely, but in due tyme and measure' (97–8). Other 'braunches' of prudence include 'providence,' 'industry;' 'circumspection,' 'election,' 'experience' and 'modestie.' 'By them,' Elyot instructs, 'the saide vertue of prudence is made complete, and is in her perfection' (104). These instruments are put to work on the governor's hyper–masculine qualities and he is to emerge as the ennobled, well tempered, governor.

As our governor must achieve a proper orientation to the feminine, so must he achieve a proper orientation to his equals, through the cultivation of the virtue of 'amity': 'a blessed and stable connexion of sondrie willes, makinge of two parsones one in havinge and suffringe. And therefore a frende is proprely named of Philosophers the other I' (164). Elyot wistfully complains that, like many good things, amity these days is in decline. He illustrates with a metaphor and simile, which between them double the association with the idealized feminine: 'amitie may nowe unethe be knowen or founden throughout the worlde, by them that seeke for her as diligently as a mayden wolde seeke for a small silver pinne in a great chamber strawed with white russhes' (161).

To illustrate the nature of the 'connection of wills' that betokens the 'amity' of which he speaks, Elyot makes a long digression to retell Boccacio's tale of Titus and Gisippus, Roman and Athenian youths whose homoerotic friendship Elyot idealizes. Hutson suggests that this tale is 'probably the first *novella* in English' (57) and certainly the narrator of *The Boke* presents the tale as narrative relief: 'But nowe in the middes of my labour, as it were to pause and take brethe, and also to recreate the reders, which, fatig[ue] with longe preceptes, desire varietie of mater, or some newe pleasaunt fable or historie, I will reherce a right goodly example of frendship. Whiche example, studiousely radde, shall ministre to the redars singuler pleasure and also incredible comforte to practise amitie' (166). Thus the tale of the pleasures and rewards of true friendship is at the same time modelling an amity between author and reader that will produce profit through pleasure.

In the story, a young Titus has come from Rome to Athens to be educated with Gisippus, the son of his father's friend, and the two boys grow and study together. Reaching manhood, Gisippus hesitates to marry as he is urged to do by his 'frendes' 'havinge his hart all redy wedded to his friende Titus, and his mynde fixed to the studie of Philosophy, fearinge that mariage shulde be the occasion to sever hym bothe from th[e] one and th[e] other' (167). Enter a worthy woman — Sophronia — found by the friends of Gisippus and whom he agrees to marry. If Gisippus is ambivalent about Sophronia, Titus burns with lust for her to the point of distraction and the decline of his health. Gisippus demonstrates his 'amity' by devising a bed trick whereby it is Titus and not Gisippus who makes a bedtime pledge with Sophronia on the wedding night and Titus and Sophronia consummate their pledge sexually: 'more estemynge true frendship than the love of a woman...[Gisippus] willyngly graunted to [Titus] the interest that he had in the damasell' (177). When the act is accomplished and then discovered by the people of Athens, Gisippus loses his position in Athens and must presume upon the kindness of his friend, now in an elevated position in Rome. Travelling into Rome as an emaciated beggar, Gisippus is not recognized by Titus, comes upon a murdered man and is charged with the crime. He readily confesses as he wishes to die. Titus attends the trial, recognizes his friend, confesses to the murder himself to free Gisippus and the real murderer comes forward and tells the truth, impressed by this display of amity. The murderer is granted clemency by the merciful Titus; Gisippus marries Titus' sister and a comedic end is achieved.

Hutson refutes the view taken by earlier critics that this tale articulates the transformation of feudal and instrumental relations between men to that of pure and affective early modern friendship. She argues instead that 'amity' is just more subtly instrumental: 'The saturation of the literature of sixteenth–century England with *De Amicitia formulae*.....may be saying less about the age's commitment to a new theory of non–instrumental male friendship, than it is about a *displacement* of the instrumentality of male friendship into the communicative action represented by the persuasive mobilization of arguments from classical texts' (63). Hutson concentrates on the fruitfulness of the rhetorical appeal made by Gisippus to convince the people that Sophronia and Titus are truly married and Titus' appeal to the court to convince them that he and not Gisippus was the murderer. Boys schooled together in the liberal arts will be able to utilize rhetoric for the maintenance of amity. Hutson observes, however, that there is a problem in that the friends' plot involves a 'shared project of deception, involving clandestine vows and mystifying rhetoric' (60). While these friends are idealized by Elyot, they are at the same time, says Hutson, 'the demonic Other of that same ideal: the "supposed husband," the histrionic imposter, whose ability to persuade a courtroom by probable argument of his guilt or innocence becomes indistinguishable from his ability to betray husbands and fathers of the chastity of their wives and daughters' (84–5).[10] Stewart picks up on Hutson's attention to the shared studies of the friends and figures this friendship as a sign of the potentially dangerous 'close reading' that holds the threat of the sodomical (as that which disturbs the social hierarchy). For Hutson and Stewart, friendship is both a necessary and dangerous mode of humanist relations. I would like to expand on the range of its necessity and to suggest that an analytics of government allows us to see that the dangers produced within humanist relations are implicated in the status of humanism as both cause and cure of dangerous masculinity. Amity must produce governors, justify their existence and be governed by them.

In his introduction to the tale of Titus and Gisippus, Elyot describes *amicitia* as 'nowe so infrequent or straunge amonge mortall men, by the tyrannie of covetise and ambition, whiche have longe reigned' (161). Logically, then, the flowering of *amicitia* is to have a tempering effect on both covetousness and ambition. *Amicitia*, in fact, is the very ground upon which civilization thrives: 'the whiche taken a way from the lyfe of man, no house shall abide standinge, no felde shall be in culture....he semeth to take the sonne from the worlde, that taketh frendshippe from mannes life' (162). Titus and Gisippus are exemplary because they place each other above both the allure of women and the attraction to political power. In this way, their male/male love tempers two forms of temptation, collapsed in Elyot's moralizing conclusion to the tale. A good governor, 'will nat preferre honoures, great offices, rule, autoritie, and richesse before frendship...For disdayne and contempt be companions with ambition, lyke as envye and hatrede be also her folowers' (185–6). Titus and Gisippus are finally governed neither by ambition nor lust but by amity. But they are governed all the same.

This is further demonstrated as Elyot expands on the problems of carnality and ambition later in *The Boke*. He dispraises ambition as 'pernicious to the publicke weale' because those who are ambitious are too 'secure' and 'wolde so be separate from other that no man shulde countrolle them or warne them of their enormyties' (244–5). Lust for sex is clearly connected to lust for money in Elyot's configuration. Sexual desire must be tempered by 'Abstinence' and 'Continence' or you will get

'Avarice and Lecherie.' Elyot refers to Aristotle's *Ethics* on this point, where continence is described as 'forberynge the unl[aw]ful company of women' (247): 'nothynge so sharpely assaileth a manne's mynde as dothe carnall affection, called (by the folowars thereof) love. Wherefore Plato sayeth that the soule of man, which by love is possessed, dieth in his owne body, and livyth in an other' (250). Titus and Gisippus' story has been an exemplum on this point. It is desirable that men should find in other men 'another I,' but the love of women does not offer the same kind of promise.Titus and Gisippus are finally a pair of well–tempered governors, bound together against adversity and the temptations of tyranny and the flesh. To accomplish this transformation and temperance, a struggle was required. To secure victory, it took the bonds of friendship; it took the voiceless Sophronia figure as an interest bearing commodity; and the fine grained work of a metaphorical maiden seeking a small silver pin 'in a great chamber strawed with white russhes' (161).

The section immediately following the tale is named 'The division of Ingratitude and the dispraise therof' and its appearance here in proximity to the tale is telling in relation to the function of amity as the site where debt and duty accumulate interest for the state: 'The moste damnable vice and moste agayne justice, in myne oppinion, is ingratitude....He is unkynde that dissimuleth, he is unkynde that recompenseth nat. But he is moste unkynde that forgeteth...In this vice men be moche wars than beestes' (186). An emotionally charged friendship may ameliorate the governor's forgetfulness, however, and thus amity's instrumentality is again made plain.

Elyot offers his student–governors some direct advice about governing. A virtue given much emphasis in this regard is mercy: 'in whome mercye lacketh and is nat founde, in hym all other vertues be drowned and lose their juste commendation' (141). Mercy is not, however, a stable positive term, but again, like homoerotic amity, functions as a relative term, as the mean between, on the one hand, the impulse in the governor for revenge in the face of personal injury 'if ye aske me what mercye is, it is a temperaunce of the mynde of hym that hath powar to be avenged, and it is called in latien *Clementia*, and is alway joyned with reason' (145); and, on the other hand, the impulse to be so sympathetic that he will tolerate counter–productive behaviour.

When mercy is not 'joyned with reason,' continues Elyot, you get instead 'vaine pitie.' It is 'vaine pitie' suggests Elyot, which has resulted of late in England in the increased tolerance of vagabonds and 'masterless' men and women:

> Beholde what an infinite nombre of englisshe men and women at this present time wander in all places throughout this realme, as bestis brute and savage, abandonyng all occupation, service, and honestie...by outrage in riotte, gamynge, and excesse of apparaile, be induced to thefte and robry and some tyme to murdre, to the inquietation of good men and finally to their owne destruction. (145–6)

Like Morison's traitors, Elyot's poor arise, not from the vagaries of supply and demand, nor from the depopulation of the countryside through enclosure, but rather from bad self–management. Their 'destruction' is thus by their own hands only. He recalls the many good statutes and proclamations that have recently declared against such vagabonds and argues that to ignore the law in these cases is to 'condemn a good and necessary law' (120). Better to condemn vagabonds than laws, argues Elyot. These 'disreputable poor' as Linda Woodbridge puts it, 'tried the limits of humanism' (109) as Elyot and others stood strongly against what they called 'vain pity' for this constituency. Woodbridge suggests, however, that 'ordinary peopled persisted in being more pitying and charitable than reformers or humanists advised' (114).

For most of this guidebook, Elyot has been offering prescriptive and proscriptive dictums for the would–be good governor; he concludes his text with advice about the actual 'practise necessary in the person of a governour' (284). He in fact has not dealt at length, as he promised he would, with the nature of 'the public weal'; here, however, he offers a remedy for the body politic:

> the universall state of a contray or citie may be well lykened to the body of man. Wherefore the governours, in the stede of phisitians attending on their cure, ought to knowe the causes of the decaye of the publike weale, whiche is the helthe of their countraye or cytie, and thanne with expedition to procede to the mooste spedy and sure remedy. (285–6)

As physician/governors, then, they must practise a forensic science. They must conduct a particular kind of investigation, of information gathering. Guided by the human sciences, governors must search their own bodies and souls for desire, temptation and all threats to the polity; so must they

> personally resorte and peruse all partes of the countrayes under their governaunce, and insorche diligently as well what be the customes and maners of people good and badde...howe the one may be preserved, the other suppressed, or at the leste wayes amended...[and to those] that have ministration or execution of justice... to taste and fele howe every of them do practise their offices...febly or unprofitably, and whether it happen by negligence, discourage, corruption or affection. (286)

Significantly, the governor is not out to locate and prosecute criminal behaviour; rather, he is conducting a far broader study about the daily lives of his people, an empirical study in which the senses are engaged. In order to fulfil this function, governors should 'repaire into divers partes of their jurisdiction or province...[and hear] what is commonly or privatly spoken' (286). Importantly, one piece of information he will discover will be whom next to promote to public office.

In his search for knowledge and truth out there in the world, he must be alert to the evils of 'Detraction' and it is with a discussion of detraction that Elyot concludes his book. For one thing, the hardworking and just man of office is particularly prone to this 'vice very ugly and monstruouse' himself (288). He cannot win, Elyot complains, itemizing the common accusations levelled at a governor by those who have been subject to his justice:

they wyll note and touche some thynge of his maners, wherein shall eyther seme to be lyghtnes or lacke of gravitie, or to moche sowernes, or lacke of civilitie, or that he is nat benevolent to hym in auctoritie, or that he is nat sufficient to receyve any dignitie, or to despeche matters weyghtye importaunce, or that he is superfluous in wordes or elles to scarse. Also if he lyve temperately and deliteth moche in studye, they embrayde hym with nygardeshyp, or in derision do calle him a clerke or a poete, unmete for any other purpose. (288–89)

Elyot's governor is a model of temperance, always a public person in that he needs to assume that he is always watched as he strives to watch others always. The very act of reading this treatise is rendered a public act, not the private act of novel reading that will so suit the sphere of women two centuries hence. And the act of reading is figured as the form and activity of governance itself.

Christopher St German, the author of *Doctor and Student*, was, like Elyot, a Middle Temple man. His most prestigious administrative position was as Master of Requests, although the dates of his tenure there are not known and he appears to have retired from legal practise by 1511. The text published by the Selden society as *Doctor and Student* consists of two dialogues which were first published separately by John Rastell. A supplement to the dialogues, *A Little Treatise Called the New Additions*, was published in 1531 by Berthelet. Berthelet's involvement supports those who argue against Elton that St German can be counted among those official propagandists of the reign.[11] The 1532 edition is the first vernacular law book and the first written for the general public. It takes the form of a dialogue between a student of the common law and a doctor of divinity about the relation of conscience to English law.[12] In his introduction to the 1974 edition, J.L. Barton calls the work 'in part an apology for English law. The author is setting out to demonstrate that the common law rather than the decrees of the Church should govern the consciences of Englishmen' (xlvi). As the Doctor concedes, 'it is clear enough that a knowledge of [English law] is highly necessary, even in matters of conscience...to all who dwell within this realm' (153). It is for the sake of all those laymen, the Student claims, that the vernacular tongue has been employed:

It is ryght necessary to all men in this realme...for the good orderynge of theyr conscience to knowe many thynges of the lawe of Englande that they were ignoraunt in....and some that can nat rede Englysshe: by herynge it redde may lerne dyvers thyngs by it....for the profyte of the multytude it is put into the Englysshe tonge....To them therefore that be nat lerned in the law of the realme this treatyce is specially made. (176–77)

The knowledge St German is disseminating is both totalizing, it is for everybody — 'for the multitude' — and individualizing, in that it clearly defines the responsibility of each legal subject to relate the law to matters of personal ethics. He envisions a situation in which every person in England will either read or have read to them, his 'treatyce specially made.'

The shift in authority from the Church to the law is immediately established. The text is introduced, somewhat awkwardly, by a fleeting narrator who sets up the dialogue between the Doctor and the Student and then disappears:

> A Doctoure of Dyvynytie that was of great acquayntaunce and famylyarytie with a Student in the Lawes of Englande sayde thus unto him/ I have had a great desyre of longe tyme to knowe wherupon the lawe of Englande is grounded....And bycause I have alwayes founde the[e] a faythfull frende to me in all my busynes....Therfore I am bolde to come to the[e]...to know...what be the very groundes of the lawe of Englande as thou thynkest. (7)

The narrator establishes that sometime in the past, prior to this meeting, the authority in matters of conscience has already shifted. The mere Student of the law has already been positioned as the one who knows and the clergyman as the one who has been seeking this knowledge out of 'great desyre of long tyme to knowe.' Their 'faithful friendship' — their amity — will make this interdisciplinary exchange possible.

As Barton suggests, St German is careful not to overload his work with overt citations from the legal canon, because 'they would puzzle rather than enlighten the intelligent non–lawyer...whom St. German has in mind' (xxi). The authorities that he does cite are ones presumably familiar to this general reader, and consist mainly, as the Selden Society *Centenary Guide* notes, of 'confessorial types of literature' (198). His principle strategy is to align himself carefully with the authority of Christian texts and tropes while avoiding direct debate about ecclesiastical matters. Nevertheless, by producing a discussion in which the notion of the Church as intermediary between the individual Christian and God is delimited in favour of a relation between the individual and the law, St German is clearly propagating secular 'policy,' whereby the state will 'shepherd' the legal subject to perfection. Thus, he is interpreted as a reformer by such conservatives as Thomas More (St German xiii).

One significant example from this 'confessorial literature' is St German's numerous citations from St. Bridget's *Revelations*. According to John Bale, St German in fact wrote a work on the saint, but if he did it has not survived (St German 51). St. Bridget, the early fourteenth–century Finnish mystic, recorded her religious visions in their immediate detail. Her confessors translated them into Latin and disseminated them widely, some versions arriving in England even before her death in 1373 (Cumming xxix). A.G. Dickens counts St. Bridget among the practitioners of the intensified late medieval mysticism named '*devotio moderna*' (14). He derisively informs us that '[t]hese were devotees who fell into foaming trances, interviewed angels, enjoyed charming if rather vapid causeries with Our lady, or were helped to roll out altar cloths by the Christ child in person' (18). St. Bridget offers to St German the attractiveness of her association with such popular faith practices, as well as with the technology of reading he is promoting in his treatise.

St German appropriates more than holy women for the purpose of authenticating his text. His history of property law is presented as a 'genesis,' the true end of which is private property: 'For at the begynnynge all goodes were in comon/ but after they were brought by the law of man in to a certayne propertye so that every man myght knowe his owne' (183). Such a manner of relating to property, the writer argues, is universal: 'diffused throughout the whole world' (33). The history of various ways of holding land is related, culminating with the category of 'fee simple,' that is freely held land which could be sold outright: 'it is contrary to the estate of a fee symple to bynde hym that hathe that estate that he sholde not alyen yf he lyst....fee simple...is the moste hyghe/ the moste free/ and the most purest state that is in the lawe' (253). As J.H. Baker argues, 'It is not improper to call [fee simple] ownership, since its continuity was no longer restrained by the claims of the lord [or through him the king] or his heirs' (301). Richard Helgerson explains the implications of such ownership: 'ownership of landed property...becomes the basis for and a type of the liberty of the subject' (*Forms of Nationhood* 93). And such a subject is clearly the *sine qua non* of contractual and liberal relations.

　　While 'fee simple' as the true end of common law is supreme and free (in that it is alienable by an individual owner) so is the landholder of property in fee simple — no longer bound by feudal obligations or kinship ties — powerful, free and increasingly worrisome to the government. The problem of ruling this liberated subject is clearly connected to contemporary concerns about language. St German explains the essentially Thomist view that there was once a pure and transparent language through which the natural law was 'wryten in the herte of every man techynge him what is to be don & what is to be fled' (15). When the Student inquires why written law is now necessary, the Doctor replies:

> byfore the lawe wryten it was greatly...blynded by evyll customes & by many synnes of the people besyde the orygynall synne/ in so moche that the inner book of the heart having been obscured and...obliterated and mutilated by divers passions it myght hardly be descernyd or read by men what was ryghtwyse and what was unryghtwyse...what good and what evyll...[what] just and what was unjust. [It was therefore] necessary that an external book should be given, containing laws and precepts delivered by God and by wise men whose hearts still remained more lucid, whether it be by heavenly illumination, or by human study. (15)

St German's Doctor and humanists like Elyot will use rhetoric as a cure, a way back even to the pre–lapsarian word. It is in relation to this fall that St German appropriates, like Elyot, terminology from the medical lexicon: 'it was necessarye that dyvers paynes shulde be ordeyned for dyvers offences as Physcyons ordayne dyvers remedyes for severall dysseases' (29). St. Bridget too, he relates claims that 'every goode lawe is ordered to the helth of the soule' (27).

　　Yet, it is words themselves that are a symptom of the fall: 'yf thou take all...the wordes of the law...thou shalt somtyme do agaynst the lawe....therfore to folowe the wordes of the lawe / were in some case[s] both agaynst Justyce & the common welth...in some cases it is good and even necessary to leve the wordis of the lawe / & to folowe that [which] reason and Justyce requyreth' (97). Because neither men's hearts nor wisemen's words can any longer be relied upon, justice and reason must sometimes be ensured by other means. St German proceeds to elucidate two such means of ensuring the true end of justice. The first is the production of a new interiority, a new law book of 'the heart' for English citizens, through which each would know themselves in relation to the demands of the state and each would act, spurned on by a sharpened conscience, for the benefit of the self and the English realm. The second means is through the expanding scope of the Court of Chancery.

To articulate the relation between the 'inner' subject and the state, St German produces a description of the operations of conscience. Throughout the dialogue, the legal subject of concern to St German has been grammatically male. St German makes the same rhetorical move as Elyot in his figuration of the dance, when he marks the conscience of his legal subject as a male stronghold where he must struggle to straddle a mean between opposing forces that are gendered female.

The highest level, or capacity, of consciousness is 'sinderesis,' a natural inclination toward the apprehension of universal knowledge, 'sinderesis is the begynnynge of all thynges that may be lernyd by speculacyon or studye' (81). Sinderesis is infallible, infinite and this capacity brings 'man' close to the status of an angel. It does not, however, in itself lead to right action. The confusion caused by temptations of the world makes it necessary to execute the operations of conscience through reason, in order to discern, through consideration of the observed phenomena, what is to be done in a particular situation. When reason is concerned with 'principles which, as soon as their terms are apprehended...cannot fail to be known, and cannot be disputed, it may then be called sinderesis....And reason taken in this sense is always virgin, that is to say it persists ever inviolate' (87). Reason through sinderesis is gendered feminine, as a virgin ever unsullied by 'man's' polluting culpability. In this way, we see again the production of knowledge about masculinity as inherently corrupt and of the feminine as 'handmaid of logic' and 'housewife of virtue.'

Reason is further divided into two territories: the higher and lower parts. The higher part is concerned with 'hevenly thynges' (85) and the lower with things temporal. The lower part of reason is employed when legal subjects consider what is proscribed and prescribed action and this fallible and lower part of reason is also gendered female, 'reason that is not ryghtwyse nor strayte...is sayd culpable...eyther bycause she is deceyved with an errour that myght be overcome or els through her pryde or slouthfulnes she enqueryth not for knowleg of the trouth that ought to be enqueryd' (87).

St German elaborates on the seven ways through which conscience comes to err: ignorance, neglect, pride, singularity, fear, perplexity and desire. Through 'decyre,' or affection to the self, the subject 'maketh conscyence to folowe his decyre & so he causyth her to go out of her ryght course according to the saying of Seneca "all judgement perishes when a matter involves the feeling"' (93). His conscience, like Isomachus' housewife in training, must be steered away from desire and 'feeling' and onto the proper path to the initiation of proper action.

St German's grammatical 'he' — the object of his explication — is logically male, as the legal subject most likely to control most transactions in which property is exchanged. His object is also intrinsically male, as the creature struggling between, on the one hand, the capacity for corporeal error, figured as a female tendency toward naivete, pride, sloth, ignorance, desire and 'feeling' and, on the other hand, a capacity for angelic truth, alien from him through its figuration as feminine virginity. 'He,' the legal subject of English common law, must precede and actively direct his passive, feminized conscience, for he is the mean between heaven and earth.

Through the operation of 'conscience,' as 'the science of knowledge,' St German's male legal subject is 'bound' to behave in particular ways and this disciplinary power of good conscience will ensure the right workings of the state. St German, like Morison, would have a 'whip in the bosom' of the legal subject: 'no punishment [he advises] exceeds the inner wound of conscience' (3); 'law byndeth all...under the law...in the courte of conscyence' (129–31). Finally, the achievement of self–knowledge and the adherence to the dictates of conscience that will emerge from the gain of such knowledge leads to the 'startling promise' of earthly reward: 'I praye the[e]...wylte always have a good conscience and yf thou have so thou shalt always be mery and...always have inwarde peace' (93–5). The Catholic examination of conscience and stoic practices of self–inspection are appropriated by St German as techniques by which each person in the realm will come to self–knowledge, self–regulation, merriment and peace as a legal subject. This is Foucault's notion of pastoral power, ' "of all and each"...an oeconomy, through its way of equating the happiness of individual subjects with the state's strength' (Gordon 12).

Just as the legal subject is bound by the 'internal forum' (3), the 'court of conscience' to the laws of the state, so are the law and its ministers bound by conscience to be sure that true justice is administered. One way that the law sought to ensure such justice is through the Court of Chancery, the court of conscience . Historically, as we saw above, Chancery was an administrative court, issuing writs to petitioners and hearing petitions to the monarch. Recognized as the most important jurisprudential achievement of *Doctor and Student* is its demonstration of how the principle of equity should be applied in relation to the principles of the common law, through an expansion of the function of Chancery.

In practice, however, as we have seen, Chancery would soon become a distinct body, separate from and with the ability to supersede the common law. The chancellor was positioned as a master interpreter with the insight to discern the intention embedded in the letter of the law, St German instructs, and the action it dictates is 'equity:' 'equytie is ordeyned...to tempre and myttygate the rygoure of the lawe...(97). Even the most sound right to the ownership of land at common law could be overturned by a 'common injunction' in Chancery, if the chancellor judged the case to warrant it. No form of ownership, no amount of rhetorical prowess in the common–law courtroom could assure absolute security from the intervention of Chancery. As St German personifies the process: 'Lawes covet to be rewlyd by equytye' (97).

St German's treatise was not disseminated quite as widely as he had hoped, although there is some evidence that the English *Second Dialogue* sold so well that a pirated version of the *First Dialogue* translated into English preceded St German's own translation. *Doctor and Student* achieved its widest affect, however, as a standard students' textbook that endured for two centuries (Holdsworth 265–9). As a pedagogical document that laid the foundations of modern equity, this 'treatise specially made' had long term governmental effects.

Both *The Book Named the Governor* and *Doctor and Student* position their masculine reader as being in a constant battle against his desire for power and pleasure even as power and pleasure are his rewards for the good governing of self and others. Elyot's oxymoronic platitude, 'measure is the feast' signals the seeming paradox I have been describing in which humanism is both cause and cure of the social ills it puts into discourse and in which the 'governed bodies' are those of the governors themselves.

Notes

1. Lisa Jardine, in *Erasmus, Man of Letters: the Construction of Charisma in Print* argues that Erasmus, especially, carefully cultivated the public persona of Erasmus.
2. English logicians, it seems, were, like the English common lawyers, bogged down in form. Lisa Jardine observes that '[i]n his disparagement of unnecessarily technical and "quibbling" logic Petrarch specifically singles out the English logicians and their technically refined formal logic for opprobrium, establishing them as the main butt of humanist ribaldry and vituperation down to the seventeenth century' ('Humanistic Logic'176–7) and Charles Fantazzi cites Coluccio Salutati on the '"barbari Britanni"', who diffused their lethal subtleties to Paris and thence to the rest of the continent' (Vives, *In Pseudodialecticos* 66).
3. Kahn suggests that for Montaigne and Hobbes 'It is no longer prudence but science that provides the "standard and measure" of political action. With this shift one can say that Renaissance humanism comes to an end' (53).
4. For Cicero and our humanists, argues Joanna Martindale, the 'human' in 'humanitas' means studies appropriate to human endeavour, specifically literary culture and the liberal arts: 'studies which...separate him from the animals, *humanitas* as opposed to *feritas* ("wildness")...The humanists liked to emphasise that their studies were concerned with man, as opposed to what they considered the futile speculations of scholastic scientists and metaphysicians.'(Martindale 18).
5. We can certainly see the economic 'motivation' embedded in the rhetoric of the humanists' own defense of their activities. For example, in his defense of ordinary language against the obscure and inaccessible language of the scholastics Vives argues that ordinary language is 'a common public coinage' (In *Pseudodialecticos* 38). Similarly, a critique of scholastic logic is offered by Lorenzo Valla. In the Aristotelian and scholastic system of logic, Valla observes, the number one is not considered a number for the purposes of philosophical argument. He offers this parable on how fundamentally esoteric, foolish and impractical the suppositions of the scholastics were:

Once two women had a dozen hens and a rooster in common and had an agreement that of the eggs laid every day one would have the odd–numbered, the other one the even–numbered. If one day a single egg is produced, which woman will get it, pray tell me? Neither one? Of course not. It will belong to the one who gets the odd–numbered eggs. And therefore one is a number. Thus foolish women sometimes know more about the meaning of words than the greatest philosophers...I–and the foolish women — deny that this is intelligible. (qtd. in Rummel 180).

In this case, it would make bad economic sense for the woman to leave the single egg to waste; Valla's humanist reasoning is thus a 'handmaid' to intelligibility.

6. Pomeroy's translation is 'ruling over willing subjects, in my view, is a gift not wholly human but divine, because it is a gift of the gods: and one that is obviously bestowed on those who have been initiated into self–control. The gods give tyranny over unwilling subjects, I think, to those who they believe deserve to live a life in Hades' (Pomeroy 209–11).

7. The Elyot cannon consists of: *The Boke Named the Governor* (1531); *Of the Knowledge which Maketh a Wise Man* (1533); *Pasquil the Playne* (1533); *The Banquette of Sapience* (1531); *The Castle of Health* (1539); *The Defence of Good Women* (1540); two dialogues on the problem of counsel and several translations.

8. I am quoting from the introduction to the Lehmberg edition of *The Boke*; citations from Elyot's text, however, are from the 1907 edition, edited by Foster Watson.

9. On the early Tudor masque in general and dancing in particular as an essentially disciplinary activity (in Foucault's sense of the word) see Skiles Howard, '"Ascending the Riche Mount": Performing Hierarchy and Gender in the Henrician Masque' in *Rethinking the Henrician Era: Essays on Early Tudor Texts and Contexts*, edited by Peter C. Herman (Urbana Illinois: University of Illinois Press, 1994).

10. This humanist trap, Hutson argues, goes a long way towards explaining the predilection in mid–century prose narratives and late century plays for distrusting male characters who understand the ability of rhetoric to seduce women and fool family.

11. J.L. Barton argues: 'We know that the bulk of Berthelet's work as King's printer was material supplied by the government, and the suspicion is strong that *The New Additions* was an early component of Henry VIII's campaign of official propaganda' (St German 22) and that '[i]t is probable that the merits of St German's theory first came to the attention of Henry VIII's government at an abortive meeting of premier clergy and lawyers at Hampton Court in October 1530. On that occasion the king solicited opinions on parliament's legislative competence' (24). Did that competence include the the authority to grant the divorce? The bodies gathered voted no and the king 'lost his temper.' Barton speculates that if St German had expressed the opinions later appearing in *The New Additions*, he would have been seen as a useful ally as the king next attempted to persuade the lawyers that parliament could indeed do what the monarch wished. As well, St German carried on a debate with Thomas More in print (also published by Berthelet). 'We must conclude,' argues Barton, 'that he was an informal adviser to Henry VIII in 1531; four of his books were published by the king's printer...between 1531 and 1534...he was an independent scholar in touch with, but not a pensioner of, the government of Thomas Cromwell' (54–5). John Guy reiterates these arguments for a consideration of St German as at least part of 'the secondary line of official propaganda' (Guy, 'Thomas More and Christopher St German' 112).

12. The 1974 edition includes material from two sixteenth century English translations of the first dialogue; the original Latin of the first dialogue; a translation by Plucknett of some Latin passages not translated into English previously; and the original translation of the second dialogue with 'a little supplementary treatise, the New Additions,' which was published in English with the second dialogue in 1531 (xii).

Chapter 3

Performing Nature in the Tudor Secular Interlude

In somer comenly upon the holy daies in most places of your realm, ther be playes of Robyn hoode, mayde Marian, freer Tuck, wherin besides the lewdenes and rebawdry that ther is opened to the people, disobedience also to your officers, is tought, whilest these good bloodes go about to take from the shiref of Notyngham one that for offendyng the lawes shulde have suffered execution. Howmoche better is it that those plaies shulde be forbodden and deleted and others dyvysed to set forthe and declare lyvely before the peoples eies the abhomynation and wickednes of the bisshop of Rome, monkes, ffreers, nonnes, and suche like, and to declare and open to them thobedience that your subjectes by goddes and mans lawes owe unto your magestie. Into the commen people thynges sooner enter by the eies, then by the eares: remembryng more better that they see then that they heere: thus spekyng of the evyll that commethe of ignoraunce and of the goode that commethe of knowlage, I have somwhat gon from my chief matier: But I nowe retyre to it.

(Richard Morison)[1]

Counterfeit countenance every man doth occupy.

(John Skelton, *Magnificence* 472)

In the first excerpt above, we see that Richard Morison, our ambitious pamphleteer, has advice for everyone and in this case the king. This passage, portions of which are often cited to illustrate the importance of the visual in late medieval and early modern theatre, is taken from an even longer aside found in Morison's manuscript *A Discourse Touching the Reformation of the Lawes of England*.[2] In this work, Morison figures forth the nation as a personified 'sicke comenwelthe' which should be 'ordred just as men ordre ther bodys whan it is diseased' (178). He interrupts his focus on the law, however, to address the problems and promises of drama in terms of the reordering project. He would reserve for the government's use censorship, as the 'deletion' of particularly troublesome plays, but he would also appropriate the pleasures and power of drama to secure the people's loyalty, love and labour. Morison's thoughts on drama contain another kind of strategizing in this regard. He urges the king to 'wynke at the small faultes' in some plays in order to make use of their 'commodyte' and 'benyfite...[such] [p]layes, songes and books are to be born withal, thowghe they payne and vexe some' (Anglo 178). This overlooking is especially important, he continues, if any such plays, songs and books contain material declaring 'eyther the abhominacion of the bisshop of rome and his adherenttes, or the benefittes browght to thys realme by your graces tornyng hym and hys out of it' (Anglo 178). In the case of dramas that may do harm, but likely more good than harm, his recommendation is to do nothing, to govern more by governing less, to let the people govern each other for the good of all. Such are the subtle workings of the governmental arts. Of course the treatise urges pro–action as well by commissioning dramas that would function as companion pieces to Morison's anti–Catholic and patriotic prose pamphlets. This chapter looks at the body of early Tudor drama that both anticipates and responds to Morison's imperative about drama and politics. I argue that the morality play turned secular interlude is a form burdened with wide and complex interests. The plays often fail as polemics and seldom is good poetry marshalled to the service of dramatic use. They are nevertheless highly theatrical plays and that theatricality undermines their political projects.

The dramas I attend to work hard to produce knowledge about and advocate for a particular relationship between English subjects, the English nation and its laws. They argue, as St German does, that subjects have suffered a second fall, a fall from a now lost state of nature and into the state of Henry VIII, where proper correctives can be applied. When Morison relates the good governance of the country to good husbandry and to the good 'ordering of the body,' he in fact naturalizes and valorizes the essence and the activities of the state. The state has risen while human nature has fallen. The dramas reiterate this view and puzzle and worry over the problem of the human.

One sign of the fallen nature of early modern subjects of particular concern to governors is their propensity for dissimulation. This propensity might thwart the investigation of what is true and also allow dissimulators to accomplish their own ends. We have already witnessed anxiety about this problem. English subjects were required to swear the oath of succession and, about their swearing, swear that they performed the oath 'without fraud or guile' (Elton, *The Tudor Constitution* 12). And the bishops were put under surveillance to ensure that they obeyed the imperatives for reform 'without...colour or dissimulation' (*TRP* 232). Henry's witty and wily subjects are fit for both governance and the dangerous activities made possible by the education of a governor. And in that the government works to conscript each and every subject in the governance of self and other, so is every subject allotted the potential to hide under the pose of obedience and the colours of rhetoric. The dramas, more than any of the documents I have presented so far, display this contradictory orientation to the free subjects of Henry's England. And of course they diagnose and display the problem using the very tools about which they show such ambivalence. The dramas are both seduced by and terrified of the capacity of subjects to use their highly developed powers of reason and their hard–earned self–knowledge to deceive through acting.

The faith and hope of these plays is in the reason of man, the 'law natural,' written on the heart. The sensual and sexual nature of man is the limit of this faith and hope, however. Women and the flesh, the plays suggest, have played a role in the second (as well as the first) fall of man. In the English tradition on the matter of natural law and gender we find the fifteenth–century legal theorist Sir John Fortescue making the case that informs our sixteenth–century treatise writers and playwrights in his *De Natura Legis Naturae*. In a chapter entitled 'In what Virtues the Male Sex excels the Female,' Fortescue states plainly that the male sex is 'made superior to the female in all that kind of moral virtue by which the world is ruled and its peace preserved'(325). Women, therefore, he implies, never did have the 'law natural' written on their hearts, as St German's imagined audience did. The dramas present the dangers posed to men by the carnality of women in this regard. Furthermore, once awakened in man, there would be no telling what kind of counter–governance passion might dictate. The interludes thus produce sexual desire discursively as an almost impossible to resist form of governance of the subject, an incendiary force — a 'fire in the blood' — as John Bale's character Sodomy describes himself in *The Three Lawes*.

The Secular Interlude

The genre that is named the 'moral interlude' dates from the middle of the fourteenth century and offers characterizations of the virtues and vices with which the Christian soul must struggle in the battle against damnation and for eternal salvation. About fifty survive, Pat McCune notes, in the century before the advent of the Elizabethan public theatre (171). They have most often been either neglected or, once considered, dismissed by critics. Glynne Wickham charged in 1962 that '[f]ew types of English drama have suffered more unwarranted neglect than Tudor Interludes' (v). In 1991 Greg Walker is still advocating for these works, which he argues 'prove on close examination to be not baldly didactic — or not *only* baldly didactic. They provide a field for a complex interplay of political arguments and strategies...[and as such] their examination is long overdue' (*Plays of Persuasion* 22, 24).[3] Theatre historians such as E.K. Chambers and A.W. Reed had certainly given them cursory attention, citing them as evidence that the Elizabethan theatre has nationalist (and not only classical) ancestry. More often, David Bevington notes, they had been disparaged. Bevington cites J.A. Symonds, for example, who in 1884 calls the morality '"an abortive side–effort, which was destined to bear barren fruit"' (Bevington, *From Mankind to Marlowe* 1); and Tucker Brooke in 1911 calls the form the '"moribund" carrier of an anemic stage convention, tedious, rambling, overly homiletic...[and finally] abandoned to the talentless efforts of "unprogressive, leisurely poetasters," largely clerics' (1). Bevington attends to the plays as theatre history, with an interest in those plays that were published and 'offered for playing.' Walker is interested in plays that he finds to have functioned as advice to the prince. Playwrights, he argues, were given license by their sovereign and noble employers to provide the 'good counsel' that such writers as Elyot and Castiglione claimed was a necessary aspect of good governance:

[T]he acceptance of good counsel was not just a moral or political duty for the governor, it was a public demonstration of his fitness to rule...The role of the scholar and artist as moral tutor, the close association between drama and religious instruction, the fool–like license of the player to take liberties not permissible in more 'serious' forms of discourse; all contributed to the freedom of the playwright to address the failings of his patron in dramatic form...the royal household and the provincial noble households were themselves in this sense 'liberties' (perhaps the most significant liberties of all in the Tudor period), paradoxically set, not beyond the reach, but under the very gaze of royal and aristocratic authority.   (Walker, *The Politics of Performance in early Renaissance Drama* 65–6)

Walker seeks to demonstrate the topicality of a selection of plays to reveal the voices of counsellors at work in the dramas. Similarly, Pat McCune is interested in courtly dramas designed to produce political pressure as 'early Tudor political culture transformed the old struggle of vices and virtues for the soul of mankind into a discourse about the balance of powers in secular authority' (171).

If Bevington culls working dramas whose theatrical playability justifies their establishment as playhouse precursors and Walker and McCune attach critical value to the interludes with discursive connections, not to others dramas necessarily, but to others genres of writing that function as advice to the prince, my principle of inclusion is to select plays which are interested in the links between knowledge about human nature, public policy and the state's strength. The interludes I include utilize virtues and vices related more to humanist and secular values than to theological ones, a change of emphasis from sin to civil imprudence and the deflection of concern about cause and effect, reward and punishment, from the next life to this life.

I argue that the secular interludes of the 1520s and 1530s display a dynamic interchange with the concerns and the imperatives of governance, anticipating them, collaborating with them and finally falling into disjunction with them. The genre begins as a voice with license to counsel moderation in thought and action and eventually becomes a vehicle for propaganda for immoderate reform. The interlude makers eventually come to be seen by the government as transgressing their poetic license and they thereby become the object of legal instruments themselves. Having worked to draw the dramatic arts out of the town and country and into the political centre of England where they could be appropriated and policed, the state had inadvertently contributed to the production of something entirely unaccounted for. In 1543, the first legislation appears that attempts to regulate the topics to be explored in, as well as the settings for performances of, theatre. As the Proclamation following the act declares:

...fforasmoche as by reason and Occasyon of the manyfold and sundrye Enterludes and commen Playes that nowe of late dayes have been by dyvers and sondrye persones more commonly and besylye set foorthe and played than heretofore hathe bene accustomed...[leading many and especially youth] to all proclyvytye and Redynes of dyvers and sondrye kyndes of vyce and synne...to the greate decaye and hurt of the common welthe...his highnes therfore straitlye Chargethe and commaundethe that no maner of person or persones from hensforthe of what soever estate degree or Condition...playe or set foorthe or cause to be played any maner of Enterlude or commen playe [unless in particular controlled situations set forth in the act]. (qtd. in Sanders et al. *The Revels History of Drama in English.* Vol.II 25–6).

Norman Sanders et al. summarize the rationale of the Act: 'Thus do the complaints against public performance, which were to be used to justify suppression for the next hundred years, make their appearance: conflict with the times of divine service, inducement to vice and idleness, corruption of youth, competition with traditional and useful pursuits, the threat to an orderly commonwealth' (26). The Tudor interlude becomes the site of what Jean Howard calls 'the historically specific social struggles and dislocations manifesting themselves as attacks on the theater and on what are described as the theatrical practices of particular social groups' (6).

I begin my study with four plays of the 1520s from John Rastell's print shop: John Skelton's *Magnificence*, Rastell's *A New Interlude and a Mery of the Four Elements* and the anonymous interludes *Calisto and Melabea* and *Of Gentleness and Nobility.* I also consider an anonymous fragment *Albion, Knight* written in 1537 in reaction to and as a part of the government propaganda about the Pilgrimage of Grace. Finally, I consider two virulent examples of John Bale's anti–Catholic interludes: *The Three Lawes* and *King John.* In the first four dramas, all composed in the 1520s, Erasmian humanism enters the court as it would become rationalized as policy and law in the next decade. These plays hail a new relationship between the subject and the state that would be motivated by a mutual desire for prosperity. In these dramas, prosperity, civility and peace are under threat from sensuality and human will and dangerous willfulness is made evident, the plays suggest, in subjects' increasing ability to deceive through dissimulation. By the end of the 1530s, however, the secular interlude had become — on the advice of such courtiers as Morison — the medium for anti–Papal polemic that was informed by a high level of anxiety about sexuality to the alarm of the King, now grown reactionary. Anxiety about 'acting' subjects is pervasive, however, and is most fully realized in the two examples with which I begin and end my study: Skelton's *Magnificence* and Bale's *The Three Lawes.*

A key figure in the theatrical history of the period is the playwright, theatrical designer and producer, printer, courtier, lawyer, and would–be new world colonizer John Rastell. Rastell's printing device bears the motto 'Justica Regat;' he clearly believed that there was a connection between access to the printed word (here at his shop, The Mermaid, offered as a commodity) and access to justice. The device presents a merman and mermaid below a god–the–father figure, all presiding over a prosperous countryside, where smart estates lie in fertile valleys. Rastell, as we will see, is in more ways than one highly invested in the dominion of man over nature and the prosperity such dominion promises.

Rastell's theatrical activities include: a design credit for 'the Field of the Cloth of Gold' in 1522; producing a pageant played near his printing house that contained 'mechanical gadgets to move scenery, suspend actors, and create special effects' (qtd. in Geritz 15); and the erection of a purpose built theatre at his home in Finsbury that Reed calls 'the earliest stage known to the historian of Tudor drama' (17).[4] He printed four and wrote at least one of the plays to be considered here and the nature of his career will help demonstrate the context within which this dramatic genre becomes viable.

Rastell's adventures include a failed voyage to Newfoundland. Funded by wealth he gained from the patronage of Cromwell and letters from the King, he set sail on *The Barbara* from Greenwich on March 5th, 1517. His interlude *The Four Elements*, which, as Romauld Ian Lakowski observes, 'contains one of the first mentions of America in English Literature' reveals that in fact Rastell's ambition had been to be the first colonizer of the new world (Lakowski par. 3). His crew mutinied and made off with the cargo, however, leaving Rastell stranded in Waterford Ireland, where he wrote *The Four Elements*.[5]

If Rastell failed as a marine adventurer who would have brought new world wealth (in the form of cod) to market in England, he was quick to anticipate the potential custom which the religious Reformation could bring him as a printer. Yet he appears to have been genuinely converted to the new religion, and in 1534 he spoke out against tithes as a livelihood for clerics just when the King and Cromwell were attempting to gain clerical support by consulting them on the tithe question. Rastell was jailed, denied a trial and his plea to Cromwell to have his '"pore carcase at lybertye"' was ignored; he died in prison in 1536 (Geritz 25).[6] Becoming a member of the humanist flock in the heady atmosphere of possibility opened up by the impetus for change, Rastell crossed the good shepherd sovereign and was turned into mutton.

Rastell's print shop at the south gate of St. Paul's produced an eclectic collection of titles including several law books (among them *Doctor and Student*), *Les Termes de la Ley* (the first dictionary of law terms) and a book of assizes and pleas of the crown. Rastell's greatest undertaking in the field of law publications, argues Axton, was his edition of *La Grounde Abbridgement de le Ley* (1516) by Anthony Fitzherbert. 'For the next fifteen years' observes Axton, 'Rastell's press continued to produce and revise the law text books that were the backbone of England's administration and legal education' (5). Among Rastell's other publications are More's *Utopia* and his life of Pico della Mirandola; Rastell's own history of England, 'The Pastyme of People;' an English grammar; a book of riddles; Chaucer's 'The Parlyment of Fowles;' music (with an innovative method first employed in England by him); and a number of maps.

Axton argues, however, that Rastell's greatest interest as a printer was in the educational possibilities of the drama and F. P. Wilson notes that of the 18 dramatic pieces printed before 1534, twelve were printed or published by him or his son (23). In *The Politics of Performance* Walker takes stock of the evidence about the cultural impact of the printing of plays, much of it derived from the extant records of Rastell's shop The Mermaid. He demonstrates from these records that 'playbooks were produced in relatively large numbers, perhaps up to 500 or 600 copies, and sold relatively cheaply, at a price analogous to that of such "popular" literature as almanacs and ballads' (15). Walker concludes, however, that the general effect of these works as printed texts is negligible. The printed playtexts' importance, he argues, is in the contribution they make as early reference books on staging for those later playwrights developing the dramaturgy of the public playhouse. I would argue that such printing for private reading or for further playing suggests that these plays were assumed to have a life beyond the immediate topical incidents which may have generated their composition and it is to an analysis of that life in discourse that I will now turn.

Piety and Policy: Skelton's *Magnificence*

John Skelton, tutor to the King when he was but a younger son, became a commissioned 'poet laureate' in 1523. Peter Happé observes, 'We cannot really determine the point at which the morality first became concerned with historical matters...but...[Skelton's] *Magnyfycence* is very different from anything that has survived from before it' (*Four Morality Plays* 21). For Happé, Walker and others, history enters in the topical allusion that these interludes entertain. Walker sees the precedent for and evidence of such allusion in the early court masques produced during Wolsey's administration. He cites Edward Hall's account of the presentation for the Emperor Charles V on June 15th, 1522. Hall offers both a description and an interpretation of that unidentified and now lost drama and his interpretation, argues Walker, attests to the topicality of such stagings: 'theffect of it was there was a proud horse which would not be tamed nor brideled, but amitie sent prudence and pollicie which tamed him, and force & puissaunce brideled him. This horse was ment by the Frenche kyng, & amitie by the king of England & themperor, & the other prisoners were their counsaill & power' (Hall 641). Walker offers the most sustained and thorough examination of this topicality in the interludes in general and joins the debate about the topicality of *Magnificence*.

Magnificence was composed around the same time as Wolsey's 'proud horse' masque, between 1516 and 1523, and was published by Rastell circa 1530. It tracks the fortunes of a prince, Magnificence, who founders in his resolve to be ruled by his wise counsellor, Measure, when a series of vices appear who are acting the roles of virtues: Fancy (who claims to be Largesse) and Foly (acting as Conceit) convince him to consider the counsel of Crafty Conveyaunce (later disguised as Sure Surveyance), Clokyd Colusyon (disguised as Sober Sadness), Counterfet Countenaunce (who appears as Good Demeanance) and Courtly Abusyon (who plays the attractive Lusty Pleasure). Magnificence is seduced by them into a life of hedonism and thus Welthfull Felycyte quits the court and Adversity enters. With Magnificence now under their rule, the vices depart and in their place arrive Poverte, Dyspare and Myschefe. Finally, Good Hope, Perseveraunce and Redresse save the day and Magnificence is reformed.

Skelton wrote satiric poems against Wolsey which stand as evidence for some scholars that the profligate Magnificence, too, refers to the Cardinal. The editor of the 1980 edition, for example, suggests that when Liberty charges Magnificence: 'covetise hath blown you so full of wind / That *collica passio* hath groped you by the guts' (290–1), this is a reference to Wolsey's well known colic (n. 84). Walker counters the suggestion of a Wolsey allusion after citing a half a dozen studies that make it. For Walker,

> the assertion that Wolsey would be recognized in any portrayal of "a perverter of justice" ill fits the evidence. As contemporary sources suggest and the research of John Guy confirms, Wolsey's problems in the legal field stemmed in part from quite the opposite perception. It was as a purveyor of swift and impartial justice that the Cardinal was probably known, with the result that the prerogative courts over which he presided became counter productively overburdened with litigants.' (*Plays of Persuasion* 64)

Instead, Walker mounts a convincing case for the play as a representation of the incident known as the 'expulsion of the minions,' in 1519. The six 'minions' were the first members of the prestigious body known as the Gentleman of the Privy Chamber, appointed in 1518. Walker relates contemporary accounts of the minion's 'frenchified' dandyism, how they, in Hall's words, "'forgat themselves'" (69) and how courtiers gave out that the king's expulsion of them was his "'coming to himself, and resolving to lead a new life'" (69). The effectiveness of this shrewd propaganda, Walker contends, can be judged by the fact that, as far away as Paris, Francis I heard that there was "'a new world in England'" now that the minions had been exiled' (69). Skelton's response, argues Walker, was to jump on the bandwagon in order to achieve the patronage he had hoped would lead from his tutelage of the prince to a position as a close courtier to the king when he had instead been given a minor living in Norfolk. And his subsequent commissions, argues Walker, prove his success. I won't rehearse Walker's intricate argument about topicality in *Magnificence,* but only want to recognize such topicality as one aspect of the play's governmental processes.

The first shift toward secularity on Skelton's stage is in his interlude's orientation to worldly wealth. In the early fifteenth–century morality interlude *The Castle of Perseverance*, by contrast, 'Bonus Angelus' instructs 'Humanum Genus' to disregard 'Malus Angelus'" promise of fortune: 'Why shuld he coveyt werldys goode, / Syn Criste in erthe and hys meynye / All in povert here thei stode? Werldys wele, be strete and stye, / Faylyth and fadyth as fysch in flode' (350–4). In the prologue of *Magnificence*, the character Felicity immediately acknowledges worldly wealth as the reward for the good use of the human capacity to reason. Wealth is evidence in fact of reason: 'Wealth is of wisdom the very true probate' (4). We might recall here Thomas Starkey's similar proposition, noted above, that prosperity 'ys a mean to set mannys mynd in that state wherby he schal attayne hyar felycyte'(Starkey 30). Wealth, however, instructs Skelton's Felicity, must be joined with 'prudence' or it will be lost. And these days, complains Felicity: 'will hath reason so under subjection, / And so disordereth this world over all, / That wealth and felicity is passing small' (19–21). Wilful subjects, having suffered a second fall into 'will' must be seduced into civil behaviour with the promise of prosperity.

This interlude argues that self–temperance, freedom and prosperity are inextricably linked. 'Liberty' introduces himself as universally desirable: 'I am Liberty, made of in every nation' (172), but Felicity aims to temper Liberty's dangerous claim that he is above the law. Measure enters and offers a homily recommending the 'measure' of all good things, especially Liberty:

Where measure is master, plenty doth none offence;
Where measure lacketh, all thing disordered is;
Where measure is absent, riot keepeth residence;
Where measure is ruler there is nothing amiss.
Measure is treasure. How say ye, is it not this? (121–5)

Here Skelton anticipates Elyot's oxymoronic epigram, 'measure is the feast,' in which bounty is associated with self–restraint. Measure reiterates to Liberty the necessity of his accepting a 'rein' and promises that accepting such temperance will bring its own reward: 'Measure continueth prosperity and wealth' (141). It takes most of the play for Liberty to acquire the self–knowledge he needs for the task of self temperance, but he finally declares: 'I am a virtue if I be well used, / And I am a vice where I am abused' (2102–3). Liberty's good or bad influence is relative to the use to which he is put by rational subjects. Felicity joins the defence of Measure, demonstrating that it is the careful administration of life in which this counsellor is interested: 'without measure, poverty and need / Will creep upon us, and us to mischief lead' (152–3). Measure unites all the above virtues in amity so that 'There is no flatterer nor losel so lither, / This linked chain of love that can unbind' (200–201).

For Skelton, one dreadful sign of the fall into human will is found in the ability with which the vice characters are able to dissimulate. Acting appears generative in this play; acting generates more acting as we see in the representation of actors playing vice figures playing virtues. Counterfeit Countenance tells it all in his 94 line introduction:

A knave will counterfeit now a knight,
A lurden [rogue] like a lord to fight,
A minstrel like a man of might,
A tappister like a lady bright:

Counterfeit earnest by way of plays;
Thus I am occupied at all assays

Counterfeit matters in the law of the land:
With gold and groats they grease my hand,

Counterfeit preaching, and belief the contrary;
Counterfeit conscience, peevish pope–holy;
Counterfeit sadness with dealing full madly;
Counterfeit holiness is called hypocrisy;
Counterfeit reason is not worth a fly
Counterfeit wisdom, and works of folly;
Counterfeit countenance every man doth occupy.   (417–72)

Cloaked Collusion brags about his thespian skills as well: 'I can dissemble, I can both laugh and groan...Two faces in a hood covertly I bear...Falsehood–in–Fellowship is my sworn brother' (698–713). Abusion's soliloquy stresses his sartorial excesses and 'newfangledness' through which station can be 'feigned.' His claims are large: 'All this nation / I set on fire / In my fashion' (883–5). 'Feigning' is figured here as powerful, and transgressive of the social order.

The foolish Magnificence is oblivious to the danger he is in; just before the onslaught of the vices, he muses: 'I dread no danger, I dance all in delight; / My name is Magnificence, man most of might' (1493–4). He is easily seduced by bad and flattering counsellors, who advise him to obey every whim of his 'wayward wilfulness' (1595); Magnificence replies, '[t]hy words and my mind oddly well accord' (1606). And if Magnificence should want to wreak wrong upon a man with whom he is not pleased, Abusion advises him to put on a show: 'feign yourself diseased, and make yourself sick' (1613). He must vomit and then cry out 'Is there no whoreson that knave that will beat?' (1619).

The vices' instruction in the art of acting mimics the playwright's own imperatives as revealed in Skelton's frequent and detailed stage directions to his actors concerning, as Hamlet would put it, 'fitting the action to the words.' The actor playing Collusion is to respond to Abusion's song by '*doff[ing] his cap ironically*' (112)[7]; Magnificence is to look at Measure '*with a very haughty expression*' (169); Poverty is to make a speech '*[d]espairingly*' (187); Magnificence should '*dolorously maketh his moan*' (188); and Crafty Conveyance and Cloaked Collusion are to enter '*with a lusty laughter*' (194). Skelton instructs his players in the proper deployment of gesture, facial expression and tone of voice even as the characters they play are set up to reveal the dangers of such thespian techniques.[8]

Finally Magnificence is, the stage directions tell us, 'beaten down and spoiled from all his goods and raiment' (179). Adversity arrives and after six lines delivered to Magnificence he addresses the audience directly, revealing the very specific message being delivered to all: 'king, prince, lord, and knight...[as well as] [m]an or woman, of what estate they be' (1884–99). Magnificence is to serve as a warning to all subjects:

This losel was a lord and lived at his lust;
And now like a lurden he lieth in the dust.
He knew not himself, his heart was so high;

Now is there no man that will set by him a fly.
He was wont to boast, brag, and to brace;
Now dare he not for shame look one in the face.
All worldly wealth for him too little was;
Now hath he right nought, naked as an ass.   (1887–94)

The individualizing imperative to develop self knowledge is once more presented as crucial to the art of self–management and Adversity's insistence on the universality of his message attests to the play's larger than topical problematic.

The play, however, finally diverges from its early modern governmental project and reverts to the morality function. Adversity makes the point that he performs randomly in people's lives, that his workings do not correlate with the bad actions of individuals. Neither, finally, does poverty result from the imprudent, wrong or foolish actions of those who suffer. Poverty, the character, reminds Magnificence about 'Fortune's Wheel': 'She danceth variance with mutability, / Now all in wealth, forthwith in poverty; / In her promise there is no sickerness [certainty]; / All her delight is set in doubleness' (2027–30). This Poverty is medieval in the capriciousness with which he enters and leaves people's lives and in his attitude to begging as a remedy, which he offers to go and do for Magnificence.

Magnificence is next visited by Despair and is rescued from a suicide attempt by Good Hope with Redress, Sad Circumspection and Perseverance. They instruct Magnificence in contrition and reformation. These are his confessors rather than counsellors, however. In the denouement, Skelton the cleric wins out over Skelton the would–be courtier. Redress instructs Magnificence in the proper attitude to the world as 'casual and transitory'(2507); it is the next life to which Magnificence should be directing his attention. Circumspection has the same message: 'A mirror encleared is this interlude, / This life inconstant for to behold and see: / Suddenly advanced, and suddenly subdued; / Suddenly riches, and suddenly poverty' (2520–23) and Perseverence continues the theme 'This treatise, devised to make you disport, / Showeth nowadays how the world cumbered is. / To the pith of the matter who list to resort: / Today it is well, tomorrow it is all amiss....Today a man, tomorrow he lieth in the dust; / Thus in this world there is no earthly trust' (2534–47). Magnificence has learned this lesson about the world: its wealth 'cannot endure' (2561). Redress offers the final lines to the audience: 'Jesus preserve you from endless woe and shame' (2568). While this is a dim view of earthly life, in some ways Skelton has taken the burden off his early modern audience. They are not self–fashioning subjects, but rather transitory souls. Magnificence and all subjects are not future makers, but rather are to have faith in the mysterious workings of providence. We are left, however, with the suspicion that any or every 'countenance' that comes within our field of vision might indeed be 'counterfeit.'

Doing Nature in *The Four Elements*

Composed during Rastell's sojourn in Ireland circa 1518, *The Four Elements* was published in 1520. The play is staged around a central prop — a large globe — and begins with a long explanatory prologue offered by the character 'Messenger.' Bevington argues that the Messenger's 'prefatory lecture is...at once a humanist manifesto extolling new learning at the expense of scholasticism, and a glorification of the intellectual rather than the decadent aristocrat as reformer of society' (*Tudor Drama* 83). The Messenger anticipates both St German and Cromwell in their arguments for the pragmatics of publishing in the vernacular:

> ...dyvers prengnaunt wyttes be in this lande...
> Whiche nothynge but englyshe can understande.
> Than yf connynge laten bokys were translate
> Into englyshe, wel correct and approbate,
> All subtell sciens in englyshe myght be lernyd
> As well as other people in their owne tonges dyd.   (Lines 29–35)

'Clerkys' might also 'in our englyshe tonge / Wryte workys of gravyte somtyme amonge' (27–8). While Rastell is no doubt plugging his trade, the production of books in the vernacular, he, like St German, saw the publication project as a means by which the governance of the many might be achieved.

Rastell's Messenger explains further that such 'workys of gravyte' will show cause and effect as they operate in the four elements. He argues that although some think these matters are 'not mete for an audyence unlernyd' (signalling that the unlearned are indeed those he hopes to reach) quite the contrary: 'Me thynke for man nothynge [is] more necessary / Than this to know' (107–8). The character Nature reiterates the importance of such knowledge by telling Humanyte, 'Remembre that thou art compound and create / Of these elementis, as other creaturis be' (205–6). Knowledge of the elements, therefore, is a form of self–knowledge. As 'Nature' explains to Humanyte, however, 'man' is more than the four elements: man's special status in the world is an 'effect' the cause of which is 'his' rationality — 'soule intellectyve' (210). For such a creature of intellect, guided by experience, the domain of knowledge is that which is apprehended by the senses and interpreted by reason. In fact, Rastell's 'Studyous Desire' defines a man by his thirst for knowledge: 'For the more that thou desyrest to know any thynge, / Therin thou semyst the more a man to be' (289–90). 'Nature' concludes: 'every thynge is made to do his nature' (295). Man's nature is not the immutable work of God, or not anymore at least. God's work, his writing in the heart, has been obscured by worldly will. Now nature must be 'done,' performed, accomplished by 'man' through rationality, in the pursuit of knowledge about the visible world and in particular, in the pursuit of knowledge about himself.

The principle purpose of the intellect, then, the Messenger further instructs, is to act as 'cause,' not the cause of the achievement of personal gain only, however: a subject 'shall deserve but lytyll rewarde, / Except he the commyn welth somwhat regarde' (83–4). The call is to responsibility for attaining knowledge of others as well as of oneself and to leading those others 'from vyce and to use good lyvynge' (89). Only then will one's 'conscyens...be discharged' (80). Humanyte must know himself and his fellow Englishmen intimately; he must work for the elimination of all vices through his wits and for the good of the state and he must do so in order to 'discharge' his 'conscience.'

Rastell's object of knowledge, 'Humanyte,' is more than grammatically male; he is figured as the male and heterosexual desiring subject who is tempted by Sensuall Appetyte into seeking the company of Nell, Jane, Besse and Rose. Woman is the temptress of Humanyte, who like Elyot's Sophronia, might lure men from their proper occupation of self–study. Upon Sensuall Appetyte's entrance to the tavern, he knocks down Studious Desyr and cries 'Well hyet! quod Hykman, when that he smot / Hys wyffe on the buttockys with a bere pott' (405–6). When Sensuall Appetyte calls for a meat light in digestion, the Taverner suggests 'a womans tounge, / For that is ever sterynge' (599–600). Women are further animalized by the Taverner's pun on 'stewed hen.' When Humanyte calls for a capon, he says he has a 'fat hen' and '[s]he lay at the stewes all nyght' (586). These mortal women, not even graced with the names of abstract vices, appear as a threat to the right workings of men's nature.

Just as Humanyte is above women, so is he above all earthly creatures: 'by reason of thyne understandynge / Thou hast domynyon of other bestis all' (211–12). Logically, then, he will have dominion over new world people who, Humanyte relates, 'lyve all bestly' (780). The promise of wealth offered by the new world is his for the taking and 'what commodytes be within, / No man can tell nor well imagin' (747–8).[9] Rastell alludes to his failed voyage, the 'dissembling maryners' (more bad actors) and his unfulfilled colonial fantasies:

> But they that were the venteres
> Have cause to curse their maryners,
> Fals of promys and dissemblers,
> That falsly them betrayed,
>
> ----------------------------
>
> O, what a thynge had be[en] than,
> Yf that they that be englyshe men
> Myght have ben the furst of all
> That there shulde have take possessyon
> And made furst buyldynge and habytacion,
> A memory perpetuall!   (754–67)

He comments on the people of Newfoundland, 'all the clothes \ That they were is but bestis skynnes' (814–15) and these comments Axton attributes to the Portugese accounts of fifty–seven Beothuks who were captured and brought to Portugal in 1500–1 (134). Rastell also enumerates the resources he has heard lay waiting for England's taking in the new world, including the bountiful cod stock (an ironic comment in light of the devastating decline in the Newfoundland fisheries in the last century): 'Fyshe they have so great plente, / That in havyns take and slayne they be / With stavys withouten fayle' (805–7).

Nature bids Humanyte to 'prynt well in thyne hert' (319) the lessons here learned. Rastell the printer would also imprint his message in the hearts of his implied audience. If each and every male subject of the realm polices himself as well as his fellows (as Rastell models here) prosperity will be a shared commodity. The 'common welth' of all Englishmen could then be built upon the intellect of men and the labour of beasts and women just as it could be harvested freely from the riches of the new world, without regard for its less than human inhabitants.

Gentleness and Nobility: 'grudgy[ng] his consyens'

Printed in 1525, this anonymous interlude takes the form of a humanist debate among a 'Knyght,' a 'Marchaunt' and a 'Plowman' about status. The question is 'who is a verey gentylman and who is a noble man and how men shuld come to auctoryte' (Axton 98). The debate frequently returns to competing claims about the characters' relation to the authority of English law. The Knight presents a view of English pre–history, a picture produced as well in St German's narration about the origins of private property. There was a time, the Knight speculates, when '[a]ll thyng was in common' (575) until an increase of people produced an increase in desire for property and the Knight's ancestors '[d]id studi to make laws how the people myght be / Lyffyng togedyr in pease and unyte' (581–2). Having made the laws and distributed the land, the Knight argues, the lawmaking class was naturally deserving of 'part of the proffet...in money an annyell rent' (587, 593). The Merchant counters that the Knight is arguing tautologically, that the Knight's ancestors did not hold their positions because of their 'gentle' qualities but because of their status in the first place: 'By the folysh maner of the worlde, we see / For that cause ever they have had auctorite' (153–4). The Merchant claims that his own authority derives from his individual qualities: he has a supply of cold cash, 'by myn own labour and wit' (25).

The Ploughman argues eloquently against the points made by both the Knight and the Merchant. Like Rastell's Nature in *The Four Elements*, he claims a potential nobility for all men by virtue of the human 'soule intyllectyve' (379); man also is able to subdue all other creatures through his intellect, 'to releve his necessyte' (382). The Ploughman calls on the authority of both biblical and English history by employing a slogan from the peasant's revolt of 1381: 'when Adam dolf and Eve span, / Who was then a gentylman?' (485–6). When the Knight and the Merchant concur with the Ploughman that 'mekenes, pacyens, and charyte...abstynens, good besynes, and chastyte...[are all] [v]erteous and gentyll propertees' (884–891), the Ploughman proceeds to argue that these are the very qualities he possesses but neither the Knight nor the Merchant possess. As such a subject of the state, only he will reap the promise of earthly happiness: '...when I am at my cart or plow / I am more meryer than other of you. / ...these covetous and ambicious wretches, / They set there myndys in honoure and ryches / So much, that they be never content; / So they lyf ever in payn and torment' (423–434). He concludes that 'no man shall acquire [joy] / Tyll he subdew his insaciat desyre' (439–440). Like Elyot, in his tale of Titus and Gisippus, Rastell suggests that ambition is an anathema to earthly happiness, that power corrupts. Rather, earthly reward will come from self–discipline, 'subdewing' ones desires and being content with one's position. An anterior subjectivity is assumed once more in a process through which one becomes the 'cause' of one's own gentility.

As in *The Four Elements,* one quality that is particularly important for the male subject to maintain is 'chastyte.' For the Knight, Merchant and Ploughman, their relation to women becomes a point of argument in relation to their gentility. The Ploughman accuses both the Knight and the Merchant of being lecherous rapists (and therefore not gentle): '[w]hat so ever she be — wyfe, wedow or mayde — / If she come in the way, she shalbe assayd' (920–1). When the Merchant responds that the Ploughman 'usyst sych vyse more then we both' (923), the Ploughman answers that, on the contrary, he is not at all interested in 'nise proude primmys...paintyd popagays' (926–7); rather, he is 'content wyth blak Maud my wyfe... / ...for all sych venereall werk / As good is the foule as the fayre in the derk' (925–31). His brand of misogyny is reiterated in his other tale of origins; he reminds the Knight that 'the beggar and thou wer both, dowtles, / Conseyvyd and born in fylth and unclennes' (519–20).

In the conclusion of the play, a Philosopher enters for the first time, taking up the position of the Platonic philosopher/king. His epilogue is a metatext that comments on the processes of persuasion the drama has been attempting to enact, as well as offering counsel to an implied audience of free subjects:

Wherfore, sovereyns, all that here present be,

...the best wey that is for one to begyn
To convert the people by exortacyon
Ys to perswade them by naturall reason. (1128–34)

In answer to *Magnificence's* attractive and clever vices who give lessons in dissimulation, this play would inculcate prudence in its audience by modelling prudent, rhetorically persuasive, reasoned argument: 'For when that a man by hys owne reason / Juggyth hym selfe for to offend, / That grudgyth his conscyens and gyffyth compuncyon / In to hys herte to cause hym amend' (1135–8). Individuals are bidden to enter into a relation with the self in order to lead themselves to virtuous behaviour. Through the technology of reason, each man will try, judge and sentence himself in the court of conscience — as Morison argues, he will 'carry his whip in his bosom' — according to a taxonomy of virtues related to the felicitous working of the state. Such is the advice the courtier/counsellors who were responsible for the composition and publication of this text would offer their monarch, their fellow governors and themselves.

Calisto and Melebea:
'Now know ye by the half tale what the hole doth meane'

This play, printed by Rastell in 1525, is an adaptation of Fernando de Roja's 'novel in dialogue' *La Celestina* and perhaps was imported by Vives (Axton 15). It is improbable that Rastell composed the text, which is transformed from a tragedy in Spanish to a satirical and comic moral tale in the English drama. Certainly, the descriptive introduction to the printed play (which might well have been provided by Rastell), clearly indicates an educational and governmental motivation for the production of the text.

To better attend to its governmental work, we might make a useful comparison with a slightly earlier anonymous interlude fragment with a similar theme — the education of rebellious youth. *Interlude of Youth* (1514) has Humility and Charity attempting to win Youth from the snares of Riot, Master Pride and Lady Lechery. Lady Lechery announces to Youth shortly after her entrance, 'My heart is yours, body and all' (106). Pride promises power: 'And all our counsel rule you by; / Ye may be emperor, ere ye die' (112) and Riot claims 'I can teach you to play at the dice...And many other games mo' (112). Charity, on the other hand, offers no promise but eternal salvation. Youth is not impressed with this promise: 'What hath God bought for me?...He came never at the stews, / Nor in no place, where I do use' (113). Charity then offers him a narration of Christ's passion and its significance for Youth, that employs a lexicon to do with law, land, credit and debt: 'When thou wast bond he made thee free, / And bought thee with his blood' (113). Youth is suddenly interested, 'Sir, I pray you tell me / How may this be: / That I know, I was never bond / unto none in England' (113). Charity replies:

> When Adam had done great trespass,
> And out of Paradise exiled was,
> Then all the souls, as I can you tell,
> Were in the bondage of the devil of hell...
> He bought us on the rood,
> And our souls did save.   (113).

Youth is immediately repentant, forsakes the vices and Charity promises him 'Then shall ye be an heritor of bliss' (115). This bliss will come in the next life, however. Humility and charity make no promises of earthly prosperity, although as a rhetorical strategy they do appropriate a lexicon to do with earthly wealth and status. *Calisto and Melebea* utilizes other and more governmental strategies, although it does not solve all the problems it stages.

Calisto and Melebea announces in its title that it is: '[A] New Commodye in Englysh in Maner of an Enterlude, ryght elygant and full of craft of rethoryk, wherein is shewd and dyscrybyd as well the bewte and good propertes of women, as theyr vycys and evyll condicions, with a morall conclusion and exhortacyon to vertew' (70). The transmission of knowledge about the nature of 'woman' is clearly an important aspect of the moral education of an audience, both young men and women and especially their parents. We are offered the example of the corrupt Celestina, a 'bawd' who employs rhetoric to convince the young Melebea that she should succumb to the lust of Calisto. Melebea is about to do so when she is rescued by the intervention of her father. Women are clearly either evil or weak; either way, they will inevitably fall. This is the conclusion uttered by Celestina herself upon winning for her client Calisto both Melebea's holy girdle and her promise of further comfort for the man. 'Now know ye by the half tale what the hole doth meane' (910), Celestina tells the audience. Melebea's weakness here, the 'half tale,' is the incident in the plot that signifies the general weakness of women — their nature — the whole tale this play would relate.

Calisto, the aristocratic 'mooncalfe' (as Axton calls him), is under the spell of love for Melebea, despite the entreaties of his servant Sempronio, who attempts to instruct him of his folly: 'thou settyst mannis dignite in obeysauns / to the imperfeccion of the weke woman' (154–5). Sempronio argues a case against all women, using Eve as the precedent. He calls women 'serpently shrewd,' 'wanton,' 'vayn,' 'folysh,' 'the dyvellys nettys and hed of syn' and significantly, 'dyssemblyng,' (187–205). In Calisto's attempt to counter these charges, he launches a defense by citing Melebea's lineage: 'Behold her noblenes, her auncyon lynage, / Her gret patrymony' (220–1). Her class supersedes her gender in the production of positive value, although Calisto is also interested in her physical attributes, such as her 'lyttyll tetys to the eye...a pleasure' (239). Sempronio concludes that once the woman has been won or taken, the danger will be overcome and Calisto will 'see here after wyth eyen fre' (260).

Calisto's weakness is a slam on the aristocracy of which he is a member. It is Danio, Melebea's father, who represents the true hope for the future. He stands before us as an enlightened humanist educator; he even believes in the education of women. Melebea confesses she had momentarily disregarded her father's 'doctryne and lessons...[and the] verteous discyplyne' (986, 991), with which he has raised her. Danio's epilogue is an exhortation to the state, a call for legislation about parental duty. Against idlers like Calisto, the first task of parents is to keep the young busy:

...ye faders, moders, and other which be
Rulers of yong folkis, your charge is dowtles
To bryng them up verteously and to see
Them occupied styll in some good bysynes. (1046–9)

The poor especially, brought up without proper instruction and suffering from want, will resort to 'beg or stele by very necessite' (1059). Danio calls for intervention by the 'hedys and rulers' (1061) of the state; he exhorts them to 'make good lawes, and execute them straytely.../ to prevent the cause before' (1062, 1066).

As in *The Four Elements*, there is a call for an intervention at the level of cause. Danio concludes by praying for the grace to make such interventions:

> To all governours, that they circumspectly
> May rule theyr inferiours by such prudence,
> To bryng them to vertew and dew obedyens.   (1083–5)

The best and wisest governance will be discreet; it will operate as subtle influence, the circumspect 'conduct of conduct.'

This play creates more than it bargained for, however, and particularly so in the naturalistic and attractive figure of Celestina, a character related by type to Rastell's Lusty Lechery, (and both are ancestors to some of the vibrant and engaging bawds who will grace the stages of the Elizabethan public theatre). When she greets Parmeo, Calisto's servant, she recognizes him as having been her charge in his infancy:

> ...thy moder was as olde a hore as I!
> Come hydyr, thou lytyll fole, let me see the.
> A! it is even he, by our blyssyd lady!
> What, lytyll urchyn, hast forgotyn me?
> When thou layst at my beddys fete how mery were we!   (507–511)

This naturalistic recollection of a warm domestic scene is a slippage that weakens the case the drama has been making against the bawdy. Nor does this play yet go so far as to promote romantic love and marriage as a strategy of prudent government. The young remain repentant, but unmarried at the conclusion of this comedy.

Albion, Knight: 'With a little inducing of reason astute'

As the tropes of humanism gave way to the exigencies of reform and rebellion, the government, having allowed drama to offer counsel to governors, itself attempted to *use* drama, as Morison advised, to counsel citizens. The annals of theatre for the 1530s includes many plays with titles that promise daring polemics. *The Revels History* provides the following list of works composed in 1537 alone (the year recorded for *Albion, Knight* as well): *Upon Both Marriages of the King; Against the Pope's Councillors; Against Adulterators of the Word of God; Against Momi and Soili; A Rude Commonalty; The Woman on the Rock; On Sects Among the Papists*; and *Treacheries of the Papists*. Perhaps these plays were the object of Marian censorship; whatever the case, of this group of plays only a fragment of *Albion, Knight* survives.

Albion, Knight is related discursively to Morison's pamphlet *An Exhortation to Styre All Englyshe Men to the Defence of Theyr Countreye*. Both were written in response to the Pilgrimage of Grace, both call for national unity and both connect a proper patriotism to a state of manliness.[10] The play, or what we have of it, however, trades in no explicitly anti–papal polemic. *Albion, Knight* is a bid for conciliation among struggling factions in the realm of England/Albion.

The fragment includes speeches by the characters Albion, Justice, Injury and Division. Mentioned, but not appearing in the fragment are Principality, Peace, Maintenance, Rest, Old Debate, Double Device and Dame Plenty. The fragment begins with an exchange between Injury and Justice. Like the vices in *Magnyfycence*, Injury is in disguise. He is posing as Manhood to cause mischief in the realm. When Justice reveals his suspicions about Injury's true identity, Injury argues that outward signs, such as his 'light apparel,' or even a 'mad visage' do not offer 'certain knowledge of nature' (120).[11] The problem of human nature and 'its certain knowledge' thus arises again in this political drama and it does so in the context of the operations of dissimulation.

In that Inury's 'light apparel' provides a clue to Justice about that dissimulation, the importance of sumptuary law to early modern forms of governance is also made plain. As Alan Hunt's argues: 'Sumptuary laws straddle the often imperceptible but fundamental divide between the pre–modern and the modern...sumptuary regulation that had been born in the heart of feudalism came to expand its range and its volume...Sumptuary projects become a standard feature of governmental activity in the early modern period' (28). In fact the greatest number of such laws came into being in the reign of Henry VIII (four) and in the preamble to the 1533 statute, we see an anxiety about the dissimulation made possible by donning the 'costume' and playing the role of one's social superior, an anxiety that is mirrored in the interlude:

[The purpose of the Act is for] the necessarie repressing avoydyng and expelling of the inordynate excesse dailye more and more used in the sumptuous and costly araye and apparell accustomablye worne in this Realme, whereof hath ensued and dailie do chaunce suche sondrie high and notable inconveniences as to be the greate manifest and notorious detryment of the comon Weal, the subvercion of good and politike ordre in knowelege and distinccion of people according to their estates, pre–emynences dignities and degrees, and to the utter impoverysshement and undoyng of many inexpert and light persones inclyned to pride moder of all vices. (*Statutes of the Realm* 24 Hen. VIII c.13)

When. Justice comments to Injury that 'thy person induce[s] no likelihood / That in thee should be any manhood...thou seemest of manhood frail, / Because so abused is thy light apparel' (119) and Injury replies that apparel should not matter, Justice continues on this theme:

O yet in apparel is great abusion
If it be framed without discretion;

> For, in apparel there may a great token be
> Of frailness, of pride, and instability,
> If common assize therein use not measure.
> For then is apparel a wanton foolish pleasure. (120)

Albion attempts to short circuit the debate, asking if he might have the friendship of both Manhood and Justice. Injury (as Manhood) replies: 'Sir, as for mine ye shall not miss; / But this gentleman, I think, will go piss' (120). A familiar civil ritual ensues as Injury swears an oath that he is indeed Manhood and Albion invokes another oath–swearing to secure a bond among all three of them. As we have seen, oath swearing was a form of truth making employed both by the government and by the Pilgrim\rebels. The plays reveals how little the oath can be relied upon.

Injury next offers a critique of justice that reads like enlightened counsel to governors. Justice should be, he argues, 'treated with due equity; / And where no favour nor meed should be; / And when reason hath tried there every deal; / That such an act were good for the common weal' (121). It is *not* the case today, however, that ethics and reason rule. Instead, he argues, self–interest only rules:

> If therein any loss may be
> To the disadvantage of Principality,
> Such an act loseth all his suit
> With a little inducing of reason astute;
> And, if it touch the Lords spiritual,
> Or be disadvantage to the Lords temporal
> Farewell, go bet! This bill may sleep
> As well as through the parliament creep;
> And, if that merchants be moved withal,
> Or any multitude of the common hall
> This is not for us, say they then,
> This bill is naught but for to wipe a pan;
> And this is all your new equity. (121–2).

Albion accepts this criticism gracefully, coming to the prescribed conclusion: 'Alas! If this may not reformed be / I shall never be sure of prosperity' (122). Injury further suggests that as things are now, 'Master Albion' is 'derided' by 'all nations'; all nations consider anyone choosing his path 'Half a man and half a wild goose!' (122). Why so, asks Albion and Injury replies that although all know that Albion can make good laws with good 'wit and reason,' these good laws are 'never in execution' (122). Albion and Justice both promise 'reformation' of their administration and depart.

This has so far sounded like a daring critique of English justice that Albion has taken under advisement with good grace. When Injury is alone, however, he shares with the audience his real name and the secret that he has been keeping up until now. Why has he put on this particular ruse? Because 'It is a part of our new experience, / When I against right make stiff defence, / That Justice in his seat may not be enstabled...[and] then of me croaketh every man' (123). He has raised the spectre of division among Albion's subjects in the hopes that he will in fact in this way produce such division, against the interests of Albion and Justice.

The character Division enters on cue, equipped, we might well imagine, like a rebel Pilgrim 'with a bill, a sward, a buckler, and a dagger' ready to cause trouble: 'To conjure a knave / Out of his skin' (124–5). Injury asks how it is that he has not been hanged with other such troublemakers as he was supposed to have been and Division replies: 'I took delay / For lack of thee to be mine attorney' (125). Injury explains his absence; he has been performing a ruse: 'I have turned the wrong side of my hood / And told them my name was Manhood' (126). In disguise he has gleaned information and caused trouble; now Division will weigh in to turn Albion's factions against one another. His spies Double Device and Old Debate will stir up contention. Rumours will fly about taxation and tax avoidance and the threat of foreign enemies. The counter–truth to this latter statement is found in Morison's hyperbolic 'exhortation' to convince his readers that no prince in history has personally worked as hard as Henry Tudor to secure the safety of England. Division's cronies will also stir up trouble between the 'lords temporal' and the 'lords spiritual.' The latter, he will tell the former, 'would rule all'(128). The same spy will of course flatter the spiritual men as well, until, predicts Injury: '[Justice] shall stand still / While I run at large, and have all my will' (130).

This Justice must be countered because, Injury relates, he would produce a well–shepherded and, most importantly, prosperous state:

> This Justice is a fellow of a far cast,
> And driveth such drifts to rule at the last;
> Peace is his brother, of one degree,
> Which hath a fair daughter that is called Plenty;
> ----------------------------------
> ...it is a common saying that Justice, Peace and he [Albion]
> Will conclude a marriage with fair Dame Plenty
> And then will Albion, that old sot,
> With Rest and Peace, so on her dote.   (130)

To thwart such well ordered rule and prosperity, the two civil vices, Division and Injury, plan to seduce Albion in much the same way that Mangnyfycence was seduced. They will play their roles and counsel Albion to 'exercise' 'mirth and prodigality' and 'take of his own good while he may / Lest all at last be bribed away' (132). It is here that the manuscript ends.

The 'division' that the vices plot to produce implies that unity is a virtue, just as Morison does when he exhorts his readers to see that 'love and dewtie bynd all englyshemen, both to say and do, al that they judge to be for noble Englandes honour, welthe, and safetie' (*An Exhortation* 1). For Morison, of course, it is the pope and his cardinals 'who without any drede of god...breake that lovely bonde, which god hath ordeyned and sette in nature' (16). Our fragment shows more restraint. Its discourse pits abstract vices, not the sexually depraved Roman clergy of Morison's pamphlet, against a unified England. Nevertheless, like the Catholic church, the vice Injury employs theatricality to achieve his ends.

The Three Lawes and King John: 'Doing His Business'

John Bale and his varied career have been a problem for Reformation historians. On the one hand, he assembled a body of writing founded on a modernist view of history; that is, he saw his own present and presence in the ethos of the reformation as a kind of end of history. Because of this, his records are compelling and important to a consideration of both the history of the Reformation and of English historiography. As well, *The Revel's History* observes the irony that 'It was largely thanks to this ex–Carmelite that many monastic records were preserved, reflecting his obsessive interest in the history and customs of the religion he hated' (Vol.II). On the other hand, his voluminous, no–holds–barred polemics included hysterical charges of sexual transgression against Catholic clergy — from English nuns to the Roman pope — that are slanderous and scandalous. They are especially embarrassing in that they so blatantly and at times gleefully repeat or, as we must assume to some degree, actually invent, the spicy, naughty and fascinating narratives of the very transgressions Bale purports to be trying to eliminate. By the end of the twentieth century however, Bale's writings had been accorded much value for scholars interested in the history of sexuality and his interest in the writings and stories of key reformation women have made him invaluable for feminist work.[12] Alan Stewart concludes that Bale's writings now 'are being recognized as the foundations of a Protestant English historiography...[and that his career is] an uncanny literary encapsulation of the English Reformation' (38).

Under the patronage of Cromwell after 1536, Bale wrote a series of plays that certainly satisfy Morison's criteria for politically useful drama. While the performance history of these interludes in general is scant, Stewart notes that: '[i]t is now generally agreed that Bale led a troupe of players patronized by Cromwell, identified as "Bale and his fellows" or "the Lord Cromwell's men," which toured the country between 1537 and 1540' (Stewart 52). The itinerary of the players, Stewart argues, corresponds with the locations where religious houses were about to be closed and the dramas were designed to win acquiescence from the people. When Cromwell fell, Bale fled to Europe where he wrote much of the historiographic material. He returned to England when Henry Tudor died and was appointed bishop of Ossory in Ireland, where he was hated by the Catholic population. He fled to Europe again on Mary's ascension, returning in 1558 when he received from Elizabeth a minor posting at Canterbury, where he died in 1563.

Schooled by the Carmelites, he attracted the patronage of Lord Wentworth and with that humanist patronage, conversion to reform. As he articulates the event in an often cited passage: "'I saw and acknowledged my deformity for the first time...And lest henceforward in any way I might be a creature of so bestial a nature I took the faithful Dorothy to wife, listening attentively to this divine saying: let him who cannot be continent marry'" (qtd. in Stewart 69–70). As we have seen in other Henrician archives, proper heterosexual, marital relations are seen as marshalling a positive tempering effect on the English subject. In Bale's interlude *The Three Lawes*, as in his take on his own marriage, there is a more directly negative (though nonetheless highly productive) impulse towards the regulation of sexuality, that is, an association between the tempering of carnal practices and civil prudence. This association is at work in the fortunes of the Tudor sodomy laws as well.

Bale's body of polemical works is driven by the assumption that England must define itself against the illicit sexuality and especially the sodomy of Rome. Stewart's argument is that 'the confused position accorded to Bale by later critics and historians is in fact a reaction to the way in which the "unacceptable" face of his output is central to the Cromwellian Reformation' (44). The 'unacceptable face' is that which fronts the disciplinary 'tempering tongue' that was busy inserting 'buggery' and 'sodomy' into civil discourse. As we saw in chapter 1, the buggery statute operated as a tactic in the propaganda machine against the Catholic orders whose jurisdiction was being dissolved. The trope of the sexually corrupt Catholic clergy was not new with either Cromwell or Bale of course; what is new is the association of the suppression of such 'corrupt' activities with the strength of the state. Novel as well is the imperative that English subjects need to practice the self–regulation of an increasingly complex set of carnal desires.

A Comedy Concerning the Three Lawes relates the attempts by God to establish control over Man through the three laws of Nature, Moses, and Christ. The laws are threatened by Infidelity (the Church of Rome) who has a staff of six vices in three pairs, each pair being aligned with one law. The Law of Moses is to challenge Avarice and Ambition, the Law of Christ is against Hypocrisy and False Doctrine, and the Law of Nature is against Idolatry and, as Stewart observes, 'for the first and possibly last time on the English stage — Sodomy' (55).

Stewart notes that Sodomy is presented always in conjunction with the feminized Idolatry, who, Bale instructs in his stage directions, should be 'decked like an old witch' (2). She is overtly associated with the witch–midwife figure who was herself the object of Henrician legislation in 1542: 'In this way, Bale conventionally collapses Catholicism and its image worship with superstition, witchcraft, and with women in general, in the body of Idolatry [and he also] describes how homosocial relations are played out through the shared idolatrous image of one woman — the Virgin Mary...the inevitable companion of sodomy...The Madonna–whore dichotomy does not exist for Bale: they are one and the same' (Stewart 58). Stewart concludes that the ideological thrust of the Cromwell campaign at this point is to convince the government to allow the marriage of the clergy, for marriage, as Stewart demonstrates, was seen as the cure for a multitude of wrongs. Marriage would reign in fornication, sodomy and witchcraft.

In its use of biblical and theological personas and its entertainment of doctrinal questions, Bale's play seems the least like a 'secular' interlude of any of the plays I am examining. In fact, Bale apparently wrote a now lost Protestant 'cycle' of plays meant to replace the Catholic mystery plays. Yet *The Three Lawes* does repeat the governmental promise of earthly prosperity and does tie religious righteousness to the state's strength. The first line of the play makes vivid the play's concern with secular politics: 'Baleus' himself enters as the Prolocutor and pronounces that: 'In each commonwealth most high pre–eminence / Is due unto laws, for such commodity / As is had by them' (3). Without laws, 'can no good order be' (3). The purpose of laws is to ensure prosperity and a sensible motivation for obedience is thus set forth. For those who obey Christ's law 'In city and field, whether he do work or sleep; / His wife shall increase, his land shall fructify; / And of his enemies he shall have victory. / The sky will give rain when seasonable time shall be; / The works of his hands shall have prosperity' (8). Those who do not obey the law will be 'cursed' and suffer from worldly want: '[o]f corn and cattle they shall have none increase; / Within their own house shall sorrows never cease; / Never shall they be without bile, botch, or blain; / The pestilence and pox will work them deadly pain' (9). Baleus offers a homily on creation, the fall of angels and of man: 'Only to angel and man we gave liberty, / And they only fell' (6–7). A bad average for God, who sends the three laws to get man back on track.

We heard from the Henrician treatise writers and the other interlude makers that the male subject's 'soul intellectyve' (210), as a reflection of the divine, precedes and finally is responsible for 'doing' this subject's own and now fallen nature. In Bale's play, 'The law of Nature' is similarly vulnerable to external operations upon it and thus 'nature' is further produced as discursively unstable. Infidelity, Baleus reports. '[c]orrupteth [the law of Nature] with idols, and stinking sodometry' (4). The beginning of act 2 finds Natural Law on stage with Infidelity, Sodomy and Idolatry. Natural Law is seemingly unaware of his own corruption, dispensing instruction about himself thus: 'A knowledge I am whom God in man doth hide, / In his whole working to be to him a guide, / To honour his God and seek his neighbour's health – / A great occasion of peace and public wealth' (10). Natural Law is to ameliorate man's 'brittle nature, his slipperness' (10). Bale's 'law of Nature' is at once a holy tendency hidden inside 'man,' and the site of the corruption that Bale would exile from man and England. The other two laws are no less defiled by Infidelity, who 'polluteth' the law of Moses with 'avarice and ambition' (4) and 'defileth' Christ's law 'with cursed hyopcrisy, / And with false doctrine' (4).

Bale's play relentlessly attributes incredible power to the vices he enumerates and personifies and I will describe in some detail how the drama accomplishes this work. He assumes that because 'under the heavens no thing is pure and clean....the people to [Infidelity's] perverse ways lean' (4). And Infidelity enters exuberantly as that most attractive of dramatic characters, the pedlar: 'Broom, broom, broom, broom...[b]rooms for shoes and pouchrings; / Boots and buskins for new brooms; / Broom, broom, broom!' (10). When he comes upon Natural Law, he announces that he could sell him 'the pax, / Or else an image of wax' (10). To his bantering, Natural Law replies 'Thou art disposed to mock; Soon mayst thou have a knock / If thou with me so game...[and Infidelity replies] Your mouth shall kiss my dock; / Your tongue shall it unlock– / But, I say, What is your name?' (11). Natural Law explains his function, 'Such creatures as want reason / My rules obey, each season...Alonely man doth fall / From good laws natural, / By a froward wicked mind' (12–13). As Natural Law keeps the sun and the moon in their ordered orbits, so man must be guided. Infidelity answers Natural Law on his own terms, arguing that in fact the sun falls out of order during an eclipse and that from 'the planets' influence / Ariseth pestilence' (13). Similarly the sea's 'rage' can swallow towns, the air brings infection and death and animals sometimes eat humans. Natural Law replies that these happenings are the signs of God's punishment and therefore the elements are always 'Doing His business' (14).

When Idolatry and Sodomy enter, they draw compelling pictures of each other for the benefit of Natural Law and the audience. Sodomy describes Idolatry as a Queen Mab type figure who can:

Men's fortunes...tell...by saying her Ave Mary,
And, by other charms of sorcery,
Ease men of toothache, by and by;
Yea, and fetch the devil from hell.
She can milk the cow, and hunt the fox,
And help men of the ague and pox,
So they bring money to the box
When they to her make moan.
She can fetch again all that is lost,
And draw drink out of a rotten post.   (17)

Idolatry expands on her powers:

Young children can I charm;
With whisperings and wishings,
With crossings, and with kissings,
With blasings, and with blessings,
That sprites do them no harm.   (17).

Dozens more lines catalogue her powers, from ruining batches of beer, to 'work[ing] wiles in battle' (18), to making stools and pots 'dance' and 'prance,' to making farms bountiful. Sodomy offers tender colloquialisms in the midst of this cataloguing 'It is mine own sweet bully, / My muskin and my mully, / My gel'ver and my cully– / Yea, mine own sweetheart of gold' (19). To this sweet talk, Infidelity takes offense, reading the sexual in the affectionate: 'Rank love is full of heat; / Where hungry dogs lack meat / They will dirty puddings eat, / For want of beef and cony' (19). Idolatry is not finished her curriculum vitae, however, and proceeds with a list of herbal remedies for various diseases, which Bale seems to be associating with Catholic saint and relic worship.

When Infidelity wants to know how they will 'overthrow' Mankind and the 'law of Nature' (21), Sodomy replies with his own resume:

> Myself I so behave,
> And am so vile a knave,
> As nature doth deprave
> And utterly abhor.
> --------------------
> In the flesh I am a fire,
> And such a vile desire,
> As bring men to the mire
> Of foul concupiscence.   (21)

He explains that he gains his power when men 'want of wives' (21). The activities associated with him are: masturbation 'I was with Onan not unacquainted, / When he on the ground his increase shed' (22); that which 'mules and horses will do' (22); being '[c]onfounded' by images; and the 'unnatural' usages of a number of Greeks and Romans, including Sophocles, Nero and Aristotle. He will endure as long as 'monkish sects renew' (23) he claims, not accounting for the fact that his classical examples bring his compulsory association with Catholicism into question. The Catholic clergy of course get the brunt of his accusations: '[m]ore rank they are than ants' (23) and he specifically mentions Pope Julius, who 'sought to have, in his fury, / Two lads, and to use them beastly, / From the cardinal of Nantes' (23). Here we might recall Morison's similar accusation against the soldier/son of the pope who defiled the bishop. Infidelity charges Sodomy and Idolatry to corrupt '[t]he law writ in [man's] heart; / In his flesh do thy part' (24). Through the interference of sexual vice and female transgression, natural law will be overwritten. 'Man' will have taken the second fall that necessitates the rule of a strong secular state and its laws.

A Comedy Concerning the Three Laws becomes a musical comedy at this point as Infidelity commands: 'Sing now some merry song; / But let it not be long / Lest we too much offend' (25). This is a very curious moment; Bale the polemicist comes into conflict with Bale the play–maker. The playwright calls for measured musical relief to entertain but not to offend his audience who, we might imagine, could well have been offended by either the blatant sexual references or the anti–Catholic vitriol they have just heard. To ameliorate offense, to keep people in their seats, he softens his play and characters with song. After the song, Infidelity immediately resumes his narration of clerical abominations: 'Shall I tell ye farther news? / At Rome, for prelates, are stews / Of both kinds' (26). When the vices exit, Natural Law reveals that he has indeed been corrupted by 'man's operation...his nature is full brittle and unsure' (26). Although he claims that he 'abhor[s] to tell the abusions bestial' (27) that are used by the clergy, he seems, like the vices themselves and like Bale, to be compelled to tell and tell he does.

In the third act, Infidelity meets the Law of Moses and sexual transgression is still foregrounded. When the two argue about the commandments, Infidelity itemizes those he will not obey, being particularly incensed about laws against 'inordinate love': 'ye say we may not love? / I defy your worst; and to you there is my glove!' (31–2). But Moses announces that it is not just the Ten Commandments, the 'precepts moral' with which he is concerned, but also 'the laws judicial; and ... the rites ceremonial' (33). As to the judicial, Moses relates that these concern '[s]uch things to command as are civil or temporal. / From vice to refrain, and outward injury, / Quiet to conserve, and public honesty' (33).

Ambition and Avarice now arrive and pick up the discourse about civil order. These two are out to 'blind the rulers and deceive the commonalty' (36). Ambition declares: 'I gape for empire, / And worship desire' (37). Avarice in turn introduces himself: 'I am insatiate. / I ravish and pluck, / I draw and I suck / After a wolfish rate' (38). They steal from the poor, rob '[r]ight heirs,' and kill fathers. They refer specifically to clerical ambition and avarice and argue that the best weapon of clerics is to keep the people ignorant, keep them at prayer so they aren't at study. Avarice tells how he will proceed, making a dig at Catholic scholasticism: 'The laws judicial, through cautels and delays, / I will also drown, to all righteous men's decays. / To set this forward, we must have sophistry, / Philosophy and logic, as science necessary' (41). Avarice recites his list of 'anti–commandments' which begins 'First, they shall believe in our holy father Pope' (42). Avarice and Ambition now get their own musical number.

In act 4, we meet Evangelium, his antithesis Pseudodoctrina and Hypocrisis. Evangelium explains that unlike the ostentatious Catholic Church: 'My church is secret, and evermore will be...By the word of God this Church is ruled only, / And doth not consist in outward ceremony' (50). His clergy 'forsake whoredom, with other damnable usage, / And live with their wives, in lawful marriage, / Whilst the Pope's oiled swarm reign still in their old buggerage' (51). When Evangelium exits, Infidelity cries out: 'God send your mother of you to have a fondling!' (53). Incest could not be omitted from this dramatic catalogue of taboos.

At the conclusion of act 4, Infidelity, in a long soliloquy, expresses his confidence in the project at which he has been working, that is to bring down the three laws. And he relates his efforts to secular as well as spiritual chaos. He observes, 'If Christian governors do not these laws uphold, / Their civil ordinances will soon be very cold' (67). Of course, Infidelity's hopes are dashed; Deus Pater finally restores the three laws to their former strength. After doing so, he offers each a set of injunctions. He instructs the Law of Nature to 'Avoid Idolatry, avoid vile Sodomy; / We charge ye no more this law to putrefy. / Keep still that same heart, [his principle prop] for a sign perpetual, / That thou wert written in man's heart, first of all' (73). Deus Pater concludes: 'Now have we destroyed the kingdom of Babylon, / And thrown the great whore into the bottomless pit...[and his 'folk'] walk to me / Without popish dreams, in a perfect liberty' (74–5). As in *Magnificence*, liberty is a reward for proper conduct, for the recovery of that which was 'written in the heart,' inscribed by Natural Law. 'Fides Christi' offers his own set of injunctions that, importantly, include civil matters. The good Christian should obey their king and his laws as well:

> Of these laws, doubtless, those laws their groundings take,
> To the public wealth, to give aid, strength, and comfort
> For preservation of all the Christian sort.
> ------------------------------------
> Have a due respect unto your country native,
> Which hath brought ye up, and given ye nourishment,
> Even from your cradles, to these days nutritive;
> So that ye may do to her wealth and preferment,
> Minister to her no hateful detriment—
> A dog to his friend will never be unloving;
> Let reason in ye not lose his natural working. (77–78).

'Your country native,' is fully personified and gendered female, while the English subject is figured forth as a metaphorical dog or a consciousness where vice and reason would forever struggle without the good graces of the good laws. This speech echoes Danio's speech about the association of parental obedience and the strength of the state, as well as providing another allusion to the complicated relationship between reason, nature and gender. The three laws review the lessons of the play and remind the audience in conclusion that it is 'valiant King Henry' who has banished idolatry, sodomy, covetousness, ambition, false doctrine and hypocrisy. Significantly, in the course of the interlude, the vices and their strategies have once more been associated with the theatre. We find Infidelity announcing, 'Now will I contrive the drift of another play...Companions I want to begin this tragedy' (53). And in the final homily, Deus Pater advises all, with a direct topical reference to a real English traitor, 'In no case follow the ways of Reginald Pole; / To his damnation he, doubtless, playeth the fool' (77).

Bale's play no doubt had what *The Revel's History* calls a "desacramentalizing effect," on at least some of its audience, especially considering that the vices were apparently costumed in the confiscated habits of Catholic clergy (*Revels* 181–2). What the play undoubtedly accomplishes as well, however, is the imbuing of sexual desire (as Sodomy's 'fire in the flesh') and women healers with incredible power. The people's knowledge of the efficacy of the types of remedies enumerated by Bale's Idolatry, with or without the relics she associates with them, would surely work against Bale's project of discrediting both the church and the wisdom of women, just as the extensive catalogue of Idolatry's powers and the rhetoric of Sodomy's lover might endear as much as discredit these characters to an audience.

Bale's *King John*, apparently played for Cranmer during Christmas 1538-9, is generally acknowledged as the first English history play and, argues *The Revel's History*, the king 'is probably the first tragic hero in English drama' (184). Certainly the ambitions of the piece are great. The play defends the idea of the English nation, the 'due supremity' (279) of the English monarch over the pope and all else and lobbies for the demotion of the old saints (in particularly Thomas Beckett, and this despite the embarrassment of Thomases in the King's administration) while championing the martyr King John as a good shepherd king. This king was once looked upon unfavorably because of his defiance of the Roman church; now his reputation must be recuperated. To accomplish this, the play takes the opportunity to question the truth value of existing chronicle histories of England. At one point, the character Nobility charges the 'Clergy': 'You priests are the cause that chronicles doth defame / So many princes, and men of notable name, / For you take upon you to wriht them evermore; / And therfore King John is like to rue it sore' (199). Further, the character Verity corrects specifically the chronicle produced for Henry VII by Polydor Virgil which 'reporteth [King John] very ill' on the advice of the 'malicious clergy' (272).

In Bale's play, the nation, as 'England' is a feminine persona who is set up sympathetically as a widow in need, to whom the vice characters are cruel and nasty.[13] Sedition, for example, charges her: 'Out with this harlot! Cock's soul, she hath let a fart!' (253). The audience is led to sympathize and identify with the character Yngland, while being encouraged to define England against that which is not English and to this end, besides the sodomical Catholics, there are several references to Turks as the limit of the civilized. At the same time, King John is congratulated by the character Verity, 'In that he exiled the Jews out of thys region' (273). Bale would similarly see the banishment of 'witchecraftes and hydolatrye' and the play provides a wish fulfilment narrative of this act of banishment. In the personification of England, the state is further naturalized and like Morison, Bale relegates rebellion to the realm of the unnatural. King John charges the character Sedition, a figure that *The Revels History* suggests came to Bale in relation to the Pilgrimage of Grace, 'I marvel thou art to England so unnatural, / Being her own child' (181) and Verity calls the clergy who were involved with the rebellion 'unnatural' (274). England is a natural woman, while the rebels will show her 'no more favour than a Turk' (230).

The play produces several interesting discursive clashes. For one thing, the defense of the feminized 'England' becomes a defense of women in general. When England complains of treasonous priests, for example, the evil character Sedition responds: 'It is a world to hear a foolish woman reason!' (258). Whether or not Bale intended to defend women's reasoning abilities, if his audience is responding on cue they will question the misogynist opinons of Sedition. The most interesting clash comes when once more we find this piece of theatre associating Catholicism with theatricality and treason with dissimulation. England calls the clergy 'Suche lubbers as hath disguised heads in their hoods' (174) and she notes that they go about 'like most disguised players' (176). King John accuses the Clergy of having 'poppetly plays' (92) and of being 'disguisd shavelings' (192). There is a lot of doubling in the play and interestingly, while warning the audience again and again about the importance of watching out for dissimulators, Bale's stage directions such as '*Go out England, and dress for Clergy*' and later '*Here go out Sedition and dress for Civil Order*'underline the potentially counterfeit nature of all countenances. The character Dissimulation reiterates this point when he advises: 'we must show a good pretence' (204) and when he admits that 'When we sing full loud our hearts be fast asleep' (206).

The King is indeed a tragic figure as he at first gives in to the rebels to spare his people the cruelties of the clergy and the sufferings of war, such as the 'Defilyng of maids' (251). He says he will 'resign' his crown, but then the Pope demands more tribute than there are taxes and he realizes that the people will still be worse off. He is torn among impossible choices and succumbs to martyrdom when he is poisoned by that virulent actor Dissimulation. When King John tells us in a soliloquy that it is the king's 'cause' to 'correct all vice' (231), we know we have a version of the good shepherd king. The clergy, however, Verity argues, are bad shepherds. He accuses: 'Ye feed not the sheep, but ever ye pill the flock, / And clip them so nigh that scarcsely ye leave one lock' (275). The King, by contrast, promises 'honour and great plenty' (197) even to the clergy, if they will only conform.

It is worth observing that it took the meeting of cultural studies and literary history to lead scholars to re–evaluate these interludes and that when we do, we do not generally defend their aesthetic value as such. Few would argue that there is much in the way of beautiful poetry to be found in the works. Yet these works are often highly theatrical. They are full of conflict, have lively and sometimes highly sympathetic or highly unsympathetic characters, employ dramatic irony and suspense (especially in their frequent employment of disguise) and most of the time song and dance. Extremely poignant and effective in *King John* is the death scene of the King where, as Jacqueline Vanhoutte observes, the visual image created by the feminine character England holding the King in her arms is Pieta–like (Vanhoutte 67). The King's farewell speech is similarly effective and tragic.

As *The Revel's History* observes, Bale's work is caught between his intention to degrade the theatricality of the Catholic Church and his project of doing so theatrically. And this has been the most significant tension in all of these dramatic works. They are greatly concerned with the human capacity for dissimulation and wish to represent this danger on the stage. They thus compromise in complex ways the truth–producing mechanisms of their own medium. Like Morison, they understand the seductiveness of visual stimuli and attempt to use it — bright costumes, bodies in motion. They attend to aural pleasures by clothing their messages in rhyme and rhythm. They then attempt to warn their audiences about the dangers of sense perception, of the power of theatricality, of how the theatricality may spill into the street as '[c]ounterfeit countenance every man doth occupy' (*Magnificence* 472). From Skelton's three CCs playing roles for the merry Magnificence to Idolatry and Sodomy seducing that theologically and ontologically unstable character Natural Law, these plays relentlessly associate theatre, sex and power. They also depend on this tripartite relationship to help them do their governmental work.

Notes

1. Sidney Anglo summarizes and offers an excerpt from Morison's treatise in 'An Early Tudor Programme for Plays and Other Demonstrations Against the Pope,' Journal of the Warburg and Courtrauld Institutes, 20 (1957): 176–9. Anglo notes that although the manuscript is dated 1542, since such practices as he recommends had been exercised several years before this date, there is reason to conclude it was written at least four years earlier (177).

2. Morison also mentions the 'Coventry Hock Tuesday Show,' as an example of the kind of folk practice which the government could appropriate or even replace for the purposes of good government. This event was a re–enactment of the English defeat of the Danes in 1012 when English women saved the day by uniting to capture the Danish invaders of their village: 'Women for the noble acte that they did in the distruction of the Danes, whych so cruelly reigned in this realme have a daie of memorye therof called hoptide, wherin it is leasul for them to take men, bynde, wasshe them, if they will give them nothing to bankett [ransom]' (Anglo 178). Some thirty–five years later, it seems that the practise had been 'put down' but not forgotten by the women of Coventry. A courtier's account describes the 'playing' of the action of a Hock Tuesday Show at Kenilworth in Coventry for Queen Elizabeth in 1575 to a very favourable reception. A description of the event comes to us in a letter by a Robert Laneham who relates that the custom was an ancient one in the area, but had been recently 'laid dooun' by preachers (Chambers 154). The locals made a 'humbl peticion untoo her heighnes, that they myght have theyr playz up agayn' (Chambers 154). As the celebration of a national victory, 'The Kenilworth production was both an offering to the Queen and a "political" act. It was appropriate because it enacted a historical event...in which women had acted with heroism' (Cawley et al, *The Revels History*, Vol.I 131). This 'play' was not dangerous theologically — it was not based on pre–Christian mythology nor any accrued Catholicism. Neither was this play, like those celebrating the activities of Robin Hood, subversive of official law and order. As such, it was viewed favourably by Elizabeth, not as ritual, but as theatre and she showed her appreciation by offering monetary reward to the 'performers.'

3. Walker has contributed four important works on the period: *John Skelton and the Politics of the 1520s*, (Cambridge, England: Cambridge UP, 1988); *Persuasive Fictions: Faction, Faith, and Political Culture in the Reign of Henry VIII*, (Aldershot, England: Scolar's Press, 1991); *Plays of Persuasion: Drama and Politics at the Court of Henry VIII*, (Cambridge: Cambridge UP, 1991); and *The Politics of Performance in Early Renaissance Drama*, (New York: Cambridge University Press, 1998).

4. One of the most interesting if scant pieces of information about the Finsbury theatre is that Rastell's wife Elizabeth (nee More, sister of Thomas) assisted in making a set of elaborate costumes used for productions at Finsbury. We know this from a law suit in which Rastell sued a servant who had let the costumes and returned them at a late date and in damaged condition. See Alfred Pollard, 'Pleadings in a Theatrical Lawsuit,' *Fifteenth Century Prose and Verse*, (Westminster: A. Constable and Co. Ltd., 1903).

5. Among the crew of *The Barbara* was 'Thomas Bercula or Berculay' and Henry Plomer maintains that Thomas Bercula is the same man as Thomas Berthelet, the king's printer with the Lucretia shingle (Plomer 224). A fascinating epilogue to the tale is the journey taken in 1536 by Rastell's son John. Reed reports that the younger Rastell, 'now a Gentleman of the Inns of Court' and the crew reached Labrador, but they 'were so beset

with hunger that they were reduced to watching an osprey's nest for the fish she brought her young...A seaman killed his mate while he stooped to take up a root, cut out pieces of his flesh and broiled them on the coals and greedily devoured him. Others joined him, and the company decreased in this way until the officers discovered the ghastly truth.' Fortunately for the Englishmen, a French ship sailed into their port and 'such was the policie of the English that they became master of the same' and returned home (Reed 27).

6. Rastell's son William kept the family name in the printing trade and his daughter Joan married the playwright John Heywood and would be the grandmother of John Donne.

7. The stage directions are cited by page numbers.

8. Robert Carl Johnson observes that the frequency of such stage directions along with the action implied in the dialogue in the Tudor interludes demonstrates that they were meant, not as debate literature to be read, as some suggest, but as plays to be performed (*Theatre Notebook* 26 (1971) October, 36–42. He makes the same case for the 'liveliness' of these dramas in relation to implied audience interaction in *Theatre Notebook* (1970) 24: 101–11.

9. Richard Helgerson has recently noted that in Rastell's play we have the first English work in which the notion of a new geography (of the new world) and a new literature (in his *New Interlude and a Merry of the Four Elements*) intersect (http://purl.oclc.org/emls/emlshome.html).

10. For the connection between *Albion, Knight* and The Pilgrimage of Grace, see *The Revels History*, Vol II 14.

11. I am citing page numbers; the J.S. Farmer edition of *The Three Law* and *King John* has no line numbers.

12. He published *The First Examination of Ann Askew with the Elucidation of John Bale*, after Askew became the first woman executed for her Protestant beliefs in England in 1546, as well as publishing in Germany in 1548 the then Princess Elizabeth's translation of a poem by Queen Marguerite of Navarre entitled by Elizabeth 'The Glass of the Sinful Soul.' Bale composed the 'Epistle Dedicatory' and 'Conclusion' to the work and renamed it *A Godly Medytatcyon of the Christen Sowle.*' Krista Kesselring argues that Bale in fact presents Askew and Princess Elizabeth as 'role models for the emerging protestant cause' (41) and most importantly that Bale implies that being a good Christian requires that women be learned: *Renaissance and Reformation* 22–2 (1998) : 41–61.

13. Jacqueline A. Vanhoutte makes some interesting connections between Bale's *King John* and some of Morison's pamphlets in 'Engendering England: the Restructuring of Allegiance in the Writings of Richard Morison and John Bale.' Her focus is on the sexism in the representation of England as a woman: 'Bale's feminization of England...allows him to present questions of invasion, of boundaries, and of possession within a familiar context of patriarchal values' (67). While this is certainly true, more related to my focus here is Vanhoutte's claim that 'Bale's play speaks clearly on the nature of the shift of allegiance demanded of English subjects, arguing for a replacement of the medieval dialectic between the local and the cosmographic with a dialectic between the individual and the nation' (64). *Renaissance and Reformation* 20–1 (1996) : 49–77.

Chapter 4

Elizabeth Barton,
Tempered Tongues and Tudor Treason

The miracle was this: the maid...was brought thither and laid before the image of our Lady... [where] her face was wonderfully disfigured, her tongue hanging out and her eyes being in a manner plucked out and laid upon her cheeks, and so greatly disordered. Then was there heard a voice speaking within her belly...her lips not greatly moving...[she spoke about] the joys of heaven, it spake so sweetly and so heavenly that every man was ravished.

(Cranmer 79–80)

If the subject is produced in speech through a set of foreclosures, then this founding and formative limitation sets the scene for the agency of the subject...[but not] the sovereign subject.

(Butler 139)

Women and Change in the Early Tudor Century

It is a premise of feminist history that women lost ground as autonomous and public persons in the early modern period and one can certainly argue that ground was lost for women in the Henrician period. Medieval women belonged to guilds, traded and ran businesses but by the late seventeenth century, historians argue, to find women so occupied, even as business partners with their husbands, was exceptional.[1] The closing of the convents at the dissolution is seen as a significant loss for women because the religious life was one of the few places where women 'exercis[ed] jurisdiction in their own right' (Loades *Tudor Government* 193).[2] Where women once may have been influential as models of devotion, mystics or prophets, such modes of being and communicating were cast into the realm of superstition.

The Henrician administration spearheaded the first Parliamentary statutes concerned with wills, prostitution, the regulation of the practice of medicine and witchcraft and such legislation affected women in particular ways. An act was passed in 1512 forbidding unlicenced medical persons from practicing in England (3 Hen 8 c, 11). Among those it addressed were '"common artificers, as smiths, weavers, and women that boldly and customarily take upon them great cures and things of great difficulty, in which they partly use sorcery and witchcraft...to the ...grevious hurts damage and destruction of the king's liege people'" (qtd. in Sim 86). While the act proved too difficult to enforce, and was nullified in 1542 (35 Hen 8 c, 8), in the same 1542 session of parliament, the first legislation against witchcraft was enacted (34 Hen 8 c, 8). And in 1546, the statute against prostitution finds the government back in the business of regulating sexuality.

With the establishment of the registration of marriages as required by the injunctions of 1538, the Tudor state and the English church collaborated in tightening their hold on the marital practices of English subjects. Other such moves are seen in the blocking of 'the intended marriage of desperately poor people whose families seemed likely to become a burden to the parish' (Cressy 312) and in the institution, early in the reign of Elizabeth, of the 'table of kindred and affinity' that defined and forbade certain unions.

In the Henrician period, the married woman (the legal persona of the 'feme covert') was further limited by such legislation as the Statute of Wills (32 Hen. 8 c, 38) which put the state firmly in charge of property issues and disqualified married women from writing wills for the first time in English legal history. Hence the English proverb: "'Women must have their wills while they live, because they make none when they die'" (qtd. in Erickson 140).[3] The Statute of Uses (27 Hen 8, c,10) restricted inheritance, disallowing women from inheriting both common law dower and assets they shared with their husbands in jointure. An Elizabethan commentator on women and the law observes as well that, according to Henrician law on petty treason and coverture, the 'Baron may beate his Wife.' '[I]f a man beat an outlaw, a traitor, a Pagan, his villein or his wife,' the author explains, 'it is dispunishable, because by the law Common these persons can have no action' (*The Lawes Resolutions of Women's Rights* 128), and he wryly comments 'God send Gentlewomen better sport, or better companie' (128).[4]

More subtle are the ways in which the government of women and the function of marriage itself become linked to national security in the Henrician period. Conduct literature for women in the early sixteenth century, while individualizing, largely relies on the strategies of discipline, that virtue demonstrated so vividly in Berthelet's image of Lucrecia. Juan Vives' program for the education of women, for example, is simple and single–minded:

> though the precepts for men be innumerable: women yet may be informed with few words. For men must be occupied both at home and abroad, both in their own matters and for the common weal. Therefore it cannot be declared in few books, but in many and long, how they shall handle themselves, in so many divers things. As for a woman, she hath no charge to see to, but her honesty and chastity.   (Watson, *Vives and the Renascence Education of Women* 34).

The primary tool in the governance of women, according to Vives, is shame or 'shamefastness,' which, with sobriety, are 'the inseparable companions of chastity, insomuch as she cannot be chaste that is not ashamed: for that is as a cover and veil of her face' given by nature. 'Of shamefastness,' he continues, comes: 'demureness' and 'measurableness,' virtues that will help her eschew vices and Vives includes a list of proscriptions in that regard. '[N]othing' for the woman, he instructs, 'shall be outrageous, neither in passions of mind, nor words nor deeds, nor presumptuous, nor nice, wanton, pert, nor boasting, nor ambitious...as for honours she will...flee them...be ashamed of them' (Aughterson, *Renaissance Woman* 70).[5] Recall Vives' similar warning tale about 'natural man' in his 'The Office and Duty of a Husband' : 'if he followeth his natural affection and appetite [he] is a proud, a fierce and a desirous beast to be revenged' and thus if women are 'common,' 'contentions,' even war, will ensue. Whereas, 'when the woman is lawfully married all such contentions do cease' which in times past have erupted when women were 'ravished' (as Vives notes was the case with Lucretia, among others). The implication is that had Tarquin the rapist been married, his fierce desires would not have gotten the better of him. Thus, Vives concludes to his audience of husbands, we see the 'utilities and profits [that] do spring and issue of matrimony' (Aughterson, *The English Renaissance* 430). Marriage in Henrician discourse clearly comes to bear a great burden as a tool of government. It is the site where the husband could exercise sovereign power and where the husband and wife each practiced the disciplinary regulation of the other. Both were to guarantee that the 'oeconomic' model of the household would serve as the template for the profitable governance of the nation.

Despite these rationales, strategies and injunctions, however, historians agree that the losses to women's autonomy in the period were accompanied by certain gains. Phyllis Mack's research on the vibrancy of women's prophecy in the late seventeenth century undercuts the argument about the absolute losses incurred by women at the dissolution. Or the research suggests, at least, that women refused spiritual limitations from the beginning. As well, the emphasis in Protestant theology on the individual's unmediated relationship with God and on the ability of all to comprehend the word of God in scripture applied to women as well as men and the educational initiatives that promoted reading for this purpose had some positive effect on the rates of reading among women of the middling sort. As Tina Krontiris observes, 'Religion actually creates one of the paradoxes of the sixteenth century: on the one hand women were enjoined to silence while on the other they were permitted to break that silence to demonstrate their faith and devotion to God' (10). Furthermore, there were juridical moves in the Henrician administration that would prove to have positive implications for women (though that may not have been their intention). The expanded scope of the equity courts, for example, would offer the feme covert more sway than did the common law.[6]

While marriage was the site of governance for both women and men, the new marriage held rewards for each as well. Marriage becomes both an arena of freedom where the 'ambitious promise' of earthly happiness will be fulfilled and a mode of containment for unruly impulses. For example, free choice in marriage is sanctioned by the state when in the 1530s we find Star Chamber hearing cases on forced marriage and finding on behalf of the youthful and often feminine complainants.[7]

Women suffered losses and enjoyed gains in the aftermath of change brought on by the Reformation, statutory reform and the widely dispersed forms of secular government in the period. Evaluating history in terms of loss and gain, however, limits our perception of the complexities of politics and the personal in early modern England. As Mack observes in her discussion of the Quaker prophets of the civil war:

> It is as automatic for feminists to point to a decline for women in the early modern period as it is for Whig historians to see progress. Indeed, the two are evidently interrelated, for the evolution of the modern nation–state and expanding capitalist economy was linked to a restriction of women's economic activities and to a conception of citizenship and public service that was emphatically masculine. Yet the experience of Quaker women visionaries, and of other religious women of the seventeenth century, makes plain the inadequacy of words like 'advance' or 'decline' for historians of gender. (412)

Karen Newman similarly argues that while women, as historian Joan Kelly argued, did not 'have a Renaissance' in the same way that a certain population of men did, historical records complain 'not only of upstart courtier–ship, a socially mobile middle class, and "masterless men," but of female rebellion. Incidents of feminine transgression crowd the historical record' (xviii). Newman reminds us that conduct writers like Vives are presenting a wish list and that it is a false premise to conclude that 'the prescriptions for female behavior in a sermon or conduct book reflect women's lived experience, which the critic can decipher to provide a true account of Renaissance women's lives' (xix). On the contrary, when Vives makes his bid for women's 'shamefastness,' he may be doing so because at least some women are seen by him to be 'outrageous' in their 'passions of mind,' not to mention presumptuous, nice, wanton, pert, boasting and ambitious.

The complexities of evaluating the domain of freedom for women is brought home as we observe governmental rationalities and practices at work. A good example of this is the Henrician law on prostitution. While this legislation may on one level seem to be aimed at curtailing the freedom of women, the novel statute against brothels may be concerned primarily with the liberty of men. Ruth Mazo Karras has shown that prostitution in medieval Europe had been tolerated and regulated. In 1546, however, the Henrician administration closes the stews and issues the following explanatory proclamation:

> considering how by toleration of such dissolute and miserable persons as, putting away the fear of Almighty God and shame of the world, have been suffered to dwell besides London and elsewhere in common, open places called the stews, and there without punishment or correction exercise their abominable and detestable sin, there hath of late increased and grown such enormities as not only provoke instantly the anger and wrath of Almighty God, but also engender such corruption among the people as tendeth to the intolerable

annoyance of the commonwealth, and where not only the youth is provoked...[but also] the true laboring and well–disposed men, for these considerations hath by advice of his council thought requisite utterly to extinct such abominable license. (*TRP* 365)

Mazo Karras comments that the same moves to curb prostitution are being made in cities across Europe, regardless of whether the countries are Catholic or, like England, in the throes of reformation. She argues that the shared impulse in these disparate lawmakers' aims is the desire to place checks on male sexuality, 'the encouragement of marriage and the criticism of male fornication reflect a change' (43). I suggest that such initiatives demonstrate the operations of governmentality at work across a Europe divided by religion, ideology and a growing imperialist imperative but united in their need for a class of well–tempered bureaucrats.

I am arguing, then, that one aspect of the governance of women in the period involves their conscription as governors of men. We have seen how conduct literature for men created elaborate taxonomies of masculine consciousness through which men were to understand themselves and work to fit themselves for public service. Elyot produces, in his discourse on the government of men, the persona of the 'housewife of virtue' as does Vives the 'handmaid of logic.' At the same time, real Tudor women were to become housewives and handmaids of the state's interest; both governed by and governors of men.

That the education and the government of women were perceived as political acts with implications for the nation is demonstrated in Richard Hyrde's preface to his 1540 English translation of Vives' *Instruction of a Christian Woman*. He announces: 'I thought at the leastwise for my part it would do well to translate this book into our English tongue, for the commodity and profit of our own country' (*Watson* 31). Hyrde authorizes the text by citing as precedents the political works of Xenophon and Aristotle, who gave out 'rules of housekeeping' 'oeconomic' rule and in Plato who in the course of writing his 'precepts of ordering the common weal, spake many things appertaining unto the woman's office and duty' (32). Women were seen as important actors in the polity. At the same time, we should not underestimate the degree of expertise and autonomy that women exercised as household managers. As Alison Sim argues, in the Tudor period women were 'formidable managers'(40): '[e]ven wealthy women were very much practical, working housewives. They may have had servants, but these were people whom they worked alongside, rather than just gave orders to as the grand ladies of later centuries did' (xxviii).

To further complicate the issue of women and freedom, we must consider that many of Henry Tudor's women subjects refused the function of guardian and instead threatened the very borders they were meant to secure. Sharon Jansen complains that '[t]he presence of so many women in the popular resistance to Henry's reforms has been largely overlooked, even in revisionist analyses of the Tudor revolution and Reformation' (*Dangerous Talk* 3). Certainly Jansen is joined by many feminist scholars in a reassessment of women's spheres of action in the Tudor period. We know, for example, that women took an active role in the rebellion of 1536 and that the 'Pilgrims' appeared to be well aware of the implications, specifically for women, of Henrician reform. One of the Pilgrims' demands in 'The York Articles,' was for the relief of the 'many sisters...put from their livings and left at large...a great hurt and discomforth to the common wealth' (Berkowitz 166–7). Most priests and monks were offered positions in the new reformed clerisy, but nuns expelled from convents were at the mercy of their families or parishes; some were left in dire poverty. Women took an active role protesting these and other changes during the 'Pilgrimage.' Jansen has collated many stories about women's activities, including a spy's report that one Lady Rhys brought 3,000 men to a rebel camp, along with '"half a cartload of plate, which they are coining among themselves"' (qtd. in Jansen, *Dangerous Talk* 25). On resistance to the commissions and the destruction of Catholic iconography, John Guy observes that 'in Exeter groups of women upbraided the iconoclasts' (Guy, *Tudor England* 179). To further examine the issue of women, their agency and politics, I will look closely at the case of one particular dissenting woman subject: Elizabeth Barton, the nun or holy maid of Kent who was executed for uttering treasonous words in 1534.[8]

Elizabeth Barton and the Word

The case of Elizabeth Barton is instructive in terms of women's history as well as in terms of the epistemological problems involved in apprehending that history. She appears to have contested the government's version of reform through her engagement with a hybrid union of European mysticism and English prophecy, both of which had been producing an increasingly politicized discourse from early in the previous century. Diane Watt has explored Barton's relation to such continental women mystics as St. Bridget of Sweden, St. Catherine of Sienna and St. Teresa of Avila, all of whom had directed their religious and mystical practices towards ameliorating injustice in the world. In his study of continental mystics during the turbulence of the reformation centuries, Michel de Certeau observes the ways in which these mystical movements were perceived as a political threat to secular powers. Humble holy people (often women) were raised to the status of erudite fonts of spiritual knowledge: 'maids, cowherds, villagers...characters, real or fictitious, were like pilgrimages to an alternative "illumination"' (26). Learned clerics, de Certeau observes, 'became exegetes of female bodies, speaking bodies, living Bibles spread here and there in the countryside or in the little shops, ephemeral outbursts of the "Word"' (26).[9] The nature of the spiritual experience made possible by these meetings, outside of churches, in private homes and humble cottages, appeared, de Certeau argues, dangerous to political and religious authorities.

If late medieval mysticism was political, prophecy in late medieval England, as we have seen, also linked communal narrative, personal inspiration and political protest. Alistair Fox concurs with Sharon Jansen, arguing that such prophecies:

had circulated in the fifteenth century and even earlier, but after the accession of Henry Tudor [Henry VII]...they seem to have been collected and refurbished with particular zeal. Indeed, several of the most important extant compilations date from the last three decades of Henry VIII's reign...political prophecy was exploited to create a myth of destiny which foreshadowed, and perhaps even promoted, the later idea of England as the elect nation. (Fox 77–8)

Fox demonstrates how the same prophecies were appropriated and reinterpreted in the interest of rival factions in the 1530s and like Sharon Jansen, sees them as a 'sub–literary genre' in need of reevaluation. Watt also consider the prophetic tradition, observing that 'prophecy could offer women a rare opportunity for direct involvement in the political sphere' ('Reconstructing the Word' 138) and she has recently linked Barton to other English women religious prophets from the middle ages through to the civil war period.[10] Mack concurs that '[w]omen as prophets enjoyed virtually the only taste of public authority they would ever know'and that 'the visionary's experience was profoundly *social*. Her enlightened condition did not imply detachment from the world but connectedness' (Mack 5,8). Jansen argues that Barton 'was very much aware of the form and language of contemporary political prophecy,' as demonstrated in Barton's use of the old prophecy '9,9,9, the reign of a king how long he shall reign' which, Barton claimed, meant that Henry's reign would end in its twenty–seventh year — 1535 (Jansen 70). Speaking a prophecy was clearly a citational act; one became a prophet by performing a novel and locally significant interpretation of a text that originates, not from a sovereign self, but from a shared history. The reading, like the prophecy, is un–authored and belongs to the community from which it sprang.

Operating within a vibrant culture of resistance, women mystics and prophets of the 1520s and 1530s, including Barton, practiced a form of Sharon Jansen's 'dangerous talk and strange behaviour' that at the very least disturbed and worried the government. Jansen makes the important observation that Barton's case was not unique, not as 'singular as it has seemed to historians' (70). What is unique about Barton, however, is the effect her 'revelations' exerted on the nation and consequently, the range of extant government documents that deal with her case.

I have presented the context in which individualizing forces that appropriated sovereign selves for government interests worked to inscribe the range of women's action in the public sphere. We also saw how notions about the feminine as a force on human consciousness, as well as real Tudor women themselves, were to join in the government of ambitious and potentially unruly men. In a counter–discourse of reform, conceived of by those clustered around Barton, their own design for reform is figured as a feminine force on the civil life of England and one with broad social ramifications. Henry Gold, vicar of Ospringe, soon to be a follower of Barton and one who would die with her, preached in 1522 that 'trew religion is wonderfully dekayed from her old state of perfection' (Whatmore, 'A Sermon of Henry Gold' 38). In a similar vein, Barton's follower Henry Mann writes to her confessor Dr.

Bocking: 'Let us magnify the name of the Lord, who has raised up this holy virgin, a mother indeed to me, and a daughter to thee, for our salvation. She has raised a fire in some hearts that you would think like the operation of the Holy Spirit in the Primitive Church' (*L&P* 6:835). The insurrection Barton generates would, her followers suggest, effect the daily and secular lives of English subjects. Reading one of the now lost pamphlets about Barton, an Elizabethan writes that she 'preached frankly against the corruption of maners and civill life' (Lambarde 171).

If gender was a potent force in the competing discourses of reform, so was the struggle conceived in relation to claims on the authority of a past that would authorize the direction of the future. The movement inspired by Barton clearly conceived of itself as a renewal, a return to a pre–lapsarian past. In his sermon, Gold complains about what are surely Wolsey's architectural projects in his reference to 'the chef devisors that be in englond of new & strawnge fascions in byldyng' (41). On the other hand, those who had been influenced by Barton are described by the Act of Attainder against her as 'inclyned to newfangilness' (25 Hen.VIII. c.12). John Salcott's sermon against Barton complains that the traitors had worked to 'distain His Grace's renown and fame in time to come' (Whatmore, 'The Sermon Against the Holy Maid' 464). The struggle at this time was over the nature of a reform that appeared inevitable, and the struggle worked itself out at the level of discourse through rhetorical claims and counter–claims about the past, the present and the future.

Barton prophesied that the house of Tudor would fall if the king married Anne Boleyn and thousands appear to have taken her at her word, that is, as a messenger from God, Mary and the saints. The government, however, saw her as either a witless and perhaps hysterical pawn of the men around her or as an equal in fraud with them. As Jansen has observed, historians generally have tried her on similar terms; they find her saintly, pitiful or full of guile. Feminist revisions of this history work to move beyond a discussion of Barton's authenticity to her agency. Nevertheless, feminist takes on Barton, like those of the Tudor judiciary and most twentieth–century historians, still tend to rest on arguments about the nature of her experience. I argue that the nature of her experience is inaccessible to us and that may not be solely the result of censorship. Barton may have actively participated in the mystification of her particularity of experience. For it is the king who would make her a sovereign subject; deep, complex, capable of considered deception.

The extant texts that make reference to Barton and which I will draw on include: reports on her case chronicled by Hall; her story according to a narrative by Thomas Cranmer; what Diane Watt calls a 'pornographic' and 'voyeuristic parody of the eroticism of mystical fervor' in the form of Richard Morison's Latin pamphlet *Apomaxis Calumniarum*; Salcott's sermon; the preamble to the Act of Attainder against her; the Elizabethan William Lambarde's observations upon his perusal of a now lost pamphlet about her (by her followers) in his *A Perambulation of Kent*; and many letters in the state papers. Lost to us are a number of printed works produced and distributed by her followers.[11]

The range of views about her is wide and irreconcilable. In November 1533, the Catholic ambassador to the Emperor Charles V writes to his employer that the king 'has lately imprisoned a nun...a good, simple, and saintly woman' (L&P 6:1419). The chronicler Hall, however, calls her a 'holy Hypocrite' (806). Our pamphleteer Richard Morison sees her as malleable pawn. He suggests about her public 'ecstasies' that she was '[o]rdered several times to fall down, distort her face and distend her jaws in the presence of the Duke of Norfolk...she fell down, distorted and distended as often as they pleased...' (qtd. in Neame 262). Further, some men are judged in relation to their estimation of Barton. In a scathing letter to Bishop John Fisher, Cromwell charges that if the nun had been plain mad, Fisher would not have been obliged to tell what he knew about her, but 'ye toke not this nunne for a mad woman' (Wright 33).

More recently, in 1944, we find L.E. Whatmore acting as an apologist for Barton; he edits a sermon about her in order to demonstrate that the 'devotio moderna' of which she was a part was an internally generated, grass roots kind of counter reformation.[12] Similarly Alan Neame's 1971 biography — *The Holy Maid of Kent: The Life of Elizabeth Barton, 1506–1534* — is hagiographical, hinting that Barton, like Thomas More, was a martyr deserving of sainthood. A.G. Dickens does count Barton among late English manifestations of the new devotion, but he finally dismisses her as a victim of the king, an epileptic and a 'psychopath' (18). J.G. Bellamy calls Barton's confessor and clerical supporters 'her handlers' (*Tudor Law of Treason* 28), suggesting that she was manipulated by men for political purposes.

Watt argues that history has been limited by a concern about whether Barton was complicit with her 'handlers' or a victim. She observes that even sympathizers have tended to see her as 'a victim of clerical exploitation rather than as an active political agent' ('Reconstructing the Word' 137). Watt's thesis is that 'Barton, contrary to being part of some larger machiavellian plan, stood instead within established traditions of female and popular prophecy which, as recent medieval and early modern scholars have suggested, had their own partial autonomy' (138). Watt also suggests that those who surrounded her were authentic followers. Jansen similarly presents evidence that Barton was familiar with the tropes of the English prophetic tradition and that therefore she saw herself as part of that tradition.

While this debate is primarily about facts, I am more interested in the function of the fact in Barton's case. I work to produce an historical narrative about Barton that does not engage in debates about the nature of her experience as a victim, charlatan, saint or agent. I do so because, on the one hand, the evidence is confounding in this regard and Barton herself seems to thwart our efforts to find her out. On the other hand, the truth of her individual experience is that which the government needed to know, prove, in order to prosecute her as a legal subject. I would also suggest that although it is an important feminist project to re–insert into history women's experience, it is not only through our internalized understanding of ourselves as individuals that we may become makers of history. I argue that Barton and her case have much to teach us in this regard. While her case illustrates the delimitation of the speaking subject through a government of individualization within the juridical sphere, I argue that Barton herself, whether saint, actor, plotter or ploy, provides a vivid example of full engagement with the new complex of government. As well, I investigate the government's attempts to discredit her by transcoding her considerable impact on the nation from the domain of theology to that of theatricality. In this way, the government inadvertently attributes great power to the human ability to act as another, to feign, to perform.

Barton's life first enters documentation in 1525, when she was working as a nineteen–year–old servant to Thomas Cobb, a steward to the Archbishop of Canterbury, William Warham. She fell ill with a disease that apparently caused her intermittent, but terrible, pain in the throat. Sick for several months, she is reported to have predicted the imminent death of a child being nursed in the same room as her. Lambarde, the Elizabethan commentator, observes about her prophecy: 'which worde was no sooner uttered, but the childe fetched a great sighe, and withall the soule departed out of the body of it...This her divination and foretelling, was the first matter that moved her hearers to admiration' (Lambarde 171). The mysterious disease and the prediction of the death of the child piqued the interest of local clergy, who sent servants to put her under watch.[13]

Barton is reported to have begun to hear the voices of Mary and angels who gave her a variety of instructions. Sequestered at St. Sepulchre's, a Benedictine foundation at Canterbury, she was placed under the spiritual direction of Edward Bocking, a local monk. When she announced that she had instructions from 'Our Lady' to attend the chapel at Court–at–Street on a certain day to be cured of her affliction, the 'falling sickness,' she apparently was followed by a crowd of between two and three thousand people of all social classes who, with Thomas Cranmer (whose response is cited at the top of this chapter), witnessed Barton's ecstasy. As the sermon preached at her public indictment puts it, 'the King's Grace's people, went in procession with this false and dissembling person...[all] singing the litany and saying divers psalms and orations by the way' (Whatmore, 'The Sermon against the Holy Maid' 465). Around the same time, Warham brought her request for a meeting with Wolsey to the Cardinal and Jansen identifies in this moment the transformation of Barton from a religious to a political prophet.

Many meetings with many prominent men are recorded, including three with the king, which Barton requested, she said, at the bidding of an angel. Her prophecy of the destruction of the House of Tudor, and indeed of every minister connected to that house, should the king divorce seems to have been reiterated to them all. The Bill of Attainder against her would claim that, in her final meeting with the king, she prophesied that 'there was a roote with three branches and tyll they were plucked up it shuld never be merye in Englond, interpretyng the roote to be the late Lorde Cardynall, and the first branche to be the Kynge, our Soveraigne Lorde, the seconde the Duke of Norfolke, and the thirde the Duke of Suffolke' (*Statutes at Large* 449).

Her feats, we learn, were wondrous. Lambarde relates that at the shrine of Court–at–Street she lit 'candels without fire, moisten[ed] womens breastes that before were drie and wanted milke, restor[ed] all sorts of sicke to perfect health, reduc[ed] the dead to life againe...finally dooing al good' (Lambarde 174). She is alleged to have performed a great many such miracles from out–of–body transport to invisibility and telepathy. A Cromwellian spy reports the story of some monkes fleeing England to join Tyndale; Barton 'by hur prayer' rendered their ship powerless to leave the harbour (Wright 16). While her secrets were not yielded up, she claimed jurisdiction over the secrets of others, from the state of Wolsey's soul (arrested in purgatory), to, as we have seen, the future of the house of Tudor. The Act of Attainder complains that 'the seid Elizabeth and Edwarde Bockyng John Deryng Richard Maister lykewyse actually travayled to dyverse places in this Realme, and made secrete relacion of the seid false feyned hypocrysie and revelacions...and gave knowlege herof to divers other sondre persons of this Realme' (450). Barton's reputation spread abroad as well and by 1528, the Lutheran and English expatriate William Tyndale included, in his *The Obedience of a Christian Man,* the claim that her visions were either feigned or works of the devil.

Her English followers included many women, some of high status such as Gertrude Courtenay marchioness of Exeter, whose family were the last Yorkist claimants to the throne. A document in the *State Papers* reports that the marchioness travelled in disguise to Canterbury to consult Barton (L&P 6:1468). Watt observes, however, that while there is evidence that she had a strong following among women '[i]t is impossible to say whether these women, evidently from quite disparate backgrounds, formed a community in any sense or were even known to one another, although it is entirely possible that many would have had connections with Syon Abbey [as did Barton] as a center of lay and religious feminine spirituality' ('Reconstructing' 155).

After the King's re–marriage in January 1533 and his subsequent excommunication, steps were taken to silence Barton. She was brought to the Tower of London for interrogation. In particular, she was to answer for her prophesy of Tudor doom, for which the king sought a case of high treason against her under the Treason Statute of 1352. A body of prestigious clerics and men of law assembled in Star Chamber and dutifully questioned Barton who, on November 18, apparently confessed herself a fraud. Following her confession, there was a three day debate in Star Chamber at Westminister about which the sympathetic Chapuys, reports:

> the principal judges, and many prelates and nobles [were]...employed three days from morning to night...[after which] the Chancellor, at a public audience, where were people from almost all the counties of this kingdom, made an oration...[saying] the Nun and her accomplices in her detestable malice, desir[ed] to incite the people to rebellion...[and] some of them begin to murmur, and cry that she merited the fire. The said Nun, who was present, had so much resolution that she showed not the least fear or astonishment.   (L&P 6:1445)

Nevertheless, having studied the evidence and debated the question of whether her activities were indictable, as 'compassing or imagining' the death of the king, the council concluded (undutifully) that there was no firm case, that her prophecies did not constitute evidence of a secret conspiracy against the king or his family, especially allowing that she had spoken them to the king in person the year before. The nun was not a traitor in the eyes of the law.

The king, his ministers and these judges did agree on one thing: that it would be in the interest of national security to launch a tour in which Barton would reiterate her confession in every corner of the realm. For the first such event, workmen erected a large wooden platform and bleachers for spectators at St. Paul's Cross. On Sunday November 23, Barton and nine men associated with her were brought to this stage where an audience of over 2,000 heard Bishop John Salcot preach the lengthy sermon narrating the government's version of the nun's history. Hall relates that as Salcott preached, he held up to view the many documents circulating about Barton and gestured to the principals who each ritualistically delivered 'with their [own] handes...to the preacher...appoynted, a bill declaryng their subtile, craftie and supersticious doynges' (807).The king did not give up on the treason charge however; thwarted by the court, in January 1534 he used parliament to bring the bill of attainder against Barton and the others. On April 20, Barton and five men were dragged on a hurdle from the Tower to Tyburn and hung. She alone was then decapitated.

The uptake of Barton's case was that immediate action was taken by the king and his ministers aimed at strengthening both the juridical arm and the rhetorical reach of the Reformation. Legislation was written that categorized certain speech acts and certain silences as actionable, even as newly designed rituals of statecraft, such as the oath of succession, were conscripted to the service of the crown.[14] As a performative, illocutionary speech act, the oath signaled the government's attempt to collapse speech into conduct, to turn speaking into doing for political purposes.

I use the word 'performative' in the Austinian sense, as that category of public, social and in a broad sense ritualized speech act which has the capacity to carry some force and accomplish some effect in the world.[15] Austin is disturbed by speech acts in which the intention of the one who performs the act is radically severed from the effect of that act and his touchstone in this regard is the example of the troublesome performative effects produced by actors on stage, who do not mean what they say and whose words and actions constitute a 'sea–change in special circumstances' where words are 'parasitic upon [their] normal use' (Austin 22). Upon scrutiny, as Jacques Derrida and others have argued, every speech act (and indeed every semiotically charged gesture) prove to be in some sense conventional, ritualized and therefore the carrier of an institutional force. Theatrical performance can be performative, just as everyday speech acts can be 'parasitic' upon theatrical and literary conventions. A consideration of speech acts within such a framework enables an appreciation of an almost inevitable incongruence among the intention of the one who acts, the historically accrued meaning of the words uttered and the effect of the words spoken in the world.

Henry Tudor and his ministers, like Austin, were grappling with the problem of intentionality and speech acts in relation to English law as they set to work drafting the new treason statute, one capable of addressing the issue of speech in such cases as that of the Barton. As Morison puts it in his Latin pamphlet *Apomaxis Calumniarum*, "'The Maid died, and a handful of monks with her; and in dying gave occasion for the making of a most valuable law'" (qtd. in Neame 347). The new statute instituted treasonous words as well as treasonous silences as a capital offense, the term 'misprision' of treason sliding semantically between words unspoken (the failure to report on the treasonous intentions or acts of others) and words spoken (words against the king, that are assumed to be conduct, to constitute a threat to his well–being or that of his family). The preamble to the Act begins with a justification of the king's divorce and a declaration that the king is legislating 'only [for the] discharge of hys conscience and for the welthe and sueritie of this hys Realme;' this law, therefore, has been brought forward '[t]o prevent the catastrophe of giving to[o] greate a scope of unreasonable lybertie...to al cankarde and traytrous hartes willers and wurkars of the same' (*Statutes at Large* 446). The law would police the space where hearts and wills dwell and to achieve this purpose, the Act declares that:

> If any person or personnes after the fyrste daye of February nexte comynge do malicyiously wyshe will or desyre by wordes or writinge, or by crafte ymagen invent practyse or attempte, any bodely harme...or schlaunderously & malyciously publishe & pronounce, by expresse writinge or wordes, that the Kynge...be heretyke scismatike Tiraunt ynfidell or Usurper of the Crowne...they shalbe adjuged traytours...[and every such offense] ajuged hyghe Treason. (*Statutes* 446)[16]

Here is an attempt to produce and delimit the early modern juridical subject as a thinking, speaking and acting being. Indeed thinking and speaking are brought under the jurisdiction of the state in novel ways as part of a complex repertoire of individualizing practices.[17]

The intention of the government to secure that area 'within' the subject to the service of its own interests is further evidenced in a report from an investigator who, in 1534, was carrying out inquiries for the *Valor Ecclesiasticus*. From Syon Abbey, where feeling against the oath of succession was particularly strong, Thomas Bedyll reports that the 'conversion'of the nuns to the 'kynges title' of head of the church had been accomplished. This notion of conversion betrays the ruler's desire for an intimate, even metaphysical relation with his subjects. This monarch in fact desires and needs 'sovereign subjects'created in his own image who are in some sense freely and willfully converted to the cult of the state. The sovereign subject of modernity is thus a subject of this particular brand of sovereign. And just as the king's words as such 'do something'in the instance of their uttering, so is the subject's word deemed to be an action that is both felicitous and culpable. The institution of state jurisdiction over speech acts, Judith Butler argues, in her instructive *Excitable Speech: A Politics of the Performative*, is a constitutive element of the founding of the sovereign nation state of modernity. '[T]he juridicalization of history' Butler concludes, 'is achieved precisely through the search for subjects to prosecute who might be held accountable and, hence, temporarily resolve the problem of a fundamentally unprosecutable history' (50).

Barton and a careful selection of her followers were severed from the religious and political history that had allowed them to speak against the actions of the government; they were then chastised for their speech acts as culpable, singular actors.

So the gentle, pastoral, personal and highly intrusive monarch is simultaneously an increasingly absolutist monarch, a monarch whose power is centred in his own person. Treason itself, as Bellamy has observed, was increasingly seen as a crime, not against the realm as it had been in feudal England, but against the ruler's own person, after the Roman fashion.[18] Executions increased, novel tortures were devised and terror had its place. Yet this is clearly a self–conscious regime that is concerned with more than rule by law; such governance is concerned with the problematics of rule, with 'men and things': '[g]overnment is the right disposition of things' (Foucault 'Governmentality' 93). Thus the Act of Succession, the Oath of Succession, the Treason Act of 1534 and the monarchy that underwrote them were complex and productive forces in the world. This legislation proscribes traitorous action, while at the same time invoking subjects with a tendency for dissension, even as new categories of traitorous action are produced. In the Commissioners' reports of the swearing of the oath and the trials of those who refused to swear and were charged with treason (such as that of Thomas More) we witness the production of 'knowable man.' The oath, with its regulation of the swearing hands, moving lips and the 'cunning wits'of every subject in England, aims to call these subjects into the service of policing their own convictions and measuring them against their knowledge of those words they have sworn before the king's deputies. Conversely, the Treason Act aims to proscribe against lips and wits, to exclude certain discourses from the domain of the sayable. An 'agonism' ensues in the tension between the forces of such governance and the inevitable dissenting counter–conduct of critical subjects, subjects whom Jana Sawicki describes as 'capable of critical historical reflection, refusal and invention' (Sawicki 103).

Barton's actions signify a refusal of the role of sovereign subject, that was cast for her by the Tudor administration. Rather, her utterances and actions are displaced by her from the sovereign centre of individualized speech where the law would situate them onto the divine as well as back onto the long history of English political prophecy. The king would foreclose on her mode of prophetic discourse, her connection to both the past and the present, in order to cite her words as individual acts emanating from a sovereign, autonomous, treasonous personage. She instead speaks from a pre– and anti–sovereigntist position, offering ritualized performatives saturated in history and community. The government was successful in censoring words by and about Barton. Through its production of Reformation discourse, it also attempted to foreclose on the truth value of some modes of public speech (such as prophecy and mystical utterance) that had allowed women and some members of the lower orders to have a voice in public affairs.

Explicit, overt forms of government censorship were thus highly successful in Barton's case. Those texts about Barton's miracles (likely in the thousands) were called in for destruction by the parliamentary act and the subsequent proclamation that convicted her of treason. There were two hundred copies of Bocking's books seized from the printers and apparently five hundred more in circulation. Yet there is no physical trace of any of these texts, nor one word that we can attribute to Barton with complete confidence. More than simple censorship is at stake, however. 'A subject who speaks at the border of the speakable,' argues Butler, 'takes the risk of redrawing the distinction between what is and is not speakable, the risk of being cast out into the unspeakable' (139). Barton herself, her words and the discourse of reform that was produced by, around and through her are indeed cast out. Yet the archive remains a record of vibrant struggle.

For one thing, by representing her miracles and her fame, these government documents are caught in their own discursive trap. Like all censors, they are compelled to reiterate the speech they would eradicate. They complain that Barton 'was brought into a mervelous fame credit and good opynyon of a great multitude of the people of this Realme' (*Statutes at Large* 448). They speak of 'sondry bokes, bothe greate and small both prynted and wrytyn' (448). The sermon claims that these documents are full of 'imaginations and lies, void of all truth and full of contradictions, one thing being repugnant to another...the said horrible terms issue from a corrupt, malicious, and mischievous mind, void of all sincerity and truth' (471). By these books, the act complains, Barton 'was brought in a greate brute and fame of the people in sondre parties of this Realme'(449), putting 'the nobles and commons of this realm in continual strife, dissension, and mutual effusion of blood' (464). The events involving Barton, relates Lambarde, were 'manifested to al men in bookes abroad'(170). If she had not been discovered, the St. Paul's Cross sermon instructs, 'this realm...might have been brought to utter confusion and destruction' (469). These references suggest that Barton rivaled the King and Cromwell in her breadth of influence and did so with far fewer resources, as either she or the array of written material about her followed the same routes around the realm as the government's many printed statutes, injunctions, articles of interrogation, circular letters, sermons, proclamations, commissioners and spies.

Even the fate of Thomas More and his carefully plotted words and silences were touched by Barton and her case. Elton says More's first slip of the well–guarded tongue occurred 'in connection with the Nun of Kent' (*Policy* 401). Like Bishop John Fisher, who was attainted with her, More seems to have found her compelling despite himself. In a letter to her, he asks her to recall that from the beginning of their acquaintance he had insisted that he would not speak of politics, 'I nothinge doubt your wisedome and the spirite of God shall keepe you frome talkinge with any persons speciallye with ley persons, of eny such maner thinges as perteyne to princes' affeirs, or the state of the realme, but onelye to [commune] and talke [about matters relating to the soul]' (Rogers 466). Barton, of course, did not heed his advice. Once she became a person of interest to the government, More attempted to explain to Cromwell why he had been a sympathizer. More relates that he once had asked Barton's advice about a young woman — Helen of Totnam — about 'whose traunces and revelacions ther hath bene muche talkinge.' Barton apparently advised the woman to assume 'that they were no revelacions but pleyne illusions of the devell' and on Barton's advice the woman had ignored the visions and they had slackened off (Rogers 484). More was impressed: 'I liked her in good faithe better for this answere, then for manye of those thinges that I harde reported by her' (Rogers 485). The king and Cromwell were not impressed with More, however. In fact, Henry wanted More charged on the Act of Attainder that convicted Barton; only his council persuaded him to desist. Similarly Salcott's sermon links Wolsey's fall to her. Salcot states that Wolsey was swayed by her truth claims, that he was: 'bent to go forth in the King's Grace's said cause...till he was perverted by this nun (467).

To counter such power, such charisma, such press, the government aimed to discredit Barton by accusing her of not being what she seemed, of being something else entirely, something secret and, predictably, something sexual, something steeped in Catholic carnality. The Attainder Act declares that when she entered the convent at St. Sepulchre, her newly appointed confessor 'had commenly hys resorte, not without probable vehement and vyolent suspicion of incontinencye, pretendyng to be hir gostly father by Godys appoyntment' (448). Hall reiterates the theory that she stole forth at night to fornicate 'for bodely communication & pleasure with her frendes' (810). She is a whore secretly playing the part of a nun. Hence she is accused of criminal 'feigning' and this verb 'to feign' becomes a keyword in government discourse.

Hall accuses Barton and her followers of travelling 'to divers places in this realme [making] secrete relacion of thesayd false fayned hypocrysie and revelacions of thesayd Elizabeth' (813). The official investigators Roland Lee and Thomas Bedyll report of their visit to Barton at her convent that '[t]he crafty nunne kept herself very secrete here, and shewed her marchaundise more openly when she war far from home'(Wright 25). The Act of Attainder lists those who knew about the many books but kept quiet while they 'traytrously beleved in theire hartys' that the prophecy had come true, that is that the king was not now the true king

> in the reputacion of Almyghty God; wherby in theire hertes and wylles they trayterously withdrewe from his Highnes theire naturall dueties of obedience, and secretely taught and moved other persons...to thyntent to sow a secrete murmur and gruge in the hartys of the Kynges subjectis agenst the Majestie of our seid Soveraigne Lorde. (449)

Richard Morison aims to reveal the trickery and depravity of Barton. In his *Apomaxis Calumniarum*, he claims that she and the friars duped the people who came to her for prayers, advice, and information, that they would be shriven by a priest who relayed their secrets to Barton. Morison inadvertently offers an intriguing scene in which the fiery Barton chastises a series of men:

> [s]he took the opportunity to rail most bitterly against the particular sins of the man she was addressing. Thus — You should not have done such and such a thing at such and such a time. — You should not have disgraced such and such widow. — You should not have ravished such and such a girl's reputation for chastity. And so [complains Morison] she

brought every one of the wretch's sins to mind. The sinner sees that nothing however hidden, nothing however secret, can be done without being known to God and to those whom God favours. (qtd. in Neame 142)

This claim on the space and time of the secrecy of the subject is usurping the jurisdiction of More's shepherd/king and the new Treason Act is a tactic to re–secure that jurisdiction, through its conceptual collapse of intent, speech and conduct.

In this discourse, theatricality becomes the play between the individual, their secret 'wish, will or desire' and the external forces that would know and prosecute those secrets and desires. Salcot claims that Dr. Bocking 'daily rehearsed matter enough unto her, out of St. Bridget's and St. Catherine of Senys [Siena's] revelations' (Whatmore 469). The claim is that she studies in order to imitate the ecstatic trances of these beloved women saints.[19] Similarly, Hall relates that she bases the gestural form of her feigned trances on her own bouts of the 'falling sickness,'as directed by Bocking and that 'when thesaid Elizabeth had used this false, feigned counterfeatyng for a ceason and was perfecte therein' they went on tour (808). Salcott's sermon claims that 'she feigned herself to be in a trance and disfigured...[that] she feigned and spake divers sentences as though she had been in another world' (Whatmore 466). The Act of Attainder accuses her of 'craftely utteryng in her seid feyned and falce traunses dyverse and many vertous and holy wordes...[and] heresies' (447). Lambarde, reading the lost pamphlet, describes how she 'fell...into a marveilous passion...utter[ing] sundry metricall and ryming speeches' (173). He concludes that '[i]f these companions could have let the King of the land alone, they might have plaied their pageants as freely, as others have beene permitted' (175). Barton's words and actions, these writers contend, were composed, scripted, studied, rehearsed and performed.

While these government writers associate theatricality with criminality in their narration of the events, at the very height of Barton's power the government attempts to use theatrical spectacle itself in order to counter what they saw as the force of dissent performed by Barton. Nowhere is this use of spectacle by the government more well marked as was Anne Boleyn's coronation. Nothing was spared for the production, as the extensive lists of purchases for the event in the *Letters and Papers* demonstrates. Hall reports that on May 29, the days of celebration leading up to the coronation on June 2 were launched by a procession on the river of fifty barges, followed by 200 smaller boats, to bring Boleyn from Greenwich to the Tower. 'The whole river was covered,' reports one writer (*L&P* 6:584). Another witness claims that '[i]t was a marvellous sight how the barges kept such good order and space between them that every man could see the decking and garnishing of each' (*L&P* 6:563). Before the first barge, the mayor's, there was 'a great Dragon continually movyng, & castyng wyldfyer...[and with] terrible monsters and wylde men castying fyer, and makyng hideous noyses' (Hall 799). After such chaos comes the order of the official personages in their stately, dazzling procession with its glorious musical accompaniment: 'Shalmes, Shagbushes & divers other instrumentes, whiche continually made goodly [h]armony' (Hall 799); this provision was 'a thinge of a nother world' (*L&P* 6:563).

The day before the coronation itself, Anne left the Tower accompanied by all the principle justices in England; one of these justices reports:

> [Her dress was] the same fashion as those of France, she mounted a litter covered inside and out with white satin. Over her was borne a canopy of cloth of gold. Then followed twelve ladies on hackneys, all clothed in cloth of gold. Next came a chariot [with the duchess of Norfolk and the queen's mother.] Next, twelve young ladies on horseback, arrayed in crimson velvet. Next three gilded coaches, in which were many young ladies; and, lastly twenty or thirty others on horseback, in black velvet...Before all, marched the French merchants, in violet velvet, each wearing one sleeve of the Queen's colours; their horses being caparisoned in violet taffeta with white crosses. In all open places...were scaffolds, on which mysteries were played; and fountains poured forth wine...On Sunday morning...she went on foot from her lodging to the church, the whole of the road being covered with cloth...the length of the garden of Chantilly...After hearing mass [she was] crowned by the archbishop of Canterbury. (*L&P* 6:584)

Despite the spectacle designed to legitimate and to produce awe, however, one reporter claims that all the people did not respond on cue:

> Though it was customary to kneel, uncover, and cry 'God save the King, God save the Queen,' whenever they appeared in public, no one in London or the suburbs, not even women and children, did so on this occasion. One of the Queen's servants told the mayor to command the people to make the customary shouts, and was answered that he could not command people's hearts, and that even the King could not make them do so. Her fool, who has been to Jerusalem and speaks several languages, seeing the little honor they showed to her, cried out, 'I think you have all scurvy heads and dare not uncover.' (*L&P* 6:585)

Order and magnificence meet the freedom within which the crowd could refuse the rhetorical force of such magnificence. The writer above also reports on her dress, but not as French fashion; rather as the livery of terror, '[h]er dress was covered with tongues pierced with nails, to show the treatment which those who spoke against her might expect' (*L&P* 6:585).[20] Tongues and torture: a more blatant association of forms of speech and state retribution could not be made. Some tongues attending the coronation did not transgress by commission, however, but rather they cleverly transgressed by omission; they offered only silence when they were meant to be crying their aves.[21]

Five months later, the government designed and produced another spectacle, this time at St. Paul's Cross, with Elizabeth Barton cast as the lead. The imperial ambassador calls this event a 'comedy....to blot out of people's minds the impression they have that the Nun is a saint and a prophet' (qtd. in Whatmore 461), and he notes that each of the principals were to 'play the same part'on the next two Sundays in different locations (*L&P* 6:1445).[22] This event, with its own scripted text, props and stage directions, announces that it is being presented so that 'you shall plainly understand the beginning, the progress, and final intent of this false, forged, and feigned matter' (Whatmore 464). Theatricality aims to show the inherent treachery of theatricality.

Finally, the king uses the occasion of the Act of Attainder to cast his 'eye of mercy' on every subject who may have been tempted by Barton's politics, who may even have acted in support of her in various ways. While the new treason law would temper the 'unreasonable lybertie' of English subjects, the Act of Attainder magnanimously offers subjects a certain freedom: 'all and every other hys subject not above convicted and attaynted by this Acte, shalbe released acquyted and clerely p[ar]doned agaynst his Hygnes hys heires and successours for...all maner of...offences...soo that none of hys seid Subjectes other than be above convicted...be impeached chalenged or trobled...but shall be by this present acte pardoned and released therof for ever' (451). His subjects are shriven by him and offered a 'reasonable' liberation from their 'trobling' guilt; now, he hopes, they are ready to invest their liberation in the new nation and its religion. As in the statute exonerating the universities from taxation so that his ambitious subjects would be free to become bureaucratic 'personages,' Henry Todor governs more by governing less in his exoneration of the vast majority of Barton's devotees.

I conclude the story of Barton by returning to Archbishop Cranmer's report of her 'cure' at the chapel of 'Our Lady of Court–at–Street' with which this chapter began. Despite himself, Cranmer is moved by this vision and chooses the word 'ravish' (a legal synonym for rape in the common law) to describe the effect of this seemingly grotesque image of a disfigured, picasso–esque body with its ventriloquised yet enthralling voice. This image calls into question the notion of an uninterrupted drive from autonomous thought to considered speech to determined effect, pointing instead to 'the torsion, the mutual perversion...of reference and performativity' (Sedgewick and Taylor 3). In speaking from her belly in rhyming verse, Barton challenges, consciously or not, the king's premise that there is an easily determinable relation between the intent and the effect of speech acts. Barton's prophetic and ecstatic voice speaks from elsewhere, like the murmur of discourse; its form precedes and exceeds the vulnerable body through which it lives. On the border of the unspeakable, Barton affects the very source that would seek to disarm her. It is her audience, in fact specifically her male audience, that is rendered passive, ravished even, in Archbishop Cranmer's figuration.

Even when Barton is reported to have been fully conscious, she herself confounds identification as a subject whose intentions are determinable. While she had confessed to fraudulence under interrogation, Barton later retracted the confession. An annunciatory angel had appeared to her, she asserted, in what she knew to be a final vision.[23] She claims to have been instructed to make the false confession because the world was not ready, the time had not come for her message. In this denial of her denial, the truth of her motivations and her estimation of these strange events is deferred once more, this time onto the angel of history, within whose jurisdiction her story still lies.

The only direct evidence pertaining to her life that either she or the Henrician administration has left us takes the form of a poignant and poorly spelled list, found in Cromwell's copious papers, of her worldly goods at the time of her imprisonment:

> Stuff received 16 Feb. of dame Elizabeth Barton, by the prioress of St. Sepulchre's — without — Canterbury, into the hands of John Antony of Canterbury....A 'coschyn blade,' an old cushion, two carpets, a mattress and other bedding. Platters, dishes, &., 12 lbs., which the prioress has bought for 4s. A white 'corter,' for which the prioress has paid 12d. A towel and three pillowberes. Two 'canstyckes,' A coat, for which dame Catherine Wyttsun has paid 5s. A piece of plank for a table. A little chest. Stuff remaining in the nunnery pertaining to dame Eliz. Barton, at the request of the lady prioress. Two new cushions given to the church; a mantle and a kirtle to the youngest nun; an Irish mantle, a cupboard with two great chests, and two stools and a 'canstycke' to the prioress; a coverlet and an old kirtle to dame Alys Colman, at the request of the lady prioress. Endd. (*L&P* 7: 192)

A testament to the dailyness of this life, perhaps to gifts given her, certainly to some status, the list tells us nothing of Barton's experience or opinion. I have worked to show that nevertheless, through an analysis of the discourse generated by Barton's case, we can extrapolate another legacy. The story of Elizabeth Barton teaches us much about the history of the subject and the nation, about the legal subject's new relation to public speech acts and performance, about how '[t]he kind of speaking that takes place on the border of the unsayable promises to expose the vacillating boundaries of legitimacy in speech' (Butler 41) and finally about the ethics of the arts of government.

Notes

1. On women and guilds see John Guy, *Tudor England* (Oxford: Oxford UP, 1988) 22 and Alison Sim, *The Tudor Housewife* (Gloucestershire: Sutton Publishing Ltd., 1996) 97.
2. Patricia Crawford answers the argument that the numbers of women who chose the religious life were on the decline at the Reformation with evidence from Yorkshire (taken during the visitation) that the twenty–four religious houses there had 'no difficulty in recruiting young women to the cloister' (22).
3. The 1540 Statute of Wills itself does not specifically mention that the feme covert could not make wills. It only notes, in section X, that the King would be granted the reversion of all land held in jointure and dower on the death of the wife. In 1542, however, an explanatory statute was passed, 'Explanation of the Statute of Wills' (34 & 35 Hen 8 c, 5) in which numerous questions were clarified, including those regarding women and wills: 'And it is further declared and enacted by the authority aforesaid that wills or testaments made of any manors, lands, tenements or other hereditaments by any woman covert...shall not be taken to be good or effectual in the law' (qtd. in Baker *Sources of English Legal History* 119).

4. *The Lawes Resolutions of Womens Rights*, or 'The woman's lawyer,' as it is titled on its page headings, was published anonymously in 1632, having been edited and amended by one T.E. The editor relates that the text was composed some time earlier by an author who is long deceased and, indeed, no statutes are cited after the reign of Elizabeth.

5. I am working with two truncated versions of this work, each containing material not in the other.

6. On this point, Constance Jordan observes that: 'In the legal thought of England the meaning of equity has a particular relevance to women, for it was in chancery and the other courts of equity that women could press for rights to own and manage their own property' *Renaissance Feminism: Literary Texts and Political Models* (Ithaca: Cornell UP, 1990) 5; see also my 'Wit, Will and Governance in Early Modern Legal Literature,' *Mosaic* 27.4 (1994): 15–34. For social histories of women in Chancery cases see Maria Cioni, *Women and Law in Elizabethan England with Particular Reference to the Court of Chancery* (New York: Garland, 1985); for women and the Court of Requests see Tim Stretton, *Women Waging Law in Elizabethan England* (New York: Cambridge UP, 1998).

7. See 'Dyon v. Sotheby, Forced Marriage,' *English Historical Documents* under the heading 'The Court of Star Chamber. Some typical proceedings,' ed. C.H. Williams (London: Eyre & Spottiswoode, 1971) 428.

8. For some recent general studies of women, religion and politics see Tina Krontiris, *Oppositional Voices: Women as Writers and Translators of Literature in the English Renaissance* (London: Routledge, 1992); Patricia Crawford, *Women and Religion in England* 1500–1720 (London: Routledge, 1993); Rosalynn Voaden, ed. *Prophets Abroad: The Reception of Continental Holy Women in Late–Medieval England* (Cambridge: D.S. Brewer, 1996).

9. The relative autonomy of women mystics, particularly in relation to their confessors, has been evaluated by Janette Dillon in 'Holy Women and their Confessors or Confessors and their Holy Women? Margery Kempe and Continental Tradition.' She argues that such women mystics are 'both dominated and liberated, living under the spiritual direction of authorised agents of the established church, yet set free to live lives of unorthodox independence by those very directors' (Voaden, 120).

10. See Diane Watt, *Secretaries of God: Women Prophets in Late Medieval and Early Modern England*, (Rochester, NY: D.S. Brewer, 1997).

11. On the topic of 'media' in the Elizabeth Barton case, see Ethan H. Shagan, 'Print, Orality and Communications in the Maid of Kent Affair,' *Journal of Ecclesiastical History* 52:1 (2001): 21–33.

12. See 'The Sermon Against the Holy Maid of Kent and her Adherents, Delivered at Paul's Cross, November the 23rd, 1533, and at Canterbury, December the 7th,' *The English Historical Review* 58 (1943): 461–75.

13. Watt observes that '[t]he link between illness and prophecy is to some extent a gendered one, as accounts of prolonged physical suffering are especially common in the lives of female saints' ('Reconstructing the Word' 144).

14. Although the Act of Succession does not appear to exclude women from those subjects who would swear the oath, the commissioners' reports found in the *Letters & Papers* contain no women's names. Historians tend to agree with John Guy who says that the oath was sworn by 'all adult males' (*Tudor England* 136). The chronicler Edward Hall, however, asserts that women did swear the oath. Of the commissions he claims, they 'were sent over all England to take the othe of all men and women to the act of succession, at whiche fewe repyned' (814).

15. Austin distinguishes between the production of meaning — 'locutionary acts' — and the force of words — 'illocutionary acts.' Illocutionary acts accomplish institutional effects in the instance of their uttering, as in Austin's prototypical example — the marriage vow. A third type of speech act is named 'perlocutionary,' as the production of force that causes an effect on a witness or witnesses and Austin makes the important observation that such perlocutionary force can be achieved by 'non–locutionary means' such as 'waving a stick or pointing a gun' (119). See J.L. Austin, *How To Do Things with Words* (Cambridge, Mass.: Harvard UP, 1972).

16. To further the scope of the secular, the Act also proscribes appeals to benefit of clergy and to sanctuary in the case of treason.

17. Bellamy observes that 'the Tudor era is remarkable in the history of treason for the large amount of legislation which concerned itself with that subject. Between 1485 and 1603...there were no fewer that sixty–eight treason statutes enacted, though there had been less than ten in the period 1352–1485' (*Tudor Law* 12).

18. See John Bellamy, *The Law of Treason in England in the Later Middles Ages*, (Cambridge: Cambridge UP, 1970).

19. In Voaden's anthology, Denise Despres and Diane Watt both examine Barton's relationship to St. Catherine of Sienna. In 'Ecstatic Reading and Missionary Mysticism: The Orcherd of Syon,' Despres argues that 'Catherine's bold maneuvring in conciliar politics, through prophecy, preaching, and mendicant *imitatio*, would have provided Barton with a model of success, or at least the validation of such evangelical activities as a testimony to visions' (159). In 'The Prophet at Home: Elizabeth Barton and the Influence of Bridget of Sweden and Catherine of Siena,' Watt suggests that 'it is the determination with which she championed the Church against bishops, the King and even the Pope, obtaining interviews with some of the most powerful people in the realm in the process, which is most reminiscent of the activities of St Bridget and St Catherine' (171).

20. The queen's daughter, when queen herself, would wear a dress with a message as well; in the famous 'Rainbow Portrait,' Elizabeth I's gown is embroidered with a multitude of eyes and ears.

21. The crowd may have resorted to violence against Boleyn earlier on. J. Christopher Warner cites a report to the French ambassador in Venice that '"a mob of from seven to eight thousand women of London went out of the town to seize Boleyn's daughter [Anne], the sweetheart of the king of England, who was supping at a villa on a river...The women had intended to kill her; and amongst the mob were many men, disguised as women"' (Warner 6). As in the case of Barton, the status of Boleyn's innocence or guilt is still much debated. For a recent contribution, see Greg Walker's 'Rethinking the Fall of Anne Boleyn,' *The Historical Journal*, 45:1 (2002): 1–29.

22. While the performance was repeated in Canterbury on December 7, a national tour did not materialize.

23. See Whatmore, 'The Sermon,' 474 and Wright, *Three Chapters of Letters*, 18.

Conclusion

This book has argued that the reign of Henry VIII saw the emergence of a new form of secular government designed to strengthen the state one subject at a time.Through innovative legislation, the dissemination of propaganda, the appropriation of ecclesiastical and pastoral modes of rule and new and sometimes spectacular rituals of statecraft, this monarch and his counsellors worked on the intimate territory of conscience, desire and speech, as intention, sexual practises and verbal performatives were forced into the domain of public discourse and the juridical sphere. I observed how gender was a fulcrum for social change and that the domestication of women took place in relation to a new 'publication' of a certain class of men. A pervasive conviction of humanist writing was that masculinity needed to be tempered but that certainly men were governable and a new economy of friendship and marriage was charged with serving this end. We saw how the governmental arts operated through the promise of freedom and prosperity for those who would pay the price of self–temperance. And such temperance necessitated the acquisition of self–knowledge. To this end, early printed books operated as self–help manuals, guides for exercising a newly secularized civil conscience. Simultaneously and ironically, the self came to be understood as a territorialized site of secret refuge. For humanist men, in fact, the self was constituted *as* property and freedom; as Thomas Elyot instructs, a man's 'soule is undoughtedly and fre[e]ly his owne...[and] [h]is body so pertayneth unto him that none other without his consent may vindicate therein any propretie' (*The Boke* 202). At the same time, the government demanded a right of special access to and jurisdiction over that newly discovered territory of the citizen self, as both intention and speech acts were increasingly deemed accountable to the law. Thus we see how the processes of individualization, although represented and perhaps experienced as liberation, nevertheless also provided a means for governing.

We saw that engagement with these modes of government was vibrant, imaginative and courageous as dissenting subjects mobilized around counter–discourses of reform given material embodiment in collective movements such as the rebellion named by its participants 'The Pilgrimage of Grace,' or in individuals such as Elizabeth Barton in her persona as the 'Holy Maid of Kent.' She (and those working with her) created a theatrical spectacle of the revelation of secrets. The government in turn worked to appropriate certain forms of representation from the repertoire of these dissenting subjects, as it sometimes desperately aimed to convince, seduce and compel (as well as to threaten) English subjects into compliance. By studying the case of Barton, I observed the relation between the increasing absolutism of the English sovereign and the juridical and 'sovereign' subject of early modernity. The king aimed to discredit Barton as prophet in order to cite her words as indictable speech acts emanating from a criminal personage. I argued, however, that an unforeseen effect of the enactment of such policy was the discursive transference of Barton's domain of operation from the realm of the prophetic to that of the theatrical. Besides imbuing the theatre with great power, the unforeseen inference is that any and all public spectacles (even the government's) could well be inherently false — merely performance.

I traced the discursive conjunctions and disjunctions between the historical archive and examples of the dramatic form that was the Tudor secular interlude. We saw that this drama was intent on examining questions about human nature and especially human sexual nature in terms of the state and its security. Like the treatises, this stage believed that reason, as the 'soul intellectyve' was a technique for the operations of conscience and temperance. Now, however, the fallen and corrupt 'will' of English citizens threatened to override reason. Enter the governmental promise of prosperity and liberty, on offer in exchange for reasoned temperance. In this regard, recall that Skelton's Felicity instructed that: '[w]ealth is of wisdom the very true probate' (4) and that Bale's Deus Pater promised 'perfect liberty' (*Three Lawes* 74–5) to those who would forsake the excesses, and especially the sexual excesses, of Rome. We found the temptations of the flesh embodied in Rastell's Nell, Jane, Besse and Rose; the Ploughman's 'nise proude primmys...paintyd popagays' (*Gentleness* 926–7), in the bawd Celistina and in Bale's Idolatry and Sodomy.

The reasonable subject was both to be a performer and to be on guard against dissimulators. Especially dangerous in this regard, we saw, are the bad counsellors posing as good ones such as Division (of *Albion, Knight*) who advises Albion to join his ruse and 'dissemble [him]self wise' (131). Dangerous dissimulation and bawdiness are conflated in Skelton's 'tappister like a lady bright' (420), one of the figures in Counterfeit Countenance's large catalogue of bad actors. We saw this dramaturgy work to contain the attractive vices it threw up in its warning tales, as its didactic imperatives came into conflict with its theatrical ones. Finally, however, the drama called for the active and highly self–conscious performance of the citizen self, because 'every thynge [advised Rastell] is made to do his nature' (*Four Elements* 295).

Thus early sixteenth–century English subjects were to harness their consciences and their desires to a new patriotism as well as to the demands of the state and its institutions for the promise of great happiness and wealth. The ethical problems with this new relationship between subject and nation, I suggested, arise in the modes of exclusion made necessary by the aims of government. Those judged incapable of managing their freedom — the poor, the sexually 'abomynable,' the cowardly, the unreformed, the foreign — would have that freedom limited; at the same time, good, self–conscious and active subjects were bidden to subordinate or exile aspects of themselves judged counterproductive to certain institutional aims. Mitchell Dean observes, for example, that because the security of the early modern state required military readiness, '[t]he ideal of civil prudence thus contains a militaristic virility at its core' (88). Certainly Richard Morison worked to cultivate just such English military virility in the readers of *An Exhortation to Styre All Englyshe Men to the Defence of Theyr Countreye*.

The new self–consciousness thus worked to produce a division between thought and action. Good governance and good statecraft might involve deliberation and the decision to 'act' in ways that may conceal one's true intentions. If one were required to exercise one's freedom to dissimulate, however, so might one's political foes. Thus, as Dean observes, in early modern writings on statecraft, we often find that 'distrust and secrecy, and bribery and dissimulation, were recognized as necessary' (87–8). This government, I conclude, anticipates and creates the conditions of possibility for the liberal rule that would prop up laissez–faire capitalism and the complex rule of populations in the future just as it inadvertently contributed to an ethos where being and the performance of being become an object of interest of the new secular theatre.

As we have seen, scholars working in the Henrician period complain that this time of immense change and cultural complexity deserves to be studied for its own sake and not merely in terms of the more historically interesting, artistically sophisticated and politically important reigns of Elizabeth I and James I. Nevertheless, I will track the future fortunes of some aspects of Henrician 'pre–liberal' rule as realized in the later sixteenth and early seventeenth centuries. Elizabeth and the Elizabethans, of course, looked on the reign of her father as a model to be emulated. She would eschew the more extreme measures of her brother and sister and attempt to pursue the 'middle way' in both religion and politics. Or at the very least, she and her ministers worked to be seen to be pursuing a middle way and this self–imposed imperative is itself a sign of the governance of government. This mode of rule required innovation and imagination, theorizing and experimentation, a think tank approach to policy that was nevertheless as often ad hoc and reactive as it was proactive and constitutional.

Elizabethan self–help becomes ever more specialized as success comes to depend on the willful performance of self–rule. Books that rationalized and promoted the governance of governors and other men of law proliferated, for example, and tended to be directed at specific actors in this domain. We find William Lambarde's *The Duties of Constables* (1582), William Fulbecke's *A Direction, or Preparation to the Study of the Law* (1600) and works which deal specifically with the application of equity and the duties of equity administrators such as William West's *Symboleography* (1593) and Thomas Powell's *The Attourney's Academy* (1623). As for the strategy of dissimulation, another Elizabethan man of law advised his fellows on the matter. In his essay, 'Of Simulation and Dissimulation,' Francis Bacon defines the degrees of 'the hiding and veiling of a man's self' (59) and he concludes: 'The best composition and temperature is to have openness in fame and opinion, secrecy in habit, dissimulation in seasonable use, and a power to feign, if there be no remedy' (60). All of these advice books, like those of Elyot, Vives and Morison tie the cultivation of character both to the strength of the state and to personal success.

Later guidebooks for women reveal the complex relation between gender and government that follows from the Henrician experiments. A key case in point is a book that advises women on legal matters, *The Lawes Resolutions of Women's Rights*. By offering women knowledge to which they had previously had no access, this text encourages women to participate in their own government for the good of the nation. On this level, *The Lawes Resolutions* is aligned with such Henrician guidebooks as Hervet's translation of *Xenophon's Treatise of Householde* and with the many other conduct books and pamphlets produced by men for the instruction of women in the later Tudor and Jacobean periods. As in these other guide books, women are bidden to be 'chaste, silent and obedient;' in *The Lawes Resolutions*, however, they are also bidden to take part in their culture by being knowledgeable, wary, and active, to be in fact 'rights bearing' citizens, as the title suggests. This book promises its readers both personal and national prosperity and in fact the two are promoted as mutually dependant.

Like Elyot and Morison, the author of *The Lawes Resolutions* is very interested in and worried about men, especially dangerous men who threaten the order of things, men who, the book warns, are often 'drunken...with their owne lusts, and the poyson of...false precept' (376), men who, in the act of seduction, 'turned themselves for loves sake into Centaurs first, and...Buls afterward' (383), and who live only to satisfy their 'brutish concupiscence' (389). As we found the key virtues personified and feminized in early sixteenth–century tales about government, and as Tudor women and marriage were conscripted to the Henrician project of governing unruly men, so in *The Lawes Resolutions* are women charged with the task of exemplarity. The advice the author offers to wives of adulterers, for example, is to bid them to react to their husbands' transgressions by creating themselves as examples of virtue for the purpose of demonstrating how the well–governed subject will win 'freedome [and] happines' (146).

We saw that the influential Spaniard Juan Vives was one of the first Henrician humanist writers to articulate the relationship between gender and government; he laid out a program for the mutual and fruitful temperance of men and women that would make possible the governmental thinking of such texts as *The Lawes Resolutions of Women's Rights*. Vives also offered productive thinking on the problem of wealth, poverty and the poor that would help make way for the great Elizabethan poor law experiments. His treatise *The Relief of the Poor*, published in 1526, is seen by historians to have influenced urban schemes to manage the poor in several European cities throughout the early modern period. While we might recall Elyot complaining about the 'vaine pitie' that led to tolerance of the shiftless poor, the unemployed and vagabonds (*The Boke*, 145–6), Vives categorizes these unproductive members of the commonwealth in order to make a set of clear recommendations for their transformation into active citizens. While it is true that the treatise was not translated into English until 1552, when it would directly influence the institution of the hospital system and later Elizabethan poor law, the ideas it promulgated are seen to have had direct influence on Henrician laws dealing with begging and vagabondage as well as on experiments in managing the poor in the city of Ypres in the early 1520s.[1] While historians track a variety of systemic reasons for the rise in poverty in the period, such reasons were not the object of study for the royal and civic administrators who would follow the models laid down by their Henrician counterparts. Rather it was often on the poor themselves that blame was placed and thus the solution to poverty and the problems poverty caused to others would be solved by such programs as the transformative training at Bridewell Prison, called in the period a workhouse, a house of occupation, a house of correction and a reformatory for vagabonds. As Jean Howard puts it, citing J.A. Sharpe, Bridewell was 'a step in the criminalization of poverty.'[2]

One recent focus of historical investigation for scholars in the social sciences (including those inspired by Foucault's thinking about early modern government) is the emergence of 'the risk society.' The identification of risk and the development of schemes for the management of that risk by national and local governments are seen by Francois Ewald, in fact, as a sign of the turn to modernity itself. The sociologist Anthony Giddens goes so far as to suggest that Elizabethan poor law was a 'risk management system' designed to mitigate the danger or imagined danger posed by the increasing numbers of poor and unconnected. The fear of the poor is tangible in our Henrician, Thomas Elyot's, rant:

> Beholde what an infinite nombre of englisshe men and women at this present time wander in all places throughout this realme, as bestis brute and savage, abandonyng all occupation, service, and honestie...by outrage in riotte, gamynge, and excesse of apparaile, be induced to thefte and robry and some tyme to murdre, to the inquietation of good men and finally to their owne destruction. (145–6)

Inspired by such fear–mongering and by faith in the 'human sciences' and their schemes of reordering and rule, Elizabeth's administration set up a complex system of 'overseeing' and correction that certainly looks and smells like risk management.

The Elizabethan stage makes hay with the complexities of this sphere of freedom and government, first made manifest in the Henrician period. I argued that the Tudor governments worked to call forth a nation of highly self–conscious subjects, subjects who would understand themselves as deep, desirous and if needs be duplicitous entities. Performance became a way to understand being in the world and the theatre the art form most capable of representing this present. Thus the stage can be viewed as the site where 'the union of erudite knowledge and local memories' allow us 'a historical knowledge of struggles' (Foucault, 'Two Lectures' 83), but not necessarily the large revolutionary struggles driven by conflicts of faith or ideology. Rather the stage serves us a representation of and commentary on the subtle, daily and local struggles around the governing practices and modes of self–government that constitute the arena of ethics.

Foucault also suggested in the lecture above that a genealogical approach to history invites us 'to make use of this knowledge tactically today.' One goal of this book has been to suggest that some techniques of government employed in that four hundred year old Tudor experiment in management can be linked in kind to those permeating our culture today. To that end, I began with an anecdote about the use of the theory of the four humours in a contemporary self–help context. I suggested that there is a logic in the appropriation of this ancient model of self–understanding in the sixteenth and twenty–first–century context. I don't mean to say that the imperative that exhorts subjects to strike a particular orientation to self conduct is identical in each case, nor that there has been a linear genesis of governmentality from the early to the post modern periods. Rather, I want to suggest that the cultivation of an intimate link between the large, secular, corporate entity that was the nation and the body, mind and heart of the figure we would call the private individual is a strategy newly recognizable in our present. For today the domain of governance for nation states and other large corporate bodies is less and less that modern entity 'society' and more and more the self–regulating, 'post–private sphere' individual. Dean observes that Margaret Thatcher herself declared in 1987 that '"there is no such thing as society"' (151) and he suggests that 'the self–determining or free subject' has become the prime object of governing schemes. This may be the death knell of nation as community, as the divisive aspects of the modern state achieve prominence giving sway to the inegalitarian nature of democracy and to what Dean calls the illiberality of liberalism (131). Now freedom is to consist of becoming 'an entrepreneur of oneself and all the innate and acquired skills, talents and capacities that comprise "human capital"' (Gordon, cited in Dean 158). Hence, the 'new prudentialism' through which we are each exhorted to calculate and manage risk to ourselves (and in fact issues to do with health have achieved a new moral valence). For example, although low income people might be labeled as 'high risk groups' in relation to health, the solution is not seen to lie in the amelioration of disadvantage but in the transformation of personal weakness. In this way, argues Dean, both '[n]eo–liberalism and neo–conservatism share this same diagnosis of the problem of the corruption of the people and the need to lead them to accept their responsibilities and become a virtuous citizenry again' (163). I have argued that in early modern England such governmental arts first emerged as a form of secular governance in the Henrician period, that before the population and society could become the focus of enumeration, epistemological exercises and management, the government required a liberal or pre–liberal subject who was capable of being understood and governed in this way.

Dean concludes that most recently governmental regimes have become 'reflexive,' that is they have turned their gaze and their programmes upon themselves. In what he calls an 'explosion of audit' professionals of all kinds and from all spheres, whether public or private, are subject to new 'calculative regimes...[such as] performance indicators [and] bench–marking' (169). Such strategies propose to be restoring trust and accountability but, observes Dean, they also 'presuppose a culture of mistrust' (169). We have thus arrived back in our present as petroleum industry middle managers are exhorted to tie the governance of self and of colleagues to success and profit. We have also arrived back in the university where we found Henry VIII tying economic support to the establishment of an instrumentalist curriculum; for of course those in higher education are included in this great swath of new management. Today governments and corporations urge us latter day humanists to justify to them the 'liberal arts and sciences' through new modes of accounting, just as corporate intervention in the academy is proving a serious challenge to what we value as academic freedom.[3]

The analytics of such governance by scholars associated with the History of the Present network, on principle, does not offer a prescription for a utopian and future freedom. Yet despite observations about the 'illiberality of liberalism' and despite the proliferation of schemes of government that we suffer and enjoy today, as Vikki Bell argues,

> Foucault's point was to show us that we are 'freer than we think we are'; that radical political and psychoanalytic thought has led us to conceptualize our freedom as curtailed or repressed, such that true freedom becomes figured as the totalized breaking out of a current state of repression or oppression, and as an absence of any determinacy. But such a zero sum conception of power is one that has limited our political visions, directing them away from the possibilities in the present and on to the hope of some future radical change. (83)

The arena of freedom of the subject is the arena of ethics. Understanding the practices through which that arena of freedom has been conscripted to the aims of various institutions and regimes becomes a kind of ethical practice itself. My aim in *Governmental Arts* has been to present the past as an archive of possibility for the now. The history of political engagement with the government of individualization by ordinary women and men in the sixteenth century speaks to the vulnerability of governmental mechanisms, to the possibility of many forms of critique and to the role of representation and performance in both governance and its refusal.

Notes

1. For a brief history of the text and its influence, see the introduction to *On Assistance to the Poor*. Renaissance Society of America Reprint Texts, 1999. Trans. and intro. Alice Tobriner, SNJM, Toronto: University of Toronto Press, 1971. On its influence on Elizabethan poor law and in particular the experiment that was Bridewell Hospital see Edward Geoffrey O'Donoghue. *Bridewell Hospital: Palace, Prison, Schools, from the*

Earliest Times to the End of the Reign of Elizabeth. (London: J. Lane, The Bodley Head Ltd., 1923).

2. See Jean Howard. 'Civic Institutions and Precarious Masculinity in Dekker's *The Honest Whore.*' *Early Modern Culture: an Electronic Seminar*, No. 1 (2000): http://www.history-journals.de/articles/hjg-eartic-j00107.html

3. For a critique of such 'calculative regimes' in the university see William Bruneau and Donald C. Savage, *Counting Out the Scholars: the Case Against Performance Indicators*, (Toronto: James Lorimer & Co. Ltd. A CAUT [Canadian Association of University Teachers] Series Title, 2002).

Bibliography

'Albion, Knight.' Farmer, *Six Anonymous*. 119–32.

Anglo, Sidney. 'An Early Tudor Programme for Plays and other Demonstrations Against the Pope.' *Journal of the Warburg and Courtauld Institutes*. 20 (1957): 176–9.

—. *Spectacle Pageantry, and Early Tudor Policy*. Oxford: Clarendon, 1969.

Aughterson, Kate, ed. *The English Renaissance: an Anthology of Sources and Documents*. London: Routledge, 1998.

—. ed. *Renaissance Woman: Constructions of Femininity in England*. London: Routledge, 1995.

Augustine, Norman and Kenneth Adelman. *Shakespeare in Charge: the Bard's Guide to Leading and Succeeding on the Business Stage*. New York: Hyperion, 1999.

Austin, J.L. *How To Do Things With Words*. Cambridge, Mass.: Harvard UP, 1972.

Axelrod, Alan. *Elizabeth I CEO: Strategic Lessons from the Leader Who Built an Empire*. Paramus, New Jersey: Prentice Hall Press, 2000.

Axton, Richard, ed. *Three Rastell Plays: Four Elements, Calisto and Melebea and Gentleness and Nobility*. Cambridge, UK: D.S. Brewer Ltd., 1978.

Bacon, Francis. 'The Essayes or Counsels, Civill and Morall, 1625: Of Simulation and Dissimulation.' *Francis Bacon: A Selection of His Works*. ed. Sidney Warhaft. Toronto: Macmillan of Canada,1965.

Baker, J.H. *A Centenary Guide to the Publications of the Selden Society*. London: Selden Society, 1987.

—. *An Introduction to English Legal History*. 3rd ed. London: Butterworths, 1990.

—. and S.F.C. Milson, eds. *Sources of English Legal History: Private Law to 1750*. London: Butterworths, 1986.

Bale, John. 'King John.' Farmer, *The Dramatic Writings* 171–294.

—. 'The Three Lawes.' Farmer, *The Dramatic Writings* 1–82.

Barnett, Vikki. 'How to Deal with Difficult People.' *Calgary Herald* 4 Sept. 1999: WS1.

Barry, Andrew, Thomas Osborne and Nikolas Rose, eds. *Foucault and Political Reason: Liberalism, Neo–liberalism and Rationalities of Government*. Chicago: U of Chicago P, 1996.

Bellamy, John G. *The Law of Treason in England in the Later Middle Ages*. Cambridge: Cambridge UP, 1970.

—. *The Tudor Law of Treason: an Introduction*. London: Routledge & Kegan Paul, 1979.

Bell, Vikki. 'The Promise of Liberalism and the Performance of Freedom.' Barry and Osborne 81–98.

Berkowitz, David. *Humanist Scholarship and Public Order: Two Tracts Against the Pilgrimage of Grace by Sir Richard Morison*. East Brunswick NJ: Associated UP, 1984.

Bernard, G.W. 'Elton's Cromwell.' *History* 83 (1998): 587–607.

Bevington, David. *From Mankind to Marlowe*. Cambridge MA: Harvard UP, 1962.

—. *Tudor Drama and Politics*. Cambridge, MA: Harvard UP, 1968.

Black's Law Dictionary. Abridged 6th ed. St. Paul, MN.: West Publishing Co., 1991.

Bruneau, William and Donald C. Savage, *Counting Out the Scholars: the Case Against*

Performance Indicators. Toronto: James Lorimer & Co. Ltd. A CAUT [Canadian Association of University Teachers] Series Title, 2002.

Burchell, Graham, Colin Gordon and Peter Miller, eds. *The Foucault Effect: Studies in Governmentality.* Chicago: U of Chicago P, 1991.

Butler, Judith. *Excitable Speech: A Politics of the Performative.* New York: Routledge, 1997.

'Castle of Perseverance.' Happé. *Four Morality Plays* 1–46.

Cawley, A.C., Marion Jones, Peter F. McDonald and David Mills. *The Revels History of Drama in English.* Vol.1 Medieval Drama. London: Methuen, 1983.

Chambers, E.K. *Medieval Drama.* Vol. 1. Oxford: Clarendon, 1903.

Cioni, Maria L. *Women and Law in Elizabethan England with Particular Reference to the Court of Chancery.* New York: Garland, 1985.

Corrigan, Paul. *Shakespeare on Management: Leadership Lessons for Today's Managers.* London: Kogan Page Ltd., 1999.

Corrigan, Philip and Derek Sayer. *The Great Arch: English State Formation as Cultural Revolution.* Oxford: Basil Blackwell, 1985.

Cowell, John. *The Interpreter.* Menston, England: Scholars Press, 1972.

Cranmer, Thomas. *The Remains of Thomas Cranmer, D.D. Archbishop of Canterbury.* Vol.1. Oxford: Oxford UP, 1933.

Crawford, Patricia. *Women and Religion in England: 1500–1720.* London: Routledge, 1993.

Cruikshank, Barbara. 'Revolutions Within: Self–Government and Self–Esteem.' Barry and Osborne, 1996: 231–52.

Cumming, William Patterson, ed. *The Revelations of Saint Birgitta.* London: Oxford UP, 1929.

Cressy, David. *Birth, Marriage, and Death: Ritual, Religion, and the Life–cycle in Tudor and Stuart England.* Oxford: Oxford UP, 1997.

Dean, Mitchell. *The Constitution of Poverty: Toward a Genealogy of Liberal Governance.* London: Routledge, 1991.

—. *Governmentality: Power and Rule in Modern Society.* London: Sage, 1999.

de Certeau, Michel. *The Mystic Fable. Volume One The Sixteenth and Seventeenth Centuries.* Trans. Michael B. Smith. Chicago: Chicago UP, 1992.

Despres, Denise. 'Ecstatic reading and missionary mysticism: The Orcherd of Syon,' Voaden, 141–60.

Dickens, A.G. *The English Reformation.* New York: Shocken Books, 1964.

Dillon, Janette. 'Holy Women and their Confessors or Confessors and their Holy Women? Margery Kempe and Continental Tradition.' Voaden, 120.

Donaldson, Ian. *The Rapes of Lucretia: a Myth and its Transformation.* Oxford: Clarendon, 1982.

Elton G.R. *Policy and Police: the Enforcement of the Reformation in the Age of Thomas Cromwell.* Cambridge: Cambridge UP, 1972.

—. *The Tudor Constitution: Documents and Commentary.* London: Cambridge UP, 1962.

—. *The Tudor Revolution in Government: Administrative Changes in the Reign of Henry VIII.* Cambridge: Cambridge UP, 1962.

Elyot, Thomas, Sir. *The Book Named the Governor.* Ed. S.E. Lehmberg. London: J.M. Dent & Sons Ltd., 1962.

—. *The Boke Named the Governour.* Intro. Foster Watson. London: Dent, 1907.

—. *The Castle of Health, Corrected, and in Some Places Augmented by the First Author.* London, 1610. University Microfilms International, reel 784.6.

Erasmus, Desiderius. *The Education of a Christian Prince*, ed. and trans. L.K. Born. New York: Octagon Books, 1936.

—. 'The Praise of Folly.' *Essential Works of Erasmus*, ed. W.T.H. Jackson. New York: Bantam Books, 1965.

Erickson, Amy Louise. *Women & Property in Early Modern England*. London: Routledge, 1993.

Ewald, Francois. 'Two Infinities of Risk.' *The Politics of Everyday Fear*, ed. Brian Massumi. Minneapolis: U of Minnesota P, 1993.

Fantazzi, Charles. *Studies in Medieval and Reformation Thought*. Leiden: E.J.Brill, 1979.

Farmer, John S., ed. *The Dramatic Writings of John Bale: Bishop of Ossory*. Guildford, England: Charles W. Traylen, 1966.

—. ed. *Six Anonymous Plays*. 2nd series. Guildford, England: Charles W. Traylen, 1966.

Fletcher, Anthony. *Tudor Rebellions*. London: Longmans, 1968.

Fortescue, John, Sir. *De Natura Legis Naturae*. Classics of English Legal History in the Modern Era. New York: Garland, 1980.

Foucault, Michel. *Discipline and Punish: The Birth of the Prison*. Trans. Alan Sheridan. New York: Pantheon, 1978.

—. 'Governmentality,' Burchell et al. 87–104.

—. *The History of Sexuality Volume I: An Introduction*. Trans. Robert Hurley. New York: Random House, 1980.

—. 'Two Lectures.' *Power/Knowledge: Selected Interviews and Other Writings 1972–1977*. Ed. Colin Gordon. New York: Pantheon Books, 1980.

—. 'Omnes et Singulatim: Towards a Criticism of "Political Reason,"' in *The Tanner Lectures on Human Value*, ed. S.M. McMurrin 2 Vols. Cambridge: Cambridge U P, 1981–82, 2:223–54.

—. 'The Subject and Power.' *Critical Inquiry* 8 (Summer 1982): 777–95.

Fox, Alistair. 'Sir Thomas Elyot and the Humanist Dilemma.' Fox and Guy, 1986: 52–73.

Fox, Alistair and John Guy. *Reassessing the Henrician Age: Humanism, Politics and Reform 1500–1550*. Oxford: Basil Blackwell, 1986.

Gee, Henry and John Hardy. *Documents Illustrative of English Church History*. London: Macmillan, 1912.

Geritz, Albert J. and Amos Lee Laine. *John Rastell*. Boston: Twayne, 1983.

Giddens, Anthony. *Runaway World: How Globalization is Reshaping our Lives*. New York: Routledge, 2000.

Glimp, David. *Increase and Multiply: Governing Cultural Reproduction in Early Modern England*. Minneapolis: U of Minneapolis P, 2003.

Goldberg, Jonathan. *Sodometries: Renaissance Texts, Modern Sexualities*. Stanford: Stanford UP, 1992.

Gordon, Colin. 'Governmental Rationality: An Introduction.' Burchell et al. 1–52.

Gunn, S.J. *Early Tudor Government, 1485–1558*. New York: St. Martin's Press, 1995.

Guth, Delloyd J. and John McKenna, eds, 'The Age of Debt, the Reformation and English Law.' 69–86.

—. *Tudor Rule and Revolution: Essays for G.R. Elton from his American Friends*. Cambridge: Cambridge U, Guth and McKenna,, 1982.

Guy, John. 'Thomas More and Christopher St German: The Battle of the Books.' Fox and Guy, 1986: 95–120.

—. *Tudor England*. Oxford: Oxford UP, 1988.

Hacking, Ian. 'Making up People.' *Reconstructing Individualism: Autonomy, Individuality, and the Self in Western Thought*, ed. Thomas C. Heller, Morton Sosna, and David E. Wellberry. Stanford: Stanford UP, 1985, 222–36.

Haigh, Christopher. *English Reformations: Religion, Politics, and Society under the Tudors*. Oxford: Clarendon, 1993.

Hall, Edward. *Hall's Chronicle; Containing the History of England During the Reign of Henry the Fourth to the End of the Reign of Henry the Eighth, in which are Particularly Described the Manners and Customs of Those Periods*. 1547. New York: AMS Press, 1965.

Happé, Peter. ed. *Four Morality Plays*. Harmondsworth, England: Penguin Books, 1979.

—. *Tudor Interludes*. Harmondsworth Middlesex: Penguin, 1972 .

Helgerson, Richard. 'Introduction.' *Early Modern Literary Studies* 4.2 / Special Issue 3 (September, 1998): 1.1–14: http://purl.oclc.org/emls/04–2/intro.htm

—. *Forms of Nationhood: the Elizabethan Writing of England*. Chicago: U of Chicago P, 1992.

Henderson, Jennifer. *Settler Feminism and Race Making in Canada*. Toronto: UofT Press, 2003.

Herman, Peter C. *Rethinking the Henrician Era: Essays on Early Tudor Texts and Contexts*. Urbana Illinois: U of Illinois P, 1994.

Hervet, Gentian. *Xenophons Treatise of Householde*. London: T. Berthelet, 1534.

Hodnett, Edward. *English Woodcuts: 1480–1535*. London: Oxford UP, 1935.

Higgins, Lesley and Marie–Christine Leps. '"Passport Please": Legal, Literary, and Critical Functions of Identity.' *College Literature*. 25.1 (1998): 94–138.

Hindle, Steve. 'Justice, Peace and Paternalism: State Formation and the Rule of Law in Renaissance England.' *Renaissance, Law and Literature* Conference Abstracts. Oxford University, Wolfson College. 2 July, 1998.

Howard, Jean. 'Civic Institutions and Precarious Masculinity in Dekker's *The Honest Whore*.' *Early Modern Culture: an Electronic Seminar*, No. 1 (2000): http://www.history-journals.de/articles/hjg-eartic-j00107.html

—. *The Stage and Social Struggle in Early Modern England*. London and New York: Routledge,1994.

Howard, Skiles. '"Ascending the Riche Mount': Performing Hierarchy and Gender in the Henrician Masque.' Herman, 1994: 16–39.

Hunt, Alan. *Governance of the Consuming Passions: a History of Sumptuary Law*. New York: St. Martin's Press, 1996.

—. *Governing Morals: A Social History of Moral Regulation*. Cambridge: Cambridge UP, 1999.

Hutson. Lorna. *The Userer's Daughter: Male Friendship and Fictions of Women in Sixteenth–Century England*. London: Routledge, 1994.

'Interlude of Youth.' Lancashire 91–116.

Ives, E.W. *Anne Boleyn*. Oxford: Oxford UP, 1986.

Jansen, Sharon. *Dangerous Talk and Strange Behaviour: Women and Popular Resistance to the Reforms of Henry VIII*. New York: St. Martin's Press, 1996.

—. *Political Protest and Prophecy under Henry VIII*. Woodbridge, Suffolk: Boydell & Brewer Ltd., 1991.

Jardine, Lisa. *Erasmus, Man of Letters: the Construction of Charisma in Print*. Princeton: Princeton University Press, 1993.

—. 'Humanistic Logic.' *The Cambridge History of Renaissance Philosophy*. Gen. ed. Charles B. Schmitt. Cambridge: Cambridge UP, 1988. 173–98.

Jed, Stephanie. *Chaste Thinking: The Rape of Lucretia and the Birth of Humanism*. Theories of Representation and Difference. Gen. Ed. Theresa de Lauretis. Bloomington: Indiana UP, 1989.

Johnson, Robert Carl. *Theatre Notebook*. (1970) 24: 101–11.

Jordan, Constance. *Renaissance Feminism: Literary Texts and Political Models*. Ithaca: Cornell UP, 1990.

Kahn, Victoria. *Rhetoric, Prudence, and Skepticism in the Renaissance*. Ithaca: Cornell UP, 1985.

Kastan, David Scott. '"Holy Wurdes" and "Slypper Wit": John Bale's *King Johan* and the Poetics of Propaganda.' Herman 267–282.

Kesselring, Krista. 'Representations of Women in Tudor Historiography: John Bale and the Rhetoric of Exemplarity.' *Renaissance and Reformation* 22–2 (1998) : 41–61.

Krontiris, Tina. *Oppositional Voices: Women as Writers and Translators of Literature in the English Renaissance*. London: Routledge, 1992.

Lakowski, Romuald Ian. 'Geography and the More Circle: John Rastell, Thomas More and the "New World."' *Renaissance Forum. An Electronic Journal of Early–Modern Literary and Historical Studies* Volume 4, Number 1, 1999, www.hull.ac.uk/renforum/v4no1/lakowski.htm, par. 3

Lambarde, William. *A Perambulation of Kent*. Bath: Adams & Dart, 1970.

Lancashire, Ian, ed. *Two Tudor Interludes: The Interlude of Youth and Hick Scorner*. The Revels Plays. Manchester: Manchester University Press, 1980.

The Lawes Resolutions of Womens Rights: Or, The Lawes Provisions for Women. Amsterdam: Theatrum Orbis Terrarum, Ltd., 1979.

Letters and Papers, Foreign and Domestic, of the Reign of Henry VIII, 1509–1547. Ed. J.S.Brewer, et al., 21 vols. London, 1862.

Loades, David. *Power in Tudor England*. New York: St. Martin's Press, 1996.

—. *Tudor Government: Structures of Authority in the Sixteenth Century*. Oxford: Blackwell Publishers, 1997.

Luborsky, Ruth Samson and Elizabeth Morley Ingram. *A Guide to English Illustrated Books, 1536–1603*. Arizona: Medieval & Renaissance Texts & Studies, 1998.

Mack, Phyllis. *Visionary Women: Ecstatic Prophecy in Seventeenth–Century England*. Berkeley: U of California P, 1992.

Martindale, Joanna, ed. *English Humanism: Wyatt to Cowley*. London: Croom Helm, 1985.

Maus, Katharine Eisaman. *Inwardness* and *Theatre in the English Renaissance*, Chicago: Chicago UP, 1995.

Mazo Karras, Ruth. *Common Women: Prostitution and Sexuality in Medieval England*. New York: Oxford UP, 1996.

McCune, Pat . 'Order and Justice in Early Tudor Drama.' *Renaissance Drama* 25 (1994): 171–96.

McKenna, John W. 'How God Became an Englishman.' Guth and McKenna 25–44.

Mills, David and Peter F. McDonald. *The Revels History of Drama in English*. Vol. I London: Methuen, 1983.

More, Sir Thomas. *Utopia*. Ed. David H. Sacks. New York: Bedford / St. Martin's, 1999.

Morison, Richard. 'A Discourse Touching the Reformation of the Lawes of England.' Anglo, 'An Early Tudor Program', 1969: 176–9.

—. *An Exhortation to Styre all Englyshemen to the Defence of Theyr Countreye.* Amsterdam: Theatrum Orbis Terrarum Ltd., 1972.

—. *Apomaxis Calumniarum.* Ms.18109. The British Library, London.

—. 'A Lamentation in Which Is Showed What Ruin and Destruction Cometh of Seditious Rebellion.' Berkowitz 85–108.

—. 'A Remedy for Sedition Wherein Are Contained Many Things Concerning the True and Loyal Obeisance That Commons Owe unto their Prince and Sovereign Lord the King.' Berkowitz 109–78.

Neame, Alan. *The Holy Maid of Kent: The Life of Elizabeth Barton, 1506–1534.* London: Hodder and Stoughton, 1971.

Newman, Karen. *Fashioning Femininity and English Renaissance Drama.* Chicago: U of Chicago P, 1991.

O'Donoghue, Edward Geoffrey. *Bridewell Hospital: Palace, Prison, Schools, from the Earliest Times to the End of the Reign of Elizabeth.* London: J. Lane, The Bodley Head Ltd., 1923.

Olivier, Richard. *Inspirational Leadership: Henry V and the Muse of Fire: Timeless Insights from Shakespeare's Greatest Leader.* Rollinsford New Hampshire: Spiro Press USA, 2001.

Oxford English Dictionary Online: http://dictionary.oed.com/ (August 6, 2003).

Parker, Andrew and Eve Kosofsky Sedgwick. *Performativity and Performance.* New York: Routledge, 1995.

Plant, Marjorie. *The English Book Trade: an Economic History of the Making and Sale of Books* London: George Allen & Unwin Ltd, 3rd ed., 1974.

Plomer, Henry. *Wynkyn De Worde & his Contemporaries from the Death of Caxton to 1535.* London: Grafton & Co., 1925.

Pollard, Alfred. 'Pleadings in a Theatrical Lawsuit,' *Fifteenth Century Prose and Verse,* Westminster: A. Constable and Co., Ltd., 1903.

Polito, Mary. 'Wit, Will and Governance in Early Modern Legal Literature.' Adversaria. Spec. issue of *Mosaic* 27.4 (literature and law) (1994): 15–34.

Pomeroy, Sarah B. *Xenophon Oeconomicus: A Social and Historical Commentary With a New English Translation.* Trans. Sarah Pomeroy. Oxford: Clarendon, 1994.

Rastell, John. *Four Elements.* Axton 29–68.

—. *Les Termes de la Ley: or, Certain Difficult and Obscure Words and Terms of the Common and Statute Laws of England, Now in Use, Expounded and Explained.* Boston: J. Johnson, 1812.

Reed, A. W. *Early Tudor Drama: Medwall, The Rastells, Heywood and The More Circle.* London: Methuen and Co., 1926.

Roberts, Geoffrey. 'An Assessment of the Views of One of Our Greatest Historians.' *The Historian* 57 (1998): 29–31.

Rogers, Elizabeth ed., *The Correspondence of Sir Thomas More.* Princeton: Princeton University Press, 1947.

Rose, Nikolas. *Governing the Soul: the Shaping of the Private Self.* London: Free Association Books, 1999.

Rummel, Erika. *The Humanist–Scholastic Debate in the Renaissance and Reformation.* Cambridge, MA: Harvard UP, 1995.

Sanders, Norman, Richard Southen, T.W. Craik and Lois Potter. *The Revels History of Drama in English.* Vol. 2: 1500–1576. London: Methuen, 1980.

Sawicki, Jana. *Disciplining Foucault: Feminism, Power, and the Body.* New York: Routledge,

1991.

Simon, Joan. *Education and Society in Tudor England.* Cambridge: Cambridge UP, 1966.

Sim, Alison. *The Tudor Housewife.* Gloucestershire: Sutton, 1996.

Skelton, John. *Magnificence.* Ed. Paula Neuss. Manchester: Manchester UP, 1980.

Skinner, Quentin. *Liberty Before Liberalism.* Cambridge: Cambridge UP, 1998

Starkey, Thomas. *Dialogue between Pole and Lupset.* Ed. T.F. Mayer. London: Royal Historical Society (Great Britain), 1989.

Statutues at Large, from the First Year of King Richard III to the Thirty–first Year of King Henry VIII, inclusive. Vol. IV. London: Charles Bathurst, 1763.

Statutes of the Realm. London: Dawson of Pall Mall, 1963. Reprint. Originally published: London: G. Eyre and A. Strahan, 1810–1828.

Stewart, Alan. *Close Readers: Humanism and Sodomy in Early Modern England.* Princeton: Princeton UP, 1997.

St German, Christopher. *Doctor and Student.* Ed. T.F.T. Plucknett and J.L.Barton. Selden Society. London: Oxford UP, 1974.

Stretton, Tim. *Women Waging Law in Elizabethan England.* New York: Cambridge UP, 1998.

Thomas, Keith. *Religion and the Decline of Magic.* New York: Charles Scribner's Sons, 1971.

Tudor Royal Proclamations. Ed. Paul L Hughes and James F. Larkin. New Haven: Yale UP, 1964.

Van Cleave, Michael Alexander. *The Growth of English Education: 1438–1648.* University Park, Pennsylvania: Pennsylvania State University Press, 1990.

Vanhoutte, Jacqueline A. 'Engendering England: the Restructuring of Allegiance in the Writings of Richard Morison and John Bale.' *Renaissance and Reformation.* 20–1 (1996): 49–77.

Vives, Juan Luis. *In Pseudodialecticos: A Critical Edition.* Intro., trans. and commentary Charles Fantazzi. Leiden, the Netherlands: Brill, 1979.

—. 'Instruction of a Christian Woman.' *Vives and the Renascence Education of Women.* Ed. Foster Watson. New York: Longmans, Green & Co., 1912, 29–238.

—. 'Instruction of a Christian Woman.' Aughterson, *Renaissance Woman,* 1998: 67–8, 137, 168–70.

—. 'The Office and Duty of an Husband.' Aughterson, *The English Renaissance,* 1998: 429–33.

—. *On Assistance to the Poor.* Renaissance Society of America Reprint Texts, 1999. Trans. and intro. Alice Tobriner, SNJM, Toronto: U of Toronto P, 1971.

Voaden, Rosalynn, ed. *Prophets Abroad: The Reception of Continental Holy Women in Late–Medieval England.* Cambridge: D.S. Brewer, 1996.

Walker, Greg. *John Skelton and the Politics of the 1520s.* Cambridge, England: Cambridge UP, 1988.

—. *Persuasive Fictions: Faction, Faith, and Political Culture in the Reign of Henry VIII.* Aldershot, England: Scolar's Press, 1991.

—. *Plays of Persuasion: Drama and Politics at the Court of Henry VIII.* Cambridge: Cambridge UP, 1991.

—. *The Politics of Performance in Early Renaissance Drama.* New York: Cambridge UP, 1998.

—. 'Rethinking the Fall of Anne Boleyn.' *The Historical Journal* 45:1 (2002): 1–29.

Watt, Diane. 'Reconstructing the Word: the Political Prophecies of Elizabeth Barton (1506–1534). *Renaissance Quarterly* 50.1 (1997): 136–61.

—. *Secretaries of God: Women Prophets in Late Medieval and Early Modern England.* Rochester, NY: D.S. Brewer, 1997.

Whatmore, L.E., ed. 'The Sermon Against the Holy Maid of Kent and her Adherents, Delivered at Paul's Cross, November the 23rd, 1533, and at Canterbury, December the 7th.' *The English Historical Review* 58 (1943): 461–75.

—. 'A Sermon of Henry Gold, Vicar of Ospringe, 1525–27, Preached Before Archbishop Warham.' *Archaeologia Cantiana: Being Transactions of the Kent Archaeological Society.* 58 (1944): 34–43.

Wickham, Glynne. *English Moral Interludes.* London: J.M. Dent & Sons, 1976.

William, C.H. ed. *English Historical Documents: 1485–1558*, Vol. 5. London: Eyre & Spottiswoode, 1971.

Wilson, F.P. and G.K. Hunter. *The English Drama 1485–1585.* Oxford: Clarendon P., 1969.

Wilson, Richard. 'Prince of Darkness: Foucault's Shakespeare,' *Measure for Measure.* Theory in Practice Series, ed. Nigel Wood. Buckingham: Open UP, 1996: 133–178.

Woodbridge, Linda. *Vagrancy, Homelessness, and English Renaissance Literature.* Urbana: U of Illinois P, 2001.

Wright, Thomas, ed. *Three Chapters of Letters Relating to the Suppression of Monasteries* London: J.B. Nichols & Son, 1843.

Zeeveld, W. Gordon. *Foundations of Tudor Policy.* Cambridge, Mass.: Harvard UP, 1948.

Index